Working Out in Japan

Working Out in Japan

Shaping the Female Body in Tokyo Fitness Clubs

Laura Spielvogel

Duke University Press Durham & London 2003

© 2003 Duke University Press

All rights reserved

Printed in the United States of America on

acid-free paper ∞

Designed by C. H. Westmoreland

Typeset in Sabon with Century Schoolbook

display by Tseng Information Systems, Inc.

Library of Congress Cataloging-in-Publication

Data appear on the last printed page of

this book.

In memory of my mother, Ruth Ginsberg

Contents

Illustrations

Acknowledgments

I would like to express my heartfelt thanks to the many people who have helped me over the course of my research. First, I would like to extend my gratitude to the Fulbright-Hays Foundation for the generous grant that enabled me to conduct my field research, and to the Prize Fellowship at Yale University for their support while writing the dissertation. I am grateful to the faculty and staff at Edwin O. Reischauer Institute for Japanese Studies at Harvard University for providing me with a valuable postdoctoral fellowship.

I thank William Kelly, whose vast knowledge on all subjects related, even tangentially, to anthropology and Japan has been a true source of inspiration. His well-directed criticism and ability to synthesize the messiness of everyday culture have proven invaluable during the process of writing a grounded ethnography. I also want to extend a special thanks to Susan Brownell, who began as an anonymous reviewer of the manuscript and later became a cherished mentor. Her extensive comments and multiple readings helped shape the ideas that lie within. I am grateful to Anne Allison, Kathryn Dudley, Merry White, Andrew Gordon, Allen Guttmann, Sheila Levine, and an anonymous reviewer from Duke University Press for their constructive comments. I would like to express my appreciation to Ken Wissoker and the staff at Duke University Press for their inspiring efficiency in getting the book into print. In the harried final stages of writing the book, Robert Ulin and the anthropology department at Western Michigan University offered me encouragement and, more significantly, granted me a course release when I needed it most.

To protect the anonymity of the field sites and the people who work and work out there, I am unable to thank the members, staff, and management at the fitness clubs by name. I would simply like to express my gratitude to the managers for allowing an outsider to come in and participate in all activities; to the staff, not only for helping me over the rough spots during training but for always including me in their after-hours parties; and to the members for literally trusting me with their bodies. I am grateful to Noriko Mizuta, Yumi Ishikawa, and the staff of Josai International University, who provided both academic and emotional support while I was in the field. I would also like to extend a special thanks to Kayoko Unno and Akio Sato, who welcomed me into their home. Fieldwork would have been a lonelier experience without them.

Finally, I want to acknowledge my wonderful family. Thanks to my sweet baby son, Drew, whose imminent birth inspired me to finish the final draft of the book with just forty-eight hours to spare. Without the encouragement and constant love of my mother Ruth, father Steve, and sister Karen, I fear I would not have boarded the plane to Japan. The daily stream of letters when I was in the field and the endless proofreading bouts over many years sustained me through the long process and went far beyond the duties of family. And to my husband, Chris: you are my inspiration and love.

Introduction

In the past decade, trendy sports clubs have cropped up in all major Japanese cities, from Sapporo to Naha. Sweating bodies move in rhythm to the strains of popular American rock music. The sing-song calls of the aerobics instructor compete with the clank of heavy weights and the noisy chatter of members relaxing over a soda or snack. Young women flock to aerobics classes suited up in colorful and strappy leotards, complete with perfectly styled ponytails, lipstick, and mascara. Fully aware of the cigarette-smoking men who cluster in the doorway, for these women fitness is not only about cardiovascular health.

Expensive beauty salons (*esute*) prey on and encourage this desire to slim down and "bust up," guaranteeing results in two weeks or less.[1] Beauty aid supply stores display *home sauna* (masks, corsets, or biking shorts made of thick, unbreathable material to cause excessive sweating), metabolism-altering diet pills, and the infamously dangerous diet tea. Popular women's magazines devote entire issues to topics such as "Let's Become a Body that Doesn't Get Fat Again!" (*an-an* 1996) and "Making a Beautiful Body in '95: Leg Slimmers" (*Can-Cam* 1995). The message of the beauty industry in Japan is unavoidable: Thin is beautiful and beautiful is thin. It stands to reason, doesn't it, that fitness clubs, aimed at building and sculpting a stronger and leaner body, would be a booming business in Japan? Well, yes and no.

Contemporary Japan seems particularly primed for the popularity of exercise and aerobics, given the state's aggressive push for increased leisure and healthier lifestyles, a precedence of widespread and enthusiastic consumption of American imports, the flourishing beauty and diet industry, and a cultural system of achievement that awards hard work, industriousness, and discipline. So why haven't fitness clubs been able to capitalize on this promising convergence of political, economic, and cultural trends? Indeed, nearly 97 percent of the Japanese population chooses not to exercise on a regular basis of at least three times a week (*Leisure White Papers* 1996). Members quit the club at alarming rates, and although some embrace the rhetoric of building strong bodies to lose weight and achieve health benefits, the majority opt for sweating in the saunas over sweating in the aerobics studio.

National statistics show that despite unprecedented increases in leisure time and state-sanctioned programs designed to improve the health of the nation, only 2 to 3 percent of the Japanese population exercise more than twice a week, as compared to 7 to 8 percent of North Americans.[2] In 1995, the year in which I began fieldwork in Japan, the Japanese fitness club industry served approximately 1.8 million people, compared to the 28 million in the United States and 6 million in Australia, the two countries in which aerobics is most popular ("Clubs Shift" 1995:20). Total club memberships have since climbed to 3.1 million in Japan and 32.8 million in the United States. Although Japan's total population is a fraction of the United States,' the fitness population, which did burgeon during the aerobics boom, has not increased significantly since the introduction of aerobics in the early 1980s.

The total number of private fitness clubs in Japan is currently 1,788 (an increase of only 136 clubs since 1995); in the United States private clubs number more than 13,000 (CMN 2001; IHRSA 2001).[3] Although the fitness industry has spread slowly throughout Japan, most of the private fitness club chains continue to be located in and around the larger cities of the Kanto and Kansai regions. Thirty percent of the private clubs are located in the Kanto area (Tokyo, Chiba, Saitama, and Kanagawa), and 20 percent are concentrated in Kansai (Osaka, Hyogo, and Aichi). The remaining 50 percent are spread throughout the rest of Japan ("Report on Fitness Trends" 1997).

The health and fitness industry in Japan has earned 303.4 billion yen (about $2.5 billion) annual revenue for the past four to five years; the U.S. industry has earned $11.6 billion in the past year (CMN 2001).[4] Although the numbers appear impressive, the recent financial recession has stymied the fitness mania that characterized Japan in the 1980s. Fitness club membership numbers in Japan peaked in 1989 but decreased dramatically in recent years as belt-tightening has forced many to limit leisure activities.[5] In the past several years, the fitness club market has been dominated by older and more established companies, with fewer new companies venturing into the field ("Slimmer Fitness Sector" 1998:8). Although industry representatives predict membership numbers to double in the next ten years, with private clubs forecast to total 2,280 by 2010 (CMN 2001), the current percentages still stand at approximately one-third that of the United States.

What accounts for this discrepancy? If we take a closer look at the fitness club clientele in Japan and the United States, both of which are made up of increasingly older, wealthy, and female members, it becomes even more difficult to understand why Japanese clubs have not generated the same enthusiasm they have in the United States. The major shift in club demographics in both the United States and Japan in the past decade has been from a younger to an older membership. In 1987, the majority of American health club members were under the age of 35 (62 percent), whereas today the majority is over 35 (55 percent; IHRSA 2001). A similar trend has occurred in Japan, where those age 30 and over made up 58.6 percent of the membership in 1992 and presently constitute 66.6 percent (CMN 2001). Fitness club memberships, particularly among the postretirement population, have slowly increased in most major clubs in Japan since the September 1997 rise in medical insurance costs, which has generated a national concern with health and wellness ("Slimmer Fitness Sector" 1998:8). This increased concern over the health of the aging population has even influenced the Japanese Ministry of Health, Labor, and Welfare to consider allowing patients of lifestyle-related diseases to claim national health insurance coverage for fitness facilities ("Japan Eyes Health Insurance" 2001).

At the same time, gender dynamics have remained relatively consistent over the past ten years in both countries. Females continue to make up the slight majority of fitness club members in both the United States (52 percent) and Japan (56.5 percent; IHRSA 2001; CMN 2001). In light of the high price of a club membership in both countries, one may assume that the majority of members are relatively well-off. In fact, in the United States, where average enrollment fees are $187 with a $57 average monthly rate, it is not surprising that the many club members (39 percent) earn more than $75,000 annually (IHRSA 2001). The annual cost of membership in Japan is equal on average to 2 percent of members' annual income, compared to 1 percent in the United States, so Japanese clubs are under pressure to lower their fees to attract the mere 3 percent of national fitness club goers ("Slimmer Fitness Sector" 1998:8). In 1996, the fees at Japan's most popular clubs averaged

30,000 yen (approximately $250) for the one-time registration fee, with monthly payments of 11,000 yen ($91). In the wake of the recent economic recession, many clubs have slashed their monthly rates to as low as 7,000 yen ($58) and, in some cases, have even eliminated the enrollment fee.

Club management and members in both countries may gloss over the low percentages, citing the "catch-up" theory, suggesting that Japan is simply behind the United States by ten to fifteen years. This notion of competition and "being behind" is intrinsic to understanding the relationship of Japanese fitness clubs, Japanese sports, and, indeed, Japan as a nation vis-à-vis the United States. Because aerobics originated in the United States and is the latest import in a long history of American sports to become popularized in Japan, it is useful to consider how the consumption of aerobics differs from and is consistent with other "modern" and indigenous sports in Japan. In Chapter 1, I analyze the history of sporting metaphors in twentieth-century Japan generally and the perception of foreign and women's sport in particular to understand how processes of globalization, cultural exchange, and consumption contributed to the popularization of the aerobics import. How do fitness clubs represent both a break from and a connection with the reception of other "Western" sport imports, the more militaristic orientation of sport in the early 1900s, and the denigration of women's sports in Japan?

Imagining Japan and the United States

Rather than examining the local consumption and, indeed, transformation of aerobics in Japan as yet another example of the "domestication" of Western culture, in which foreign imports are altered to better suit the local context (Tobin 1992a), I have chosen to focus on the way the consumption of aerobics in Japan reflects the synthesis and, more often than not, the contradictions between Japanese and Western ideology. That is, I look not only at transformations but also at points of intersection and contradiction between the rigid dichotomy of Japan and the West. I want to emphasize that I am using the binary categories of Japan and the West as ideological constructions as opposed to essentialist distinctions. In this age of globalization, diaspora, and cultural exchange, geographical boundaries, cultural borders, and national identities are dissolving (in fact, it could be argued that they never existed in the first place). I assert that despite the obvious pragmatic impossibility and theoretical complication of the reductionistic separation of Japan from the West, it is undeniable that certain practices, behaviors, and paradigms are considered culturally and historically Japanese in orientation, while others are considered Western. Japan and the West as cultural categories have been and continue to be defined against each other in a dialectical tension but are by no means mutually exclusive or explicitly tied to geography.

I have taken the fitness club as the institutional framework with which to examine monastic and/or militaristic tactics of discipline; intertwined and dualistic relationships between mind and body; cross-cultural distinctions among definitions of work, home, and leisure; and transnational and patriarchal assumptions about gender, beauty, and power. Beyond these introductory background statistics, I do not continue to explicitly compare the fitness industry in the United States and Japan, but rather use the long-standing and complicated relationships between these cultural paradigms to underlie and inform my understanding of the discipline and display of the female body in contemporary Japan.

Why Fitness Clubs?

At first glance, a research project centered around fitness clubs would not seem to rate as the most serious site of academic inquiry. In fact, many anthropologists who give their undivided attention to scholarship on initiation rituals and birthing rites in other cultures might view a project on body practices in Japanese fitness clubs as commonsensical or even trivial. In the face of this skepticism, I demonstrate that the fitness club serves as the ideal location in which to explore the intersection of globalization and consumption, of bodily discipline and display, and of constructions of health and illness in contemporary Japan. The fitness club presents a unique window on Japanese cultural conceptions of work, play, marriage, sexuality, aging, beauty, community formation, education, identity, power, and gender, or, in other words, how everyday life is given meaning and relevance. One may venture that this is a sizable burden for the lowly fitness club to shoulder, but I argue that it is precisely because the clubs are located in the everyday and fall beyond the radar of cultural critique that they are so aptly situated for study.

Although the body has been the topic of much theoretical and ideological critique, several scholars have suggested that, with certain significant exceptions (e.g., Klein 1993; Wacquant 1995), extended field research on how these images are consumed or rejected on the ground has been conspicuously absent. Turner asserts, "There is a general anxiety that the sociology of the body has been confined to theoretical speculation and elaboration without creating a strong research tradition or research agenda" (1996:32). This ethnographically based study of fitness clubs in contemporary Japan addresses this gap in the literature by providing a grounded analysis of the way local bodies interpret, challenge, and submit to the normative ideals of leisure and labor, mind and body, and health and beauty.

The dual focus of this book—that is, the tension between the local and the ideological or, in this case, the grounded practices of the club and the larger constructions of beauty, health, and leisure—lends itself to two possible organizational styles. On the one hand, foregrounding the specific history, spaces, and disciplinary techniques of the fitness club provides a window on cultural assumptions regarding gender, beauty, and identity. On the other hand, by laying out the more abstract ideological constructions initially, the local particulars of the fitness club then offer concrete examples of how these theoretical issues play out on the ground. After much consideration, I decided on the former approach, because I felt that the specific history and disciplinary spaces and tactics that characterize fitness clubs in Japan could serve as a tangible "way in" to understanding how fitness has been created and used to represent gendered notions of beauty, health, and diet for and by women.

Normative Standards of Beauty

How is beauty defined in contemporary Japan? Coherent yet complicated, current standards of beauty revolve around an unobtainable combination of wholesomeness, youth, sex appeal, cuteness, and thinness. Shifting definitions of health, purity, and attractiveness target distinct audiences of students, office workers, and housewives, and thereby make it impossible to pin down a single ideal of beauty. The current ties between beauty and fitness and their respective industries are not stable or even long-standing, varying over time and across age group, class, and region. Clammer illustrates how the wide variety of age- and class-specific magazines in Japan reflect and even create this breakdown of a homogeneous ideal (1995:218).

But local variation does not preclude image standardization. Bordo reminds us that "to focus only on multiple interpretations is to miss important effects of the everyday deployment of mass cultural representations of masculinity, femininity, beauty, and success" (1993:24). In the past ten years, fashion magazines, beauty salons, and fitness clubs have contributed to the creation and projection of normalizing and highly gendered messages about body image, weight, fashion, and femininity. And it is these normalizing images that help define the desired and desirable body in contemporary Japan. I do not intend to assert that practices of consumption, the potency of mass media, or the fitness club is exclusively responsible for determining normative standards of beauty, but rather that they are collaborative and, at times, contradictory (but not conspiratorial).

Although men must also conform to a certain body type, it is the women who have been consistently subjected to rigorous standards of perfection that focus on size, symmetry, and appearance (e.g., Bordo 1993; Wolf 1991; Chernin 1981). As Bartky (1990) asserts, conforming to these standards requires time-consuming disciplinary practices on the body. Hair care, skin care, movement management, makeup, diet, and exercise "are part of the process by which the ideal body of femininity—and hence the feminine body-subject—is constructed; in doing this, [the disciplinary practices] produce a 'practiced' and 'subjected' body, i.e., a body on which an inferior status has been inscribed" (70). It is no coincidence that the contemporary feminine ideal in Japan plays up bone-thin skinniness, wide-eyed innocence, cuteness, and youth. The frail, prepubescent ideal poses little emotional, intellectual, or sexual threat to the patriarchal status quo, and this ideal can only be achieved with strict self-control of appetite, wild emotions, and independent thoughts. Most women are all too aware of the paths to success in Japan. The discrimination against women deemed unattractive is evident in this revealing, albeit dated, memorandum recovered from a major Japanese corporation's personnel department: "Be wary of young women who wear glasses, are very short, speak in loud voices, have been divorced, or are the daughters of college professors" (quoted in R. Smith 1987:17). Jeannie Lo (1990), in her work on *office ladies*, describes a similar favoritism toward attractive women who brighten the office with their beauty.

Feminists have outlined the psychological, social, and physical dangers of the narrow beauty standard in the West. The second wave of feminism launched attacks on beauty pageants as contributing to the objectification and sexualization of women. However, Banet-Weiser (1999) has argued that although pageants do contribute to the harmful representation of women, they also offer women a unique opportunity to participate in the pleasure of pageantry. When women perform exaggerated femininity through costumes, hairstyles, and evening gowns, she argues, desire is empowering (12). She points to the agency of these women as a way to avoid rendering them simply as commodities and passive victims. In this book, I use the vignettes and voices of female club members and staff to illustrate that, although images of beauty are undeniably powerful and persuasive, the choices women make to conform or contest these images are ultimately their own. As Brumberg (1997) asserts, controlling the appetite, either through fasting or feasting, can be used as a voice to challenge gender roles and ideals. But Bordo warns that "the anorectic's protest, like that of the classical hysterical symptom, is written on the bodies of anorexic women, not embraced as a conscious politics—nor, indeed, does it reflect any social or political understanding at all. . . . *As a feminist protest, the obsession with slenderness is hopelessly counterproductive*" (1997:237, 241; emphasis added). Is the pursuit of youth, balance, and skinniness in the context of sport and physical activity similarly counterproductive?

The literature on aerobics and fitness in the United States is divided between exposing aerobics as a form of cultural domination that sexualizes women on the basis of physical beauty and praising aerobics as a form of empowerment for women who have historically been excluded from sport. S. Willis (1991), Cole (1994), and other feminists convincingly argue that the privatized and commercialized fitness clubs in the United States emphasize an unobtainable look and encourage "body rivalry" among women that negates any of the benefits of achieving self-discipline. I demonstrate that in Japan, by contrast, the fitness clubs make attempts (albeit unsuccessful) to counter the hegemonic beauty ideal by privileging health over appearance. Although the clubs enable women to gain self-confidence from moving and strengthening their bodies, to enter into a supportive community, and to indulge personal desires during limited periods of social and economic freedom, the clubs ultimately cannot satisfy their members. In the end, the pursuit of effortless and impossible beauty standards tempers, and at times eclipses, this unique opportunity for empowerment in the fitness club.

In the past few years, a wave of feminist critique, both popular and scholarly, has been aimed at the deconstruction of the buxom, wasp-waisted ideal of female beauty in North America. The high incidence of eating disorders, the "waif" models who grace the pages of fashion magazines, the increasing popularity of liposuction, and the prejudice against and disdain for women who "let themselves go"—all these characterize contemporary North America and seem unimaginable in any other context. But as numerous authors point out, eating disorders and a fixation on body management are not exclusive to white, middle- to upper-class, postindustrial North American society (e.g., Bynum, 1987; B. Thompson, 1994; Brumberg, 1988). With the exception of Kawahara's (1995) brief essay on fitness in Japan, the ties among beauty, fitness, and femininity have yet to be investigated in any serious sense, although many gender specialists have examined the construction of the female body in other Japanese contexts (see Lock 1993b; Allison 1993, 1994; Buckley 1991; Funabashi 1995). Thus, there is clear necessity for an explanation of exercise, chronic dieting, and body ideology in the cultural context of an affluent, image-conscious, postwar Japan.

To accomplish this task, I have conducted over thirteen months of participant observation and interviewing at two popular health club chains, one in the heart of downtown Tokyo and one in the quiet suburbs outside of the city. I began research in the summer of 1995 and was employed as a full staff member at both clubs during the year 1996–1997. On one level, this is an ethnography of Japanese fitness clubs and their history, programs, and personnel, but on another level, it is a project on the expanding service industry, ideological contradictions and interplay between Japan and the United States, the symbolic construction and discipline of the female body, and the changing complexions of work and leisure in late-capitalist Japan and, more recently, in the severe economic recession. By examining, in tandem, the larger discourse on health, leisure, beauty, diet, and fitness, and the on-the-ground rejection or consumption of this rhetoric, I illustrate some of the ways workplaces, bodies, and lifestyles are constructed in postindustrial, consumer-driven Japan.

1. An evening aerobics class at a popular downtown Tokyo fitness club.

The Sophisticated and the Country:
Downtown Fitness and Chiba Club

At certain times of the day and in certain locations, the fitness club business in Japan does seem to be quite successful. Fitness clubs *are* booming in downtown Tokyo locations. Aerobics studios in Roppongi, Shibuya, and Shinjuku are built to hold from eighty to one hundred members, and the weekend and night classes are filled to capacity (Figure 1). The foggy glass and mirrors, the vibrating floor, and the waves of heat that greet latecomers as they squeeze into the small squares of space in the back of the room attest to the popularity of aerobics in downtown Tokyo clubs. How do we reconcile this picture with struggling fitness clubs in the suburban and rural outskirts of Tokyo?

At midday, the staff, outnumbering the members in the weight room, fill their idle hours by lowering the shades a fraction of an inch and scrubbing the already spotless equipment (Figure 2). Management of these local clubs fret over stagnant membership numbers. The one suburban club where I conducted research has maintained an unchanging membership of two thousand since its opening in 1991. The managers introduce trendy aerobics programs in an attempt to stir up interest, but then watch them fail, expressing envy and dismay over the evident

2. The spacious facilities are underused at this suburban fitness club.

success of downtown chains. There is a definite ranking of clubs, and the top chains attract the most talented and inspirational instructors. I intentionally chose two clubs, one in the urban center of Roppongi and one in suburban Chiba, to illustrate how regional differences influence the construction of identity, conceptions of work and leisure, notions of health and aging, and ideals of beauty.

In selecting the clubs, I paid particular attention to the reputation and popularity of the aerobics program. The remarkable expansion of fitness clubs in the 1980s is inextricably linked to the import of aerobics to Japan. Although a few scattered fitness clubs predated the aerobics boom in the mid-1980s, the earliest sports clubs were quite unlike the trendy and spacious clubs of the 1980s and 1990s. Marketed as swimming clubs, the original fitness clubs attracted primarily the very young and the very old. The transformation from the low-end swim center to the flashy, high-tech fitness club of today was enabled by the successful import of aerobics. In fact, the fitness club of the 1980s and 1990s became synonymous with aerobics.

Although fitness centers tend to attract a self-selected and specific group of members, those who have both the means and the motivation to exercise, the two fitness club chains I chose cater to quite different clientele. The first club, which I call Downtown Fitness, has thirteen branches located in the most exclusive and trendiest areas of downtown Tokyo.[6] Although I spent time in several of the branches, I chose to center my research in their Roppongi branch, located in the heart of the cosmopolitan section of downtown Tokyo, just minutes from the Roppongi subway station. The Roppongi club opened in an area surrounded by exclusive boutiques and upscale restaurants. Renowned for its nightlife, Roppongi is bustling after seven o'clock and packed on weekend evenings.

With facilities all over Tokyo, from the trendy and youthful Shibuya area to the finance and business district of Shinjuku and the more upscale Gotanda district, Downtown Fitness has had great success, enabling the management to build in some of the priciest and choicest locations available. One upper-level manager explained, "The first [Downtown Fitness] branch opened in Shibuya ten years ago. At that time, Shibuya was the 'in' place. It has gone downhill since, but at that time, it was a cool area and we took advantage of that. We built an open-air aerobics studio and the boom of aerobics in the late 1980s was happening right there. Aerobics became synonymous with [Downtown Fitness]."

Centrally located near the business and retail districts of Tokyo, Downtown Fitness clubs appeal to office ladies and *sarariiman*[7] who exercise after work, before returning home or taking on the bar scene. Downtown Fitness members tend to be quite homogeneous: primarily young men and women who are unmarried and in their mid- to late twenties and early thirties.[8] Every member is entitled to use any of the thirteen facilities, a flexibility unique to Downtown Fitness, as most other chains restrict members to the single branch where the member joined initially. The competitive rates and the convenience and flexibility of using downtown locations, combined with a nationally renowned aerobics program, make Downtown Fitness one of the most popular clubs in Japan.

Aerobics classes are the main attraction at Downtown Fitness, and the management boasts that among its members are, in fact, many of the aerobics instructors who teach at competing clubs. Most branches offer a wide variety of high-impact, stretch, and dance classes, for a total of more than a hundred classes a week at some of the more popular locations. The facility layout reflects the club's attention to aerobics. Each branch of Downtown Fitness has two aerobics studios, as compared to the single studio in most of their competitors' clubs. Unlike the suburban clubs, which cater to a much broader age range of members, offering family rates and special *silver*[9] and junior programs, Downtown Fitness does not allow members younger than 18. Urban locations, with a membership limited to men and women in their twenties and thirties, have enabled Downtown Fitness to lower prices and, more important, to narrow its focus exclusively to aerobics and weight training. Small and spare, Downtown Fitness runs a "bare-bones" operation, offering adequate but far from luxurious facilities for its nevertheless booming business of young single professionals interested primarily in improving their appearance.

But what about the silver and junior potential members? Is fitness constructed and enjoyed in the same way in areas outside the metropolis? To answer these questions, I selected a second sports club, located in Chiba Prefecture, which turned out to differ from Downtown Fitness in almost every way imaginable. This club, which I call Chiba Club, is a suburban branch of one of the largest fitness club chains in Japan, with over 150 branches from Hokkaido to Okinawa.[10] Although the chain is managed in a central office in downtown Tokyo, the branches differ tremendously in terms of location, clientele, facilities, and membership fees. Because of this diversity, the Chiba Club chain, unlike Downtown Fitness, tends to limit its members to a single club and does not allow reciprocity with other centers in the chain.

Chiba Prefecture, although well within commuting distance of Tokyo, is still considered by many to be *inaka*, a derogatory term meaning local or "country." This characterization reflects the larger ideological hierarchy between the urban and the periphery in Japan. The metropolis of Tokyo is widely regarded as the cultural and financial center, from which all trends—fashion, music, and otherwise—radiate to the rest of the country. The manager of Chiba Club was acutely aware of the image of Chiba and the competition between urban and suburban fitness clubs. He was embarrassed when I informed him that I was also researching at Downtown Fitness in Roppongi and said, "Roppongi is about ten years behind the United States, but we are about twenty years behind, because we are so inaka. Roppongi attracts young members, but here, we get the middle-aged. Housewives and retired people . . . this club is for the talkers [*oshaberi*]. Some women come and talk for hours, as they are getting changed, and then they sit on the exercise bikes and just talk for one or two more hours. In Roppongi, people come with a goal, that is, to go to their favorite class or favorite teacher, or to lift weights or something. Here, the people have no goals. They talk about unimportant things, but perhaps it relieves stress."

Nevertheless, the slower pace, cheaper housing, relatively short commute to downtown, and lower cost of living attracts many salariiman and their families to the Chiba suburbs. I chose to live near the Chiba Club for precisely these reasons. There are several express trains that run back and forth from Chiba City through the intervening suburbs to downtown Tokyo and, during rush hour, these trains are packed with commuters. Chiba Club is located in one such suburb along the express train line, approximately thirty minutes from downtown Tokyo. Residential neighborhoods, quaint fruit markets, and green open spaces characterize the suburb, which is commonly referred to in Japanese as a *bedtown*, a place where commuters return from work to sleep.

This Chiba suburb is serviced by two train lines, one private and one national. Although the area surrounding the public train line station is fairly bustling—home to department stores, restaurants, and bars—the neighborhoods around the less convenient and more expensive private line are quieter and less commercialized. Chiba Club rents three floors of a hotel that stands directly outside the ticket gates of the private train line. The national success of the chain overall, as well as the relatively low rents and amount of available real estate in Chiba Prefecture, permit the luxurious and spacious layout of Chiba Club, nearly three times the size of Downtown Fitness in Roppongi. With full-court basketball, squash courts, golf practice ranges, a weight room, an open-air aerobics studio, an Olympic-size lap pool, a fifteen-foot-deep diving pool, and a Jacuzzi, Chiba Club has all the amenities of a posh country club.

Originally constructed as a swimming club for children in 1969, the Chiba Club chain eventually expanded its facilities to become more fitness-oriented. Twenty years later, their total membership has exceeded three hundred thousand. True to their origins, the emphasis remains on families and swimming, and most of the clubs include aqua aerobics, junior classes, swimming lessons, scuba diving, and snorkeling. The club sponsors quarterly trips to exotic islands for diving practice and certification, and all of the fitness instructors are qualified and enthusiastic swimmers. Catering to families, the chain offers discounted rates and special gymnastics programs and swimming lessons for children. Even so, men and women in their late fifties and early to mid-sixties make up a large percentage of the membership at these same suburban branches of Chiba Club (Figure 3).

3. The *silver* clientele stretch together before their exercise class.

The time of day determines the age and occupation of the clientele in most fitness clubs but especially in suburban areas.[11] Housewives and retired men and women frequent the club during the morning and early afternoon, schoolchildren swarm in during the late afternoon, and later the working crowd takes over until the club closes. One staff member expressed misgivings about the sleepy location selected for Chiba Club and the type of clientele who were attracted as a result:

I have a female friend who told me that she is embarrassed to exercise near her work and her home, for fear of meeting men that she either works with or went to school with. She's not so much embarrassed in front of other women as in front of the men. Therefore, she goes to a club a few stops away from her house. Although there is a branch of Chiba Club near her home, she chooses to go to this one, a few stops away. I told the Area Director that he should have built the club not in a well-populated suburb, nor near a workplace, but rather near a *norikae* [train transfer station]. It depends on the members you want to attract. If you want to attract men, you should build it near the company, as they are not embarrassed to be seen by people at work. Our club was built for the older women, and so was built in a bedtown with little attention to attracting the younger crowd.

By combining research at Chiba Club with that at Downtown Fitness, I was able to examine the tensions between the urban and the periphery as well as encounter a diverse group of members, ranging from families and housewives to students and office workers.

Working In and Working Out:
Negotiating Participant-Observation

Participant-observation has been recognized as the methodological bedrock of anthropology for almost a century. It is less appreciated, though, that it embodies a fundamental contradiction. Participation implies knowledge, being enough of an insider to know how to behave. Anthropological observation, on the other hand, begins in deliberate ignorance, checking one's cultural baggage in order to see things from a different point of view. Inevitably then, most anthropologists do far more observing than participating.

When conducting fieldwork in Japanese metropolitan fitness clubs, I tried to create a research role that was more fully participatory. In the fitness club, a site where bodies are on display and members pay large fees for the expertise and privacy afforded by the club, a lurking, notebook-touting researcher is far from welcome. Gaining access proved, in fact, to be quite difficult, and I spent a good part of a preliminary six-week trip to Japan securing permission to research in two of the biggest and most well-known fitness club chains in Japan. After a series of faxes and phone calls, I finally was granted an interview with the decision-making managers at the main downtown office. Anticipating questions regarding the details of my research, I prepared my résumé and cover letter in Japanese, stressing my Japanese and U.S. university affiliations as well as explanations of proposed methodology. But as it turned out, the upper-level managers were far more interested in my aerobics instructing credentials and experience than they were in my academic affiliations and aims.

"You teach aerobics in Washington, D.C.?" the managers exclaimed as they pored over my résumé. "And are certified by AFAA?[12] That's wonderful. Why, you could teach a special American aerobics class in our clubs. You could introduce the latest American steps and could be our special guest instructor." As a foreigner, I would also function in the club as, in the words of Creighton, a "living advertisement" of foreign style, fashion, and fitness (1995:150). By hiring a white Westerner, the management could take advantage of the exoticness of the United States while also "taming" a representative from the originator of fitness and aerobics. One manager expressed relief that I had taught aerobics in popular fitness clubs, local community centers, and individual homes on previous trips to Japan. As they rattled off the numerous roles and responsibilities they envisioned for me at the club, I was simultaneously pleased and alarmed.

My initial relief that my research was being considered seriously and that I would be able to offer aerobics instruction in return for the opportunity to study in the club was soon tempered, as I imagined the time that I would be able to dedicate to my project being rapidly whittled away. Hours spent creating special "American" choreography and the pressure to perform as a guest instructor would leave me precious little time or energy to devote to interviews, field-note writing, and observation. In the end, although my schedule did not prove to be as hectic as I had feared, I did work two to three eight-hour days a week at each of the two fitness clubs, juggling the cleaning, training, and instructing responsibilities of a staff member with the additional research challenges of an anthropological fieldworker.

I entertain no doubts that it was because of my credentials as a U.S.-certified aerobics teacher and my status as a foreigner, rather than the academic rigor of my proposed project, that I was "hired" as an unpaid instructor and, ultimately, was able to enter the field not only as a participant but also as an expert participant. I do not think that being female particularly assisted or hindered me in gaining access to the fitness club. I believe that a young male anthropologist who was similarly qualified to teach aerobics would have entered the field in much the same way. On the other hand, being the same age as most of the fitness club staff and instructors was extremely important not only for securing access but for gaining the trust and confidence of management, members, and fellow staff.

Wearing the staff uniform gave me the access and authority to interview club members. Certification in aerobics instruction also provided me with the specialized knowledge and experience both to be able to evaluate fitness instruction abroad and to provide a desired service as an instructor in exchange for the opportunity to study in a sports club. Furthermore, my previous experience teaching aerobics in both the United States and, more important, in Japan assured the management that I was accustomed to working in an exclusive club setting, where protecting the privacy of members is of the utmost importance.

As a full member of the staff, I was able to move freely about the club, thereby gaining access to the "hidden" information, private relationships, and unguarded confidences that took place at club meetings, at after-hours parties, and behind the swinging door of the staff room. As a foreign anthropologist, this unrestricted access to the "backstage" enabled me to learn what Goffman terms the clubs' "inside secrets, whose possession marks an individual as being a member of a group and helps the group feel separate and different from those individuals who are not 'in the know.' Inside secrets give objective intellectual content to subjectively felt social distance. Almost all information in a social establishment has something of this exclusion function and may be seen as none of somebody's business" (1959:142). Protected and private information about the social structure, organization, and relationships at the fitness club gave me insight into understanding public practices and appearances.

At the same time, however, my expertise in American fitness and aerobics closed down certain avenues of inquiry. Some members were embarrassed that Japanese aerobics would fall short when compared to the source, the United States, and it often proved difficult during interviews to get full explanations, when I was assumed to be the expert.[13] Aerobics instructors assume an almost celebrity-like charisma and mystique; therefore, some members feel a certain degree of intimidation when confiding in an instructor, foreign or Japanese.

Choreographing aerobics routines and giving lessons was extremely time-consuming and took away from the hours that could be spent interviewing and observing. Even when observing, I could no longer stand anonymously in the back of the weight room but always felt that my presence was duly noted and, hence, influential. To broaden my perspective and to more fully understand the complexity of the fitness clubs, I felt it was important to position myself on both sides of the microphone, so to speak—as an instructor and also as a member. Thus, I complemented my participation as an instructor in two popular clubs with observations in a third fitness chain where I remained merely a member. This allowed me to assume an appropriate naïveté, but it rendered serious conversations with fellow members futile. When I wasn't dressed in the familiar club uniform, many of the members betrayed the terrified look of a deer caught in headlights as they struggled to position the foreigner asking probing questions.[14] To initiate conversation with perfect strangers, I was forced to resort to asking ridiculous or self-evident questions, such as, "I like your sneakers. Where did you get them?" Initially, many members found my questions about exercise and aerobics off-putting and intrusive. As my position in the club became more known and my presence more familiar, separating and isolating the dual roles of member and instructor proved to be somewhat artificial and difficult to sustain.

My long acquaintance with the fitness industry also had the unfortunate consequence of producing a false sense of security and overconfidence. At times, I felt that I understood far more than I did, a direct result of my overlaying Western standards onto the Japanese experience. I am hesitant to admit that I found myself jumping to conclusions, hastily dismissing certain practices, and dispensing unwanted advice. But, in my defense, I was often forced into this role. Countless people, both at home and abroad, asked me to provide sound-bites summing up the differences between the United States and Japan with regard to fitness. In an effort not to bore my audience, I supplied simple and entertaining anecdotes and was reluctant to delve into drawn-out comparisons that touched on the complexity or contradictions of the scene. Learning to juggle the distinct and often contradictory roles of insider and outsider, expert and novice, and participant and observer is a challenge central to anthropological fieldwork, whether in a fitness club, farming community, or funeral parlor. Although my experience teaching and taking aerobics and working and working out in fitness clubs made me particularly well-qualified to undertake a research project on body image, fitness, and diet in Japan, this expert knowledge also made it very difficult to intellectually and socially distance myself from the field.

I acknowledge the undeniable usefulness and necessity of questioning one's perspective, as proposed by feminists in the 1970s and later explored in the tautological debates of Clifford (1988), Marcus and Fischer (1986), Geertz (1988), and others. But these debates, while conceptually provocative and undeniably eloquent, render ethnography and fieldwork subjective, relativistic, and ultimately without meaning. How to position one's research and authoritative voice, exposing cultural biases without dissolving into crippling cultural relativism, is the postmodern problem that faces all scholars of culture and social behavior.

Escaping one's own cultural and life experiences, which unavoidably color one's perspective, is not only impossible but ill-advised. In fact, it is the author's particular and unique perspective, when made explicit, that makes the project that much more meaningful and persuasive. When writing the first draft of the dissertation, I found myself making repeated explicit and implicit comparisons to the United States, the source of my knowledge and experience. I consciously and often unconsciously constructed the United States as the standard by which Japanese fitness clubs and classes were being evaluated. Distancing myself from the rhetoric and experiences in which I was raised and trained proved (and continues to be) quite difficult.

When writing later drafts, I came to realize that fully purging the book of these comparisons would not only render the book lifeless, but would also deny the project the value of my experience in the United States. It is precisely because I taught and took aerobics in the United States for over ten years that I had the vocabulary, experience, and credibility not only to gain access to the field and offer my services in return but to evaluate fitness and aerobics abroad. Here, in the introduction, I have chosen instead to make explicit my voice (and my inherent biases) in the text, as well as the experiences that have contributed to coloring my particular and specific perspective. With an attempt at disclosure at the onset, I hope that the explicit and implicit comparisons in the book will be understood, for better or worse, in the context of my particular history as a 20-something (and now 30-something) female anthropologist, trained and certified to teach aerobics in the United States.

The Labor of Leisure: Corporate Discipline

Regardless of their diverse membership, all private fitness clubs in Japan are expensive. To satisfy their high-paying clientele, the clubs of the twenty-first century must mask the necessary hard work and discipline of exercise under a veneer of relaxation and luxury. Serving ice cream and beer, sponsoring after-hours parties, and offering professional massage, the fitness clubs attempt to find success in normative terms of leisure. By promoting a rhetoric of improved health and appearance, stress release and relaxation, and entertainment for all ages, clubs try to entice potential customers away from golf courses, department stores, and even family room television sets. Hard work is what distinguishes the fitness clubs from the rest of the leisure industry and may account for their comparative lack of success in Japan.

The word *fitness* (written in katakana) is vague in Japan, just as it is in the United States. Fitness clubs often exaggerate the multiple meanings of the word to extend the role that the club can play in its members' lives. Fitness clubs can satisfy the need to relax, lose weight, or gain energy. It is significant that these clubs are never referred to as "health clubs" in Japanese. Sometimes called "sports clubs" (*supoutsu kurabu*), they are most often referred to as "fitness clubs" (*fuittenesu kurabu*). The term *sports club* conjures up a more athletic and serious image, whereas *fitness club* connotes beauty, health, style, and trendiness. This is not merely semantics, but a key to understanding the distinctions among health, sports, and fitness in Japanese culture. As one instructor explained, "The word *fitness* is not Japanese, but comes from English, so many Japanese don't know exactly what it means. Many see the commercial posters and the advertisements of a thin pretty woman and assume that fitness equals good and attractive. Or perhaps others think it means sports or health or strength. Fitness has multiple meanings, and that's why [the members] come, to find out more about it."

The ambiguity of the term reflects the multiplicity of meanings attached to notions of health and leisure in Japan. Just as fitness is synonymous not only with exercise but also with entertainment, the pursuit of good health implies a desire to be not only self-sufficient and productive but also energetic and balanced. Eating a piece of cake while talking about one's diet or sipping a beer after an exhausting workout is not contradictory so much as an expression of well-being and equilibrium. In Japanese, there are several words used to speak of health. The noun *kenko* translates directly to "health" and is used to speak of being in good health (*kenko de aru*) or poor health (*kenko de nai*). In the fitness club, this word is used as a catch-all for mental and physical well-being. When I asked members why they were working out at the club, many responded succinctly "For my health" (*kenko no tame*). Kenko denotes a medical and physiological expression of well-being, whereas the word *genki* is used more colloquially to refer to an upbeat feeling or overall high energy level. As one instructor explained, "Most young women think of fitness as aerobic dance and healthy food and not the same as kenko, which has a medical image."

To inquire about someone's physical health, one would use the phrase "*Kenko wa do desuka?*" In response, complaints of specific ailments, such as sore shoulders or a stiff leg, would be acceptable and even expected. Ohnuki-Tierney (1984) notes that direct questions and detailed responses about one's health are not unusual in Japan and reflect a proclivity to discuss one's bodily habits with little reticence. On the other hand, the phrase "*Genki desuka?*" while also translating literally to "How is your health?" is used more colloquially in salutation to mean "How are you?" In response, a simple affirmative is expected ("*Hai, genki desu*"), just as in English, where a reply of anything other than "Fine" would be inappropriate. When speaking of health, energy, or vigor, the word genki is usually used. Gurgling babies and energetic children are labeled genki, just as enthusiastic aerobics instructors and spry older members are praised for exhibiting a genki attitude.

In Japan, to be healthy, in the genki sense of the word, is not only to be in good physiological health but to be well-adjusted, enthusiastic, self-sufficient, and passionate. Fitness clubs aim to improve the physical health of their members but also to encourage enthusiasm and a zest for life. As one manager noted, "The main difference between American clubs and Japanese clubs is that the Japanese clubs are set up more for entertainment, that is, not so much emphasis on health and hardcore fitness. We try to create a full lifestyle or way of entertainment with seasonal themes, such as summer dances and winter ski activities. We also sponsor a lot of beer parties and provide ice cream and beer in the club. It is about enjoying oneself."

As Park points out in her review of the recent literature on health, fitness, exercise, and sport, " 'Health' and 'fitness' are by no means unambiguous terms" but must be considered products of a specific culture and history (1994:60). I show that definitions of health in Japan continue to be tied to independence, efficiency, and productivity, characteristics that were (and continue to be) necessary for sustained economic growth. But the contemporary definition of health is also inseparable from the notion of a balanced "modern lifestyle," which stresses equal doses of leisure and labor and is intrinsically tied to consumption practices. The concept "unhealthy," therefore, implies not only sickness, dependence, and a lack of stamina or strength, but, at the other end of the spectrum, a dangerously overworked lifestyle. To work out single-mindedly, without taking the time to enjoy a drink with friends or a relaxing cigarette, is considered unhealthy. In Japan, just as there is concern about becoming ill and dependent, there is also a wariness about being *kenko sugiru,* or too healthy.

Institutionalized Discipline:
Monastic and Militaristic Practices

Smoking cigarettes, sipping beer, and avoiding strenuous workouts at the fitness club as a way to avoid becoming "too healthy" may seem to be an oversimplification of the diversity of motives and experiences in the club. For in fact, this resistance to hard work in the club is quite remarkable not only in light of the ideological and historical emphasis placed on effort (*gambaru*) and endurance (*gaman suru*) but also in the face of the institutionalized structure of discipline at the club itself. Scholars of Japan have discussed how discipline, effort, and self-sacrifice are some of the central themes in ethnographies of Japanese corporate offices (e.g., Kondo 1990; Rohlen 1974), schools (e.g., Rohlen 1980, 1983), and even psychoanalytic therapies (Reynolds 1980). The rigorous mental and physical discipline required to achieve spiritual growth and a responsible relationship between the individual and society is referred to as *seishin kyouiku,* or spiritual training.

With its historical roots in Zen Buddhism and later manifested in military and apprenticeship training, discipline and composure of the spirit (*seishin; kokoro*), as well as cooperation and service to others, constitute the path to personal growth. Spiritual education, in its contemporary form, strives to build character through acts of emotional, mental, and physical hardship. The central characteristics of seishin training intersect with and diverge from Foucault's description of the micropolitics of control and an emphasis on detail and minutiae. Few scholars have made explicit the cross-cultural similarities and differences between the militaristic discipline tactics of Foucault and the monastic discipline of seishin kyouiku.

The Japanese fitness club, located at the intersection of Japanese and American philosophy and inspiration, presents a unique site in which to examine this enactment of emic and Foucauldian discipline. The emphasis on training the body while simultaneously training the spirit resonates with other monastic spaces in Japanese culture, such as the daily practices of Zen nuns (Arai 1999) and the psychoanalytic methods of Morita therapy (Reynolds 1980). Like the Zen nuns, the fitness club staff are encouraged to engage in self-reflection, respect for hierarchical order, and precision cleaning, although to strikingly different ends. For the nuns, the "rules of a monastery are designed to show nuns how to act like a Buddha in everyday life" and how "to retrain one's focus upon oneself" and learn to be selfless (Arai 1999: 85, 84). Cleaning the monastery, therefore, becomes a way to purify not only one's surroundings but also one's mind.[15]

Similarly, Rohlen has suggested that this Zen-derived notion of hardship is responsible for the extraordinary diligence required to attend *juku*, or private cram school, after a full day spent at elementary or secondary school (1980:217–218). Following the same principle, corporations require employees to attend hardship training courses, in which running barefoot on gravel and dousing oneself with icy water, with nary a complaint, is considered a sign of a strong character (Kondo 1990). Even women in the throes of labor are denied anesthesia and are discouraged from uttering any noise, as vocalizing pain would be regarded as weakness. As one woman explains, "If you can't put up with that kind of pain in labor you are not going to have the [strength] to be a good mother" (quoted in Jordan 1997:B5).

The physical management of bodies in the fitness club, then, is culturally familiar. Aerobics instructors, in particular, as company employees are held to an unrealistic ideal that is intended to shape them from the inside out. Bodies are measured, outfitted, and programmed not only to appear but also to move in particular ways. Fitness club members, on the other hand, as paying clients, although managed to a certain degree, have far more freedom to be undisciplined. In Chapter 2, I analyze the way the division of space in the fitness club along lines of private versus public, clean versus dirty, and male versus female orders and organizes the bodies in the club. At the same time, as I illustrate in Chapter 3, regular body measurements, uniforms, standardized movements, adherence to timetables, recorded confessions, and criticism of others characterize the fitness club and bear a resemblance not only to the creation of selfless disciples observed in other examples of seishin kyouiku but also to the militaristic production of "docile bodies" seen cross-culturally and historically in institutions such as prisons, hospitals, and schools (Foucault 1979; Goffman 1961).

It is the methodological training and control of fitness club employees from their appearance to their language to their demeanor that most clearly highlights the consequences of corporate discipline in the Japanese workplace and, more particularly, in the service industry. Evident in other company work spaces in both Japan and elsewhere, the control of employees in the name of productivity and efficiency is as commonplace in its ubiquity as it is striking in its thoroughness. Derivative of both monastic and militaristic tactics, the fitness clubs incorporate strains of both Japanese and Western philosophy. Weighing the relative significance of these two paradigms requires reflection on competing global influences and the relationship between sport and discipline in Japan and the United States.

The Relationship between Mind and Body: Cartesian Dualism and Mind-Body Synthesis

Scholars of Asian culture have analyzed the role that sport plays in the discipline and training of minds and bodies. Brownell (1995), in her work on the People's Republic of China, has brought Foucault's work to bear on the training of athletes' bodies as reflective of the state's desire to instill a sense of progress and high culture in the general population. Alter (1992) examines how the strict diet, exercise, and massage of North Indian wrestlers are used as a way to express moral, spiritual, and social discipline. In both cases, the synthesis between mind and body allows for the training of the mind to follow the training of the body. The drills, songs, slogans, and self-evaluation diaries required of Chinese athletes are designed to induce a nationalistic spirit, just as the thousands of jackknifing push-ups and deep knee bends demanded daily of Indian wrestlers aim to produce enlightenment, self-confidence, and strength of character.

The ability to simultaneously train the body and the mind is predicated on the notion of a mind-body synthesis. The few scholars who have addressed the cross-cultural implications of the relationship of mind and body propose that most Asian philosophies do not recognize a sharp distinction between mind and body (Becker 1995; Kasulis 1993a, 1993b; Yuasa 1987). Kasulis, for example, compares the relationship between mind and body in Japan to a marriage of love, in which the mind and body are interdependent and intertwined (1993b:305). Although the fusion of mind and body is evident in multiple institutional examples of seishin training, I am not entirely convinced that the rather unproblematic intertwined relationship between mind and body plays out quite as neatly in the fitness club.

Fitness clubs, perhaps more than any other institution in Japan, have both the economic incentive and the technological means to churn out physically, socially, and economically "fit" bodies to complement the interests of the state. One might expect that the corporations that take advantage of the hardship training courses I described above, which require company employees to endure cold water baths and marathons, would also purchase fitness club memberships for their employees to build stamina and teach discipline.[16] But the physical challenges of the hardship training courses are simply a means to an end. The idea is not that the company employees come out better runners, but that through physical exertion, they undergo spiritual or mental transformation. Fitness clubs, despite ritualistic similarities to Zen monasteries and psychoanalytic therapies, emphasize physical accomplishments for their own sake and fail to make explicit the link between disciplining the body and disciplining the spirit.

The fitness club presents a vexed space, where control over the body is subjected to contradictory and ambiguous forces. On the one hand, because aerobics is a product of the West, where the Cartesian alienation of body from self plays out in sport, one might expect to find that this dualistic relationship endures in the Japanese context. But as I illustrate in Chapter 6's discussions of thinness and the social body, where identity and selfhood are tied up with relationships to a social network, this antagonistic relationship between mind and body is not consistently upheld in the club. At the same time, because the clubs do not take a strong position on the intertwined relationship between mind and body, their demands for effort and exertion ring hollow. While not explicitly suggesting the Cartesian-based separation of mind and body that characterizes the West, the clubs also do not reinforce conceptions of a mind-body synthesis that have been ascribed to Japan.

The Leisure of Labor: Consumer Display

Competition for leisure time is fierce and, in many ways, the fitness club serves as a serious contender. The prohibitive costs of housing in downtown Tokyo force many to live some distance away or in more conveniently located but tiny company apartments (*danchi*; Figure 4). Entertaining friends or colleagues at home is simply not a feasible option for most, and the service industry in late-capitalist Japan has accelerated to satisfy this tremendous need for outside-the-home entertainment. The economic recession that began in the early 1990s, sparked by the bursting of the securities and real estate bubble, has eroded the resources and free time of many. But the prior period of affluence, which peaked in the

1980s, has left its mark on the habits and expectations of consumers, who now feel a sense of entitlement to material wealth and goods. Unlike the reckless spenders idealized in the 1980s, the potential fitness club member of the 1990s and the twenty-first century carefully weighs his or her options before making the substantial time and money investment in a club.

In an effort to counter the lure of downtown nightlife, most clubs sponsor parties, extend closing hours until midnight or even 3:00 A.M., offer special "midnight memberships" at reduced rates, and sell ice cream and beer in the lounge. In the late-night hours, many members are found swimming laps, riding exercise bikes, or, more often than not, relaxing in whirlpools and saunas. For members who do not want to disturb their neighbors with the noise of late-night showers, the fitness club offers amenities similar to that of a more luxurious public bathhouse (Takabe and Miura 2000).[17] One club even sponsored a Christmas party in conjunction with a local disco, attracting nearly five hundred people (Kotani 1998:10).

Unlike clubs in the United States, Japanese health clubs emphasize relaxation, stretching, and massage, offering courses such as visual relaxation (complete with aromatherapy and a vibrating floor), yoga, and Taichi. In the last ten minutes of a typical aerobics class, the instructor massages the feet, calves, and even buttocks of the members as they relax (Figure 5). As one instructor explained, "Because the fitness population in Japan is only about 2 percent and fitness consciousness is low when compared to the United States, we need to sponsor special events, parties, and trips to bring people into the club and to make fitness fun. All of the trips are sport-based, such as scuba diving, snowboarding, or marathons. Of course, members can also enjoy shopping and eating, but the main purpose is sport."

But despite efforts to emphasize entertainment, fitness clubs, unlike many other leisure activities, are about exercise, moving the body, and athleticism. Working out is work. As one staunch non–fitness club member aptly put it, "Why should I pay someone to make me tired?" Although the clientele is self-selective, limited to members with a desire to move their bodies, many of the members dislike the very difficult and intense cardiovascular workout. As I note elsewhere the U.S. idea of "going for the burn" or working out to the point of exhaustion (or even pain) simply does not appeal to most Japanese fitness club goers (see Ginsberg 2000).[18]

4. A crowded yet conveniently located company apartment building in Tokyo.

5. An aerobics instructor gives a postworkout foot massage to the members.

As an instructor in Japan responsible for teaching classes and demonstrating exercises to members, one of the first things I noticed was the initial negative reaction of a member when faced with a difficult exercise or class. Often, the tendency was to say "I can't" rather than "I can." All of the instructors frequently had to coax healthy men and women to "just try" a beginner aerobics class or a heavier set of weights, as many seemed hesitant to try anything new, wary of overexerting themselves and embarrassed to look awkward or uncoordinated. Surveys compiled by both clubs indicate that the majority of members have had little previous experience with exercising at a fitness club and many have not exercised in any capacity since club sports in junior high school.

A large percentage of club members at the downtown clubs are office ladies and sarariiman, who sit at a desk or in front of a computer screen all day and confess to opting for the escalator rather than the stairs. Many complain about "not having enough time to exercise" (*undou busoku*) and spend most of their precious free time lounging in front of the television or eating and drinking with friends. With the sedentary lifestyle on the rise and a general lack of experience in sports and physical activity, many members come to the club having never held a dumbbell before. Most are extremely wary about trying anything new, and the staff (consequently or causally) tends to coddle the members by suggesting lower weights and not challenging them to push themselves. Even the most popular clubs like Downtown Fitness are teeming with half-hearted and low-commitment members. Although the general Japanese population statistically has a relatively low fitness consciousness when compared to that of the United States, it is the young women who are particularly criticized for their lack of commitment to exercise.

Power and Beauty:
The Intersection of Patriarchy and Consumerism

A large number of men in the clubs, members and managers alike, went out of their way to explain the "problem with the typical Japanese young woman" and her reluctance to exert herself. One 30-year-old male member, like so many of his fellow male members, commented derisively, "My opinion is that young women go to the fitness clubs for a fad. They have never done sports before, never participated in the tennis club or volleyball or anything in school, but decide to join a fitness club as a fad. They don't realize that it's hard work. At first they like the newness of it, they like to sweat, they think it's fun or they see a guy and say 'He's cool!' But then they decide that it's messy and hard work and a pain. They think, 'Why am I doing this?' and they quit after only a couple of months. . . . The people who continue for longer than a year are the serious ones. It's like when a new restaurant or club opens, tons of people go to check it out and then stop going soon after."

Certainly one must consider the source of the criticism and recognize the generalizations as stereotypical, patronizing, and misogynistic. During my first few months of research I was given countless male interpretations of the "problem" with Japanese women and their bodies, and it was only after several months of my constant presence in the gym that the women began to approach me as well. At the same time, the male perspective on the female body should not be dismissed out of hand, for it sheds light on how the single, independent female is constructed in Japan.

With a disposable income and untethered to children and a husband, the unmarried young woman has the freedom to sample a variety of activities. After the rigors and restricted freedom of high school, a female graduate who does not immediately marry has one of two choices: either to pursue a higher degree at one of the comparatively lax and undemanding universities and junior colleges or to gain financial independence by working for the first time. For women, both scenarios represent a small period of freedom between the demands of high school and the responsibilities of marriage and children. During this five- to ten-year window, most women take advantage (but often with no other choice) of living rent-free at home while also earning a salary, and then spend their entire paycheck on the latest trends, purchasing designer bags and clothing, traveling internationally, dining out, or taking up a new hobby, such as snowboarding, English lessons, or aerobics classes.

Single working women have the tendency to spend more money on leisure, recreation, and travel than do men at the same stage of life (Horioka 1993:288). The Hakuhoudou Institute of Life and Living has labeled these women, with their increasing desire and means to consume, the VIPs, which stands for variety, venture, independent, instant, pleasure, and peace (Skov and Moeran 1995:36). The young women recognize the imminent responsibilities of marriage and motherhood and want to make the most of their freedom now, dabbling in a variety of activities. Criticism of their so-called flightiness or noncommittal nature may be a commentary on or backlash against their newfound financial and social independence (see Chernin 1981; Wolf 1991; Faludi 1991). In fact, White indicates that some consider these young women "short-term feminists. . . . They live independently, self-sufficiently, take on lovers, and have relationships based on equality" (quoted in 1992:71).

Since the aerobics boom of the mid-1980s, aerobics has been the passion and pastime of young women who, because of increased economic and social independence, have become primary contributors to consumer spending in contemporary Japan. As Skov and Moeran explain, "Women have been, and still are, key figures in Japan's consumer culture—not only because they are their country's greatest spenders, but also because they form a group which has been most carefully observed, analysed and defined in marketing discourses" (1995:3). The linking of women and consumption intensified in the 1980s, when the number of women entering the workforce increased dramatically. Despite evidence that women have been participants in the labor market since before the turn of the century (see Tsurumi 1984, 1990), women began to take a more visible position in the labor force during the postwar era of high-speed economic growth.

But as Skov and Moeran explain, women's labor was and continues to be characterized as "an extension of the domestic role," and the fruits of this labor are minimized as pin money, "determined by a desire for personal development, self-fulfillment, and pleasant ways to spend their days" (1995:27). Women's work is often (mis)constructed as a leisurely choice, in effect another form of consumption, rather than a financial necessity. Skov and Moeran emphasize, however, and I agree, that work and consumption practices are mutually determinant, for "it is the decision-making power of their own salaries which is the main factor allowing women and marketers to create space for individualized consumption" (27). The import and subsequent popularity of aerobics and fitness clubs coincided with the height of the bubble economy, the growth of the service sector, and the emergence of the female-oriented and female-driven consumer culture in the 1980s.

I explore the links between consumption and the popularization of aerobics as it is experienced through and projected on the female body. Even as women gain more economic independence and buying power, they continue to be subjected to the impenetrable glass ceilings that characterize the corporate workplace and the increasingly limited standards of beauty that revolve around thinness, good proportions, and youth. As low-level employees in Japan's hierarchical service industry, young female aerobics instructors cast themselves in socially familiar roles as mother figures, daughters, or coquettes as a way to disguise their knowledge and authority regarding health and fitness. Sandwiched between the demands of an older and wealthier clientele and a cadre of male managers, the instructors learn that to effectively coach the members, they must conform to the deferential feminine stereotype. As I explore in Chapter 4, despite this onstage acquiescence, many of the instructors, when off-duty, co-opt the traditionally masculine vices of smoking and drinking as a way to subvert or at least blur gender biases in the workplace.

Similarly, dieting and food refusal become alternative ways for young women to manipulate stereotypes of femininity that revolve around the selfless care of others and an overt concern with appearance. In Chapter 5, I explore the damaging ideals of female beauty in Japan that equate beauty with subservience, complicity, and social and intellectual inferiority, paying particular attention to the social and economic implications for the status and power of women in contemporary Japan. Although refusing to eat can be read as conformity to a feminine ideal that revolves around skinniness and selflessness, dieting also can be interpreted as a way to express dissatisfaction with familial dependence and societal expectations of women. By rejecting their mother's cooking or refusing to eat at all, young women use the medium of the body to simultaneously declare their independence from their family, postpone the caregiving role associated with adult women, and alienate themselves from a larger social network.

The fitness club serves as a contradictory space where effort and leisure and beauty and health prove to be incompatible. In an attempt to contribute to the extensive body of literature that theorizes the body, I have chosen to ground my analysis in the specific reasons Japanese women choose and, more important, choose not to work out. I turn now to an ethnographic account of the ideology and practices of the Japanese fitness center that will illuminate the contradictory debates over the relationship between mind and body, discipline and leisure, empowerment and constraint, and masculinity and femininity in contemporary Japan.

The History of Aerobics in Japan

The Sexy American Import

Aerobics is American. Although Japan has trailed by a mere two to three years, the United States is, without a doubt, the original source of aerobic dance and fitness clubs and the continued inspiration for new trends and techniques. And it is this Americanness, which has been emphasized and exaggerated by Japanese and Westerners alike, that must be understood and deconstructed as "fitness" products and concepts are introduced, interpreted, and altered in the Japanese context. How has the fate of aerobics differed from or been similar to that of other Western sport imports in the twentieth century? How has the shift from the militarization of the body to the consumption of the body through sporting styles created a niche for Japanese fitness clubs in the late twentieth century? Finally, what does the import of aerobics and the definition of health and beauty tell us about Japan's identity as a nation vis-à-vis the United States?

1

To understand the role that aerobics plays in contemporary Japan, I begin by historicizing the myriad roles that sport—specifically, Western sport—has played in Japan since the early 1900s. Anthropological studies of sport in Japan are becoming increasingly popular, as evidenced by the several edited volumes released in the past three to five years (e.g., Linhart and Fruhstuck, 1998; Treat, 1996: Wagner, 1989) and the recent comprehensive analysis of Japanese sport by Guttmann and Thompson (2001). The sociology of sport in Japan is fairly well developed (see, e.g., Kyozu 1967), although the studies produced tend to focus on quantitative and empirical analyses of sport participation and sports facilities, with a financial or business-minded audience in mind (e.g., Hata and Umezawa 1995; Oga 1998; Oga and Kimura 1993). Not surprisingly, those published ethnographic accounts of sport in Japan tend to revolve around male-dominated sports such as baseball and Sumo. It is not that women have not or do not compete in sports, as the women's volleyball team who took home the gold in the 1964 Tokyo Olympics indicates, but rather that, even today, there has been little written on female participation in sport in Japan.

In this chapter, I illustrate that the enthusiastic import of aerobics and fitness clubs in the 1980s was paved by cultural assumptions about sexualized femininity, conceptions of "American" popular culture, demands for leisure time and space, and consumption practices that uniquely characterize contemporary Japan. The liberated sexuality symbolized in the leotard and choreography, the Western flavor of the clubs, the layout of the club as a hygienic and enclosed space, the financial resources required not only to sustain a club membership but to keep up with the equipment and clothing required, and the emphasis on exercise for exercise's sake are only a few of the qualities that distinguish aerobics from earlier styles of sport popularized in Japan.

As the latest import in a long history of popularized Western sports in Japan, such as baseball, golf, and professional wrestling, the American-ness of aerobics has been exaggerated and capitalized on. But I assert that in the fitness club, this exaggeration, in addition to reifying cross-cultural difference, serves to highlight local inconsistencies and discrepancies over definitions of body, health, and beauty. Whereas the consumption of foreign sport in Japan and elsewhere often has been used as a way to simultaneously imitate and best the competition, the Western flavor of the fitness club serves as a backdrop against which ideological debates between Japan and the West *and* within Japan play out. I also focus on the way the relatively brief history of aerobics in Japan was made possible by a national (indeed global) transformation in sporting metaphors, from an approach that connected athletic performance to militaristic tactics and patriotism to an emphasis that linked sport to conspicuous consumption, lifestyle choices, and beauty. Finally, I argue that the fitness craze, when considered historically against the reception of other women's sports in Japan, does indicate some strides toward the empowerment of female athletes and the demasculinization of sport in Japan, but that these advances are undercut by the continued sexualization and marginalization of women's sports.

Foreign Sport in Japan in the Twentieth Century

Scholarly and popular characterizations of sport in Japan typically divide individual sports into two opposing categories: traditional versus modern, Japanese versus foreign, and domestic versus international. Sumo, judo, karate, and the like are classified as homegrown Japanese sports, whereas baseball, soccer, and, most recently, aerobics are acknowledged to be foreign imports. In the case of Japan, to speak of a homegrown sport is to speak not only of origins but also of an ascribed national character. Sumo and judo did not simply originate in Japan: these sports are thought to embody an essence of Japan, in which stereotypes of "the Japanese"—as disciplined, passive, and cooperative—are associated with the sports themselves.

As Kelly synthesizes, "For reasons both domestic and international, the national stereotyping of 'sporting styles' is a pervasive and powerful rhetoric for reifying intersocietal differences (hence, the talk about U.S. baseball, Dominican baseball, Japanese baseball, etc.) while masking intrasocietal differences of gender, class, ethnicity, and region" (1998:108). Sport becomes a way to exaggerate domestic solidarity in the face of international antagonism and competition. At the same time, Guttmann and Thompson (2001) remind us that tradition is often reinvented as a means to reassert a threatened national identity in the face of Westernization. The fate of foreign sports in Japan offers a window onto the politics of globalization, tensions between patriotism and internationalism, and notions of the self vis-à-vis the other.

Although sport more generally has served as an arena in which international powers jockey for dominance, the reception of American sports in Japan, in particular, provides one of the most cogent examples for understanding the negotiation of international power and position. Professional wrestling, for example, illustrates how competition on the field or in the ring becomes symbolic of competition at the national level. Rikidouzan, the professional wrestler who popularized the sport in Japan in the 1950s and 1960s, was celebrated as a Japanese man who was able to hold his own against the mighty Americans. The years of humiliation in which Japan had been defeated, occupied, and finally democratized by the United States culminated in a triumphant series of battles in the wrestling ring. Rikidouzan, through his ingenious wrestling moves (most notably the deadly "Japanese karate chop") was able to level the playing field and restore national pride to the Japanese people (Igarashi 2000:122–129; A. Thompson 1986).

In much the same way, the avid consumption of baseball in Japan has led more than one sports commentator to remark that baseball "is more the national sport of Japan than it is of America" (quoted in Guttmann and Thompson 2001). Kelly (1998) has examined how baseball serves to level class, gender, and ethnic differences by uniting a potentially diversified team of players against a common opponent. There is no question that sports had served as a metaphor for enacting international tensions over land, power, and cultural domination. Does aerobics play into this debate, and where is the line drawn between imitation as the passive result of cultural imperialism and imitation as a form of agentive co-optation?

Domesticating the West?

The history of aerobics and fitness clubs in Japan and the United States is nearly parallel; the late 1970s and early 1980s roughly mark the starting point in both countries. Nonetheless, many have simply dismissed Japan's role as an equal participant and innovator in the fitness and aerobics boom. The characterization of Japanese popular culture as mere imitation of U.S. culture relies on a strict separation of the West and Japan, foreign and local, self and other. Imitation, or mimesis, suggests powerlessness and the dependency of the other on dominant discourse (see Taussig 1993). From this imperialist perspective, Japanese fitness clubs are evaluated on the basis of their success or failure in approximating the U.S. ideal. Is aerobics in Japan authentic? Scholars in cultural studies have criticized such questions, which rely on the strict dichotomization of Japan and the West, as essentialist, Orientalist, and increasingly inaccurate (Said 1993; Chow 1993; Rosaldo 1989).

In a postmodern and postcolonial context, where strict borders between countries are increasingly undefined and the flow of information traverses national boundaries, the original or self is no longer distinct from the imitation or other. Rather, self and other, or, in this case, the United States and Japan, are interdependent and defined in relation to one another. Benjamin illustrates how the modern, mechanical duplication of artwork has accelerated to such a degree that conceiving of the "original" is no longer relevant (1969:217–251). Rather than asking if aerobics in Japan is authentic, the question becomes: How can one give voice to cultural difference without dissolving into essentialist dichotomies or cultural relativism? Chow echoes this concern in her discussion of the inauthentic "native": "We are left with the question of how cultural difference can be imagined without being collapsed into the neutrality of a globalist technocracy (as the possibilities of mechanical reproduction imply) and without being frozen into the lifeless 'image' of the other" (1993:48).

The collection edited by Joseph Tobin entitled *Re-made in Japan* has been readily accepted as a useful way to conceptualize the interdependent process of cultural export and import in Japan. In his introduction, Tobin explains the analytical framework for the collection of essays: "I have chosen the word *domestication* as the central theme of this introduction to indicate a process that is active (unlike westernization, modernization, or postmodernism), morally neutral (unlike imitation or parasitism), and demystifying (there is nothing inherently strange, exotic, or uniquely Japanese going on here). *Domesticate* has a range of meanings including tame, civilize, naturalize, make familiar, bring into the home. This book argues that the Japanese are doing all of these things vis-à-vis the West" (1992a:4). In other words, the domestication of a foreign product, fashion, or phenomenon is the transformative process by which an import is made recognizably Japanese, while the lure of the foreign is still preserved (see, e.g., Creighton 1992). Is this notion of domestication useful for theorizing the way "American" fitness clubs and aerobics have been created and recreated in the Japanese context?

There is no doubt that the Americanness of fitness clubs and aerobics has been exploited, exaggerated, and even invented by management and members alike. Fitness club managers and aerobics instructors in Japan play up the "American" quality of aerobics and capitalize on the perceived delay of imported styles and products. The Americanness of aerobics and fitness in Japan is useful in luring curious new members into the club or lending credibility to a previously unknown form of exercise. Club managers play up the mystique surrounding American products and programs and purposely choose to stock their clubs with more expensive American-brand exercise bicycles, despite cheaper versions made in Taiwan. A well-known American name brand, such as Schwinn, is seen as important in marketing a certain image of fitness to the public as up-to-date, high-tech, and "cool." One manager chuckled over the fact that some clubs call Step Reebok classes *furidai*, the literal Japanese translation of "stepping bench." He claimed that "using Japanese in this context is ridiculous and outdated."

In addition, many Japanese claim that the United States serves as a test market for new products, machines, and techniques, enabling Japan to pick and choose from a variety of options. The aerobics director of Downtown Fitness explained, "As we are years behind America, we have the chance to look at the good things and the bad things. . . . After all, once you progress, you can't go backwards, right?" And, as I explained in the introduction, the fact that I was American was integral to my receiving permission to research in the fitness club. In fact, the very first clubs that opened in Japan played up the American flavor of aerobics and fitness by featuring instructors from Los Angeles and New York.

If we accept the theoretical model of domestication, a process that ultimately transforms an object, experience, or phenomenon into something that is more recognizably Japanese, the question becomes: What is Japanese? As I researched the Japanese fitness club in more detail, trying to understand emic conceptions of health, beauty, and the body, I was not surprised to discover that the more time I spent in the field, the more contradictions I observed. Local constructions of the mind-body experience, conceptions of discipline, and definitions of health were neither consistently Western nor wholly Japanese. As I demonstrate throughout this book, even in the relatively bounded space of the fitness club, I routinely observed practices such as the profound emphasis on thinness and the insistence on timetables and uniforms that reflected aspects of Japanese culture at the same time they were consistent with cultural institutions in the West.

Rather than examine the consumption of aerobics in Japan as yet another example of the way Western cultural imports have been domesticated and recreated in Japan, I choose to focus on the ideological tensions that not only polarize Japan and the United States but complicate emic conceptions of health, leisure, gender, and beauty. When we maintain that the fitness clubs are *either* American *or* Japanese (or even some combination of the two), we assume that American and Japanese cultures are consistent and uncontested belief systems that can be transposed onto an import. I assert that the myriad local Japanese cultural notions and assumptions often reveal more contradictions among one another than those observed between the imagined Japanese and Western monoliths. As this is a key theoretical point that is played out throughout the rest of the book, I do not go into the specifics here beyond asserting that conceptions of mind and body, discipline, and beauty are far more complicated than the theoretical model of a "Japanized" Western import leads us to believe. Although local contradictions and inconsistencies make it impossible to pin down precisely what is American and what is Japanese, this difficulty in no way prevents nations from creating imaginary national boundaries and a sense of patriotic solidarity through the use of sport.

The Militarization of Sport: Imagining Japan and the United States

To understand the reasons aerobics took off in Japan in the late twentieth century, we must first contextualize aerobics within the longer trajectory of sport and the construction of health and the body since the turn of the century. There is no question that the Japanese government used and continues to use sport and restrictions on the physical body as a way to create patriotism and a sense of nationhood. From the regulations on diet, institutionalization of the mentally and physically infirm, and nation-building calisthenics that characterized the 1930s and 1940s to the more recent projection of Japan as a clean and competitive nation through the display of Japanese athletes in the 1964 Tokyo Olympics, the physical body has served as an extension of the nation. In Igarashi's (2000) recent historical account of the transformation of bodily practices since the postwar period in Japan, he examines the role that sport and, more generally, bodily practices have played in the recasting of Japan's identity vis-à-vis the United States.

Igarashi (2000) asserts that during Japan's militaristic period in the early part of the twentieth century and most intently during World War II, the Japanese government recognized the potential of sport to mobilize the nation and began setting rigid standards of health and body fitness. With attempts to link physical fortitude to spiritual loyalty, calisthenics were used as a way to instill nationalist propaganda. Igarashi notes, "Toward the end of the Asia Pacific War, participants in a popular radio calisthenics show exercised to the jingoistic slogan, 'Bei-Ei-geki-metsu' (destroy, perish America and England)" (49). In this extreme example, the militaristic government played on Zen-based notions of the interrelationship between body and spirit, in which a nationalist spirit is encoded in the body through a repetition of form.

Sport became an expression of physical strength, national unity, and combative and competitive spirit. Frykman describes a similar radio program aired in Sweden at the beginning of World War II, which led listeners in a fifteen-minute gymnastics routine, designed "as one of the most successful means of synchronizing the many bodies of a diverse culture into a unified nation. By means of voluntary exercise people would be physically coordinated and by their own will subjugated to society" (1993:265).

In 1940, the passage of the National Physical Strength Law (Kokumin tairyoku hou) and the National Eugenic Law (Kokumin yuusei hou) exemplified the codification of bodily control at the state level. By setting strict standards on what was considered healthy and fit versus ill and unfit, the Japanese government advocated a particular vision for a nation at war that revolved around productive and reproductive bodies. Robertson has explored how the Ministry of Education advocated sports as part of the mandatory curriculum for girls schools during the 1930s—"as a means of forging healthy bodies, the rationale being that stronger females produced more and bigger babies" (1997:7).

We continue to see strains of this association between health and productivity in the late capitalist era, but recent constructions of a healthy and fit physique tend to revolve more around consumption practices than militaristic mobilization. As Japan moved further away from the sacrifices and losses of the war toward an era of high-speed economic growth, the body became a site on which to project images of progressive and competitive sophistication. Clean, efficient, and, above all, fit, the idealized Japanese body of the 1960s, 1970s, and 1980s reflected a vision of a new and progressive nation.

In an attempt to cleanse the sordid past of the war and to instill a new spirit of democracy, the American Occupation forces used scientific knowledge, medicine, and Western notions of health and illness to prescribe a new idealized body: hygienic, efficient, and committed to democracy and modernization. The diseased and starving bodies of World War II were nursed back to health with the aid of food supplies, vaccines, antibiotics, and the widespread spraying of DDT. But this aid carried with it the humiliation of defeat and the loss of a sense of national pride. Cast in the inferior role of the ill and infirm, Japan was dependent on the more advanced medical and scientific knowledge of the country that had defeated it in the war.

As Igarashi's (2000) book makes abundantly clear, the long-standing and complex relationship between the United States and Japan historically has played out on the physical body. Memories of the war and the push-pull relationship between competitors and allies become manifest in the arena of sports and body politics. To import a sport from the United States and then defeat them at their own games serves as a symbol of Japan's profile as a nation to be reckoned with. The consumption of aerobics in the past twenty years represents the latest stage in the long process of power negotiation between the United States and Japan enacted through notions of health, beauty, and fitness.

The Shift to Consumption:
The Aerobics Boom (1982–1985)

The consumption of leisure services is a relatively recent phenomenon in Japan's postwar history. The era of high-speed economic growth directly following the war (1955–1973) was characterized by tremendous booms in shipping, real estate, and wholesaling, as goods were produced, exported, and, ultimately, domestically consumed. After years of thriftiness and deprivation, the opportunity to purchase much-desired imports was welcomed by a majority of the population. The decades of consumer catch-up following the war centered around material consumption, as can be summed up by the mnemonic formulas described by Kelly in his discussion of technology and social change: "These have included the three Ss of the late 1950s and early 1960s: *senpuuki, sentakuuki,* and *suihanki* (fan, washing machine, and electric rice cooker); the three Cs of the late 1960s: *kaa, kuuraa,* and *karaa terebi* (car, air conditioner, and color TV); and of the three Js of the late 1970s: *juueru, jetto* and *juutaku* (jewels, jetting, and a house)" (1992:78–79).

As the Japanese population became sated with the material benefits of their newfound affluence, consumers of the 1980s began to direct spending away from product purchases toward lifestyle-enhancing investments. Havens explains that "consumer demands shifted from material and quantitative to personal, qualitative fulfillment: matchmaking and wedding agencies, home-delivery firms, golf club memberships, cultural activities, and travel" (1994:10). "Keeping up with the Suzukis" (and now the Joneses as well) began to take a different path, as the consumers of the 1980s longed to distinguish themselves from their neighbors, friends, and competitors abroad through various hobbies, travel, entertainment, and leisure experiences. If rural Japan in the 1980s continued to be characterized by a drive for materialism, as Kelly (1992) convincingly argues, Japanese urban consumers displayed a newfound shift away from product acquisition and conformity toward diverse individual experiences, best described by the three Ss cited by Havens (1994): study, sports, and social life.

Wealth and success in the 1980s meant more than owning the latest model car or wall-to-wall carpeting, and consumers began to crave more than material satisfaction. They were seeking personalized attention, service, and the buying and selling of lifestyles as allowed by late capitalism. The emergence of leisure services, activities, and spaces directly coincided with a national predilection toward spending increased time at home with one's family or devoted to personal development, a phenomenon dating back to the 1960s that was termed *mai-houmuism* (my-home-ism). Revolving around family and personal expression, leisure is not about taking "time out" but rather, as Havens (1994) asserts, incorporating family-oriented or self-indulgent activities into one's everyday life, as "time in."

The postwar "economic miracle" produced a normalizing vision of social standing, wealth, and leisure that assumed a base level of "middle-class" affluence for the entire Japanese population. The so-called New Middle Class ideology was derived from a skewed interpretation of the now well-known public opinion survey conducted annually by the Office of the Prime Minister. The results of the survey indicated that 90 percent of the population classified themselves as middle class, but, as Kelly (1993) illustrates, the details of individual lives give evidence to the falsity of this claim of undifferentiated equality. The state has benefited financially and politically from this ideal of a homogeneous population and therefore contributes to the perpetuation of a normalizing vision of class, entitlement, and consumption.

The gap between the ideal of middle-class entitlement and the reality of differentiated class-based resources plays out in the leisure industry, specifically in fitness clubs. The clubs are inherently selective, and although they have become less expensive in recent years, the cost is nevertheless prohibitive to a certain percentage of the population. For better or worse, television has had a tremendous influence in Japan, playing an important role in the dissemination of exercise to all age groups and all social classes. Ivy asserts, "Television, along with the older media of radio and newspapers, showed the consumers what they should be, what they should aspire to, what they should consume in order to confirm their middle-class status. . . . And television quickly became the primary means for the codification and dissemination of the conception of the middle class as a consumption category" (1993:247, 249).

Television, while marketing the standardizing vision of middle-class leisure and luxury, also made exercise affordable, available, and convenient for nearly everyone. From early-morning stretch programs to the latest Akino Yoko (*Perfect Body* 1995; *Back in Shape* 1994) or Claudia Schiffer exercise video, exercise could be integrated into the daily routine of anyone who owned a television. Home exercise videos and televised exercise programs expand the base market of potential fitness club members in Japan by exposing a larger audience to the benefits and enjoyment of engaging in a regular exercise program and by reinforcing the activities and teachings advocated by the fitness club instructor. The aerobics boom capitalized on this burgeoning awareness of leisure and exercise after years of hard work and economic catch-up.

With more vacation days, less overtime, and shorter work weeks, the Japanese consumer of the 1980s had not only the money to purchase a new lifestyle but, suddenly, the time to enjoy it. The Japanese government introduced a five-year economic plan in 1988 to reduce long working hours and increase leisure time and domestic spending. The Health, Labor, and Welfare Ministry proposed to reduce annual working hours from over 2,000 to 1,800 as a way "to guarantee creative free time, to enhance satisfaction in family life, to promote participation in the community, to guarantee health and creativity, and to create a workplace environment that is comfortable for the workers" (quoted in Harada 1994:280). One journalist sums up, "With the coming of affluence in the 1980s, the work ethic might be loosening its grip on modern Japan. At least some workers who once stayed late or ducked vacations now put as much energy into spending money as they do into earning it. The country famous for its workaholics now has a new class of free-spending leisure-holics, particularly among its well-educated young" (Aim 1989:LO1).

The youth of the late 1980s, who longed to distinguish themselves from their hard-working and self-sacrificing parents, were symptomatic of a more affluent and carefree Japan. Riding the crest of economic success, but perhaps cognizant of approaching global and domestic down-turning, many young people rejected the conventional responsibilities of prior generations. The Japanese media, renowned for classifying and even inventing new trends, breeds, and social illnesses, made much of the so-called irreverent and irresponsible youth, categorizing this new generation as *shinjinrui,* or the New Breed. Simultaneously villainizing and hyping and even creating images of the youth, the media played an essential role in the invention, sustainment, and dissemination of the "new breed." The shinjinrui, in a dramatized and criticized split with convention, alternated between working at well-paying part-time jobs for several months and subsequent weeks of partying, dining out, drinking, and shopping until the money ran out in a seemingly never-ending cycle (Allinson 1997:154). The young women, who opted for spending and socializing over the responsibilities of marriage, were tagged *oyaji gal, yenjoy* girl, or *anmarikun* ("unmarrieds") by the media (see Green-lees 1994).

The 1980s obsession with cute (*kawaii*) paraphernalia, style, and appearance was also characteristic of the noted rebellion against authority, tradition, and responsibility. As Kinsella explains, "Cute is anti-social; it idolizes the pre-social. By immersion in the pre-social world, otherwise known as childhood, cute fashion blithely ignores or outrightly contradicts values central to the organization of Japanese society and the maintenance of the work ethic. By acting childish, Japanese youth try to avoid the conservatives' moral demand that they exercise self-discipline (*enryou*) and responsibility (*sekinin*) and tolerate (*gaman*) severe conditions (*kuou, kudou*) while working hard (*doryoku*) in order to repay their obligation (*giri, on*) to society. Rather than working hard, cuties seem to just want to play and ignore the rest of society completely" (1995:251). Still another, perhaps more threatening rebellious youth group of the 1980s was the motorcycle-racing *bosozoku.* On noisy, souped-up motorcycles, these young men, sometimes accompanied by their female sidekicks, zoomed through city streets after midnight. With their flamboyant uniforms, tattoos, and hairstyles, the *boso* youth expressed their desire to stand out and be noticed (Sato 1991).

Rebellious, individualistic, and materialistic, the values of the younger generations of the 1980s were completely alien to the mores of their grandparents and parents, who sacrificed personal comfort and freedom for the sake of the nation during the hardships of war and the efforts of subsequent rebuilding. In postindustrial, late-capitalist Japan, consumerism began to replace production as a determinant of social status and self-worth. A person's tastes, clothing, and activities distinguish him or her from the masses while guaranteeing inclusion in a certain group. Lifestyle choice became increasingly important in determining self-identity and displaying status. In the particular context of late capitalism, assuming a healthy lifestyle became a way of "organizing and manipulating social identity" (Chaney 1996:101).

In the private and removed space of the fitness club, mountain resort, or movie theater, the service staff prioritizes relaxation, personal enjoyment, and self-indulgence, keeping pain, effort, and exertion to a minimum. The half-hearted fitness club members and their unwillingness to endure and persevere in the club are symptomatic of larger social changes that began to occur at the height of stable economic growth and the subsequent attention to consumption practices. As Skov and Moeran confirm, "Consumption came to be viewed in a positive light. Replacing a postwar version of the Neo-Confucianist attitude which saw primary social value in endurance, the smothering of personal desires, and hard work for the development of the Japanese economy as a whole, younger Japanese opted for a more relaxed outlook which permitted, accepted, and highly evaluated pleasure" (1995:31). This desire for pleasure, characteristic of the 1980s, may have manifested itself in disdain for exertion, even in exercise. Therefore, the fitness clubs created themselves as trendy sites of leisure, where young people could express individuality and fashion.

Fitness clubs found their niche by offering consumers a healthier lifestyle, a more balanced alternative to the media-hyped *karoshii* syndrome (working oneself to death). The clubs were particularly well-positioned to profit from the government's simultaneous push for greater leisure activities and an increasing concern over the perceived poor health of the population. Striving to secure their position as key competitors in the limited consumer market, many fitness clubs expanded the variety of programs offered, explicitly offering members a new "lifestyle." A pamphlet of Downtown Fitness illustrates this trend: "Our goal is to make your fitness life more comfortable. Not just for your figure, it is for your living. We believe Workout and Relaxing can help you to have most comfortable life [*sic*]."

In 1982, aerobics studios began to open in downtown Tokyo; before long, they could be found in the suburban and residential areas surrounding Tokyo and eventually all over Japan. Veteran instructors reminisce about the early days, when all of the classes were packed to capacity and reservations had to be taken by phone. Members would even line up at the front desk to wait for cancellations. Kyoko, a full-time staff and former aerobics instructor at a popular downtown club, mused about teaching in the mid-1980s:

> Ten years ago, most of the members had never been to a fitness club before. I remember that there was this instructor from America. He gave about ten lessons a week and all the *maniacs*[1] came to his class. At that time, they all wore colorful and showy outfits and dressed in the trendiest clothes. Each season, they would get new clothes, and you couldn't be seen wearing an outfit from last season. Animal prints were in, but now all you see are plain outfits. Ten years ago, the [Downtown Fitness] membership card was really cool, and it was really fashionable to be a member. [Downtown Fitness] was really a special place. Now there are many more fitness clubs, so it's not so special as it once was. Now it's more about doing fitness, moving the body, but before it was about fashion, not exercise. Now people come to [Downtown Fitness] to get thin, but before, you had to be thin before becoming a member!

In 1984, the first big fitness club chains began to open affordable and yet flashy clubs to satisfy the waves of younger members. The already established fitness clubs, which had opened five years earlier, tended to be more up-scale and catered to a wealthier and older clientele. These new chains, the first of their kind, promised lower entrance and monthly fees compared to their competitors. Furnished with extensive machine gyms, indoor/outdoor tennis courts, golf practice ranges, pools, and squash courts, the new chains became an instant success. The housing of both an aerobics studio and a machine gym in the same building at a manageable price proved to be innovative and lucrative. Members were attracted by the advertising campaigns promising workouts that were "Fun, Healthy, Affordable." Chains opened branches at breakneck speed, with some of the biggest chains opening a new club every month.

Boasting headlines about the newly opened sports clubs and the sweeping health mania, fitness magazines, modeled after exercise magazines in the United States, began publication in 1984 and were read by instructors, instructors-to-be, and aerobics enthusiasts. *Fitness Journal,* for example, contained articles entitled "I Love Aerobics" (1986: 2–3) and "Wise Women's Schemes and Places for Tea-time and Lunch-

6. These well-stocked boutiques are found in most fitness clubs.

time Fitness" (1989:10–11). Sporting goods stores began to open in 1985, and Reebok began selling athletic shoes and attire in Japan shortly thereafter. The fitness clubs continue to capitalize on this desire to consume by stocking boutiques of exercise clothing, shoes, and vitamins, with occasional sales to clean out inventory and jump-start business (Figure 6). During initiation at Downtown Fitness, new members receive 10 percent off all purchases made in the club boutique during their first three months. Coupons redeemable at local boutiques, hair salons, and restaurants can be picked up at the check-in counters of many clubs.[2]

While the larger chains were beginning to set down roots in downtown areas, regional and suburban towns and cities began to offer aerobics classes in local community centers. Although these classes, taught by former jazz dance instructors, differed in content and flavor from urban aerobics, aerobics fever was contagious. The former dance instructors were neither trained nor prepared to teach the high-impact, calisthenics-inspired exercise classes and could not compete with the aerobics instructors imported from the United States. Fitness club management recognized that they would have to begin training Japanese instructors to take over the classes, and the first aerobics instructor training schools were established a couple of years later.

In the late 1980s and early 1990s, luxurious fitness clubs designed to cater to a wealthier and older clientele began to be built in prime spots in downtown Tokyo. As land values skyrocketed, individuals and corporations rushed to take advantage of building opportunities. The bubble economy supported the construction of many high-end fitness clubs, and the number of clubs increased more than six times in a twelve-year period, from 246 in 1980 to 1,564 in 1992 (*Marketing Data of Leisure and Daily Life* 1995:120; Kawahara 1995:40). Following the collapse of the real estate bubble, many of the chains and individual studios found that they had overextended their operations and were forced to compete for a diminishing membership pool. The constant threat of bankruptcy compelled clubs to continue to update technology and to introduce new programs and added amenities. The latest statistics available suggest an estimate of nearly 1,800 clubs in operation in Japan today, as compared to a low of 187 in 1972 (CMN 2001).

The economic recession that began in the early 1990s marked the first time in fifteen years that the percentage of people with less leisure time than the year before outnumbered those with more (*Leisure White Papers* 1996:12). Nevertheless, a 1991 survey of 5,000 Japanese adults demonstrated that only 13 percent thought work was more important than leisure, a significant drop of 16 percent since 1989 (cited in Havens 1994:11). Logic would suggest that restricted finances inevitably led to a decreased attention to leisure, but several scholars propose that exerting control over the physical body through exercise and fitness can be constructed as a solution to restricted freedom in spending or loss of control on the job (Chapkis 1986:12). The power afforded by gaining control over an expanding waistline or unused muscles can help compensate for a shrinking wallet or the threat of downsizing. This relationship between the body and the economy is explored in the work of Mary Douglas (1966), who asserts that the central values, problems, and vulnerabilities of the social body are symbolically projected onto the physical body.

With an ever-increasing array of available recreational options, ranging from club-hopping to dining out, together with an ever-expanding desire to consume, the youth of the late 1980s did not remain loyal to the fitness clubs. The clubs continued to open branches, but they recognized that their programs needed inducements for membership to increase. Club staff discuss the so-called waves that characterize the fitness industry, which, one instructor explained, "change as often as the width of ties." Although high-impact aerobics continues to be the unequivocal favorite, aqua aerobics, cardio funk, muscle sculpting, and Step aerobics have begun appearing in more and more clubs. Most of the U.S. trends and exercise programs are brought over to Japan almost as soon as they appear. Even though (or perhaps because) all programs are imported with as little variation as possible, some catch on at a tremendous rate, becoming even more popular in the Japanese market than in the United States (funk and hip hop); others do not fare quite as well (Step aerobics and Spinning).

The fitness clubs present modern spaces where consumption practices and lifestyle choices are enacted and experienced through the body. Presenting an entirely new metaphor for sport, aerobics fits neatly into the shift toward modernity that has distinguished the late twentieth century. Modernity can be characterized by emergent consumerism, suburbanizaton, and globalization on the one hand and secularization, privatization, and anomie on the other. David Chaney (1996) asserts that in this context of simultaneous homogenization and isolation, discourse about lifestyles becomes a way to distinguish oneself from neighbors and peers while still maintaining affiliation with a common group. One's status may have been determined by work or occupation in the first half of the century; modern and particularly postmodern identity is predicated on patterns of consumption and leisure. Lifestyles are created and performed in the context of the development of mass leisure and entertainment. Shopping malls, amusement parks, and fitness clubs provide the stage, props, and scripted vocabulary for the performance of collective (yet individualized) identity and status. At the same time, these lifestyle choices, consumption habits, and patterns of leisure are displayed on the physical body, particularly the female body (see Turner 1996; D. Lowe 1995; Bordo 1993).

Sex Sells: The Marginalization of
Women's Sports in Japan

As mentioned earlier, aerobics was first introduced to Japan in the early 1980s, when it became an immediate national fad, attracting young women and men alike. Jazz dance and yoga were popular in the years prior to the introduction of aerobics, and the success of the women's volleyball team in the 1964 Tokyo Olympics encouraged women's active participation in sport and athletics. Touted as "the Witches of the East" (*Touyou no Majo*), players on the women's volleyball team were praised for the grit and determination that was needed to beat the Soviet team. Embodying qualities that defined success for postwar Japan, the female athletes demonstrated dedication and resilience. Although some critics felt that the women's coach, Daimatsu Hirofumi, was an overly cruel taskmaster who modeled practices on his experiences as a soldier in World War II, the majority of the public respected his drive and, more important, his impressive results (Guttmann and Thompson 2001:198).

Similarly, Hitomi Kinue, who excelled at track-and-field at the 1926 International Women's Games in Gothenburg and the 1928 Olympics in Amsterdam, and Hisano Eiko, who climbed to the top of Mount Everest in the 1970s, were two of the more well-known female athletes who garnered a certain limited degree of respect for professional women's sports (Guttmann and Thompson 2001:221). But, as Guttmann and Thompson illustrate, these isolated incidents unfortunately did not filter down to the average woman's experience in sport, which continues to be marginalized and restricted. Despite a marked gender gap in women's sport participation in the 1970s and 1980s, the situation is generally improving. Although the phenomenal success of aerobics in the 1980s was due in part to the gradual increase in support for women in sport during Japan's economic boom, this success has been hampered by the sexualization of aerobics both in the United States and Japan. In this section, I examine the early introduction and reception of aerobics in Japan to illustrate the historical underpinnings of the present denigration of aerobics as a sport.

Aerobics was single-handedly introduced to Japan by Kenneth Cooper, Ph.D., a name known to every aerobics instructor and serious aerobicizer in Japan and the United States. The author of the best-seller *Aerobics* (1968), which has been translated into thirty-nine languages and is in its forty-second printing, Cooper is credited with being the expert on and originator of aerobics theory. Since the Meiji era, individual "experts" have been called on to dispense advice, creating and hyping new trends with a foreign flavor.[3] As one upper-level manager at Chiba Club explained, "Cooper is like a god to the Japanese instructors. If he says something, everybody stops to listen carefully. He has had tremendous influence."

Cooper was initially invited by the Asahi newspaper to head the

Asahi Aerobics Seminar, which kicked off the aerobics boom in Japan. In a country where jazz dance and yoga dominated the fitness world, aerobics had yet to appear on the scene. Because both jazz dance and yoga require technique and skill that comes from years of training, many potential participants found them too difficult and too specialized. The timing was perfect for aerobics to enter the scene. The director of the first aerobics instructor training school in Japan explains: "Moving to the music was fun, it had a dance appearance, anyone could do it, and it made you healthy and pretty. So the big aerobics boom began" (quoted in Yamaoka 1996:14).

Kawahara notes that during the entire year of 1979, the words "aerobics" and "fitness" did not appear once in the popular women's magazine *an an*, but just three years later, the magazine began to run cover articles on the aerobics and fitness boom (1995:40). In an interview with *Fitness Journal* magazine, a representative from Asahi newspaper explains why Cooper was invited to Japan, a country where most people had never heard of aerobics: "The number one reason is that two years before, a recreation division was made in Asahi Shinbun Co. The recreation division was struggling with building up employee health and the existing methods were felt to be unsatisfactory, and then this aerobics theory was encountered. At this time, the jogging boom in Japan was heating up and people with knee problems were numerous. . . . It was not only Asahi that wanted to learn more about this remarkable theory, but many people did" (quoted in "Fitness Now and Then" 1991:8). After more than two decades of intensive labor, personal sacrifice, and a single-minded dedication to rapid economic growth in Japan, long working hours, little free time, and an overtaxed labor force continued to characterize Japanese corporations in the early 1980s. Management recognized that the mandatory morning stretches, instated immediately after the war, were both outdated and insufficient for improving employee health.

Nihon Housou Kyoukai (NHK) recently celebrated the forty-year anniversary of a nationally known, ten-minute stretching program entitled *Calisthenics*, which has aired twice daily since 1957. As a publicly owned radio and television broadcasting agency, NHK, much like the BBC in England, is independently operated yet has connections with the government in ways that the commercial agencies do not. Broadcast in the early morning and again in the afternoon, the program consists of four women who goose-step, pound their fists up and down their legs, and demonstrate a series of back and side stretches. Playing on the militaristic vision of sport that characterized the early part of the century, this style of exercise proved to be the inspiration for the mandatory early-morning stretches popular at most Japanese corporations. Despite cosmetic changes, such as updating the costumes of the women from the sleeveless shirts and shorts of the 1950s (which were scandalous in their time) to the tight Spandex leotards that became popular in the 1980s, the content of the program has remained little changed since its inception forty years ago (Matsuzaki 1997:18). Indeed, many of these stretches have been incorporated into the types of stretches taught at the fitness clubs.

The introduction of aerobics to Japan, spearheaded by the corporate initiative of Asahi newspaper to improve employee health and productivity was not initially directed exclusively at women. In fact, given that corporate Japan recognized the athletic benefits of aerobics, it is striking that the sport so quickly became sexualized and feminized. What was responsible for the shift in the reputation of aerobics, from being exalted as a serious and athletically demanding sport to being denigrated as an eroticized dance trend?

News coverage following the Asahi seminar and other lectures given by Cooper during that year relied on images of scantily clad women in leotards to attract the attention of the general public. Sexiness and beauty upstaged the physiological theory that had been the intended purpose of these guest lectures. As an official from the Institute of Health and Body Strength, which participated in organizing the Asahi Seminar, explains, "The seminar's main point was to make sure people understood aerobics theory, but after [the news coverage], only the dance part was emphasized, and unfortunately the basics of how people should do the exercise safely was missing. This theme still continues to remain unchanged even now" (quoted in Matsuzaki 1997:18).

In 1982, the year following Cooper's visit to Japan, a television program imported from the United States entitled *Aerobicize* was aired. This program set off the aerobics boom in Japan. The executive director of the Japan Aerobics Fitness Association (JAFA) explained the introduction of aerobics to Japan: "Aerobics in Japan was ignited because of a TV program. I don't know whether you have heard of it or not, but it was a U.S. program called *Aerobicize*. It was brought into Japan in 1981–1982 and was shown on late-night TV, from 11:20 P.M.

until 11:25, after pro baseball news. The program was shot by a professional photographer, I forget his name, but the portrayal was really, how should I say? . . . sexy. The women wore sexy leotards and the camera angles were sexy as well. Because of this portrayal, everyone was very surprised and everyone wanted to know what it was. Not just the men, but the women as well, and that was how the interest in aerobics got started."

Although the *Aerobicize* program aired for only five minutes nightly, those few minutes were enough to catch national interest. Backed by *Playboy* magazine and filmed by Ron Harris, a man who later became an entrepreneurial pornographer on the Internet, the show featured American women in high-cut leotards with bare legs who lunged and stretched, arching their backs and pursing their glossy lips. The outfitting of these women was especially provocative in the Japanese context, where bare legs, left uncovered by tights or biking shorts, was considered quite risqué. Even today, in the more suburban and rural fitness clubs, women wear flesh-colored tights under their biking shorts for modesty and to encourage weight loss and purification through excessive sweating. The camera angles dissected or, as Trevor Millum writes, "photographically cropped" (1975:83–84) the women into breasts, buttocks, and legs, zooming in for close-ups on a particular body part or coming in from below. Janice Winship explains, in her evaluation of advertising campaigns that rely on sexy photography, "Women are signified by their lips, legs, hair, eyes or hands, which stand metonymically — the bit for the whole — for in this case, the 'sexual' woman" (1987:25).

Intentionally and overtly provocative, *Aerobicize* became a hit virtually overnight. "Even though the appropriate explanation [for the program] came from aerobics theory, the next morning's news was: 'Blond Beautiful Women Spreading their Legs' or 'Sexy Foreign Women'" ("Fitness Now and Then" 1991:9). The program was extremely popular not only with men, who enjoyed the sexy style, but with women, who found the dance intriguing and the performers attractive. In particular, the high-cut and colorful leotards caught the eye of many female viewers. Two U.S. movies released in Japan in 1983 and 1984 had an enormous impact on the fitness world. *Flashdance* and *Heavenly Bodies* both featured female leads pursuing a dream of dancing and physical fitness and inspired many young women in both Japan and the United States to hit the gym. The sexy costumes and choreography typical of popular images of aerobics and dance in the 1980s attracted many young office ladies who wanted to sweat and work out just like the heroines in the movies.[4]

Although the United States was the original source of aerobics, once the exercise hit Japan, the Japanese media were responsible for the dissemination and, more important, the selection and exaggeration of certain aspects of aerobics. It is significant, although not surprising, that the sensationalism and sexiness of the television program rather than the medical theory and physiology of academic lectures catapulted aerobics into the national spotlight. The sexy image of aerobics continues to characterize participants, particularly aerobics instructors, and serves to undercut feminist gains that might have been made from the empowerment of sporting practices.

Women in Sport: Scholarly and Popular Neglect

The way aerobics has been sexualized and marginalized is symptomatic of how women's sports have been neglected in popular and scholarly discourse on sport and leisure (Vertinsky 1994a, 1994b). Historically, the conspicuous absence of literature on female participants in sport, the relative undercompensation of female athletes, and the accepted relegation of female athletes and spectators to ghettoized "feminine" sports, such as aerobics, gymnastics, figure skating, and synchronized swimming, has been rooted in narrow and sexist definitions of sport. Feminist scholars of the sociology and anthropology of sport have criticized the way women have been excluded from leisure and sport, either through explicit economic and temporal constraints and a lack of opportunity for women's leisure (e.g., Scraton 1994), or through leisure activities that reinforce gender inequality and structured power relations in society (e.g., Shaw 1994).

The first approach assumes that leisure, as a positive and desirable activity, has been denied to women because of a lack of opportunity or inadequate facilities, time, or funding (e.g., Shank 1986; Deem 1986). Marginalized and subordinated in other arenas of social life, women experience similar discrimination in sports and leisure. Furthermore, as Shaw points out, leisure research that focuses on conspicuous consumption—"the public world, the tourist gaze, hyper-realities of Disney World, theme parks, heritage"—neglects the private world of women's leisure (1994:259). Trips to the park, stretching to an exercise video, and an early morning swim at the local fitness club constitute equally important, albeit less immediately visible, realms of leisure.

The second feminist approach focuses on what Shaw terms "leisure as constraining" (1994:12), in which the leisure activities themselves reproduce unequal gender relations. Television, as perhaps the most pervasive example, prescribes and naturalizes "appropriate" gendered behavior, roles, and appearances (see Mankekar 1993; Kaplan 1987). At the same time, the types of sports deemed acceptable for women are those that emphasize aesthetics, physical attractiveness, and body shape—complementing rather than challenging current definitions of femininity (e.g., Lenskjy 1986; Scraton 1992; Brackenridge 1983). As I have illustrated, the athleticism of aerobics as a sport is downplayed in favor of the sexiness of aerobics as dance. Aerobics is considered outside the realm of the exclusively male preserve of sport, which requires a mastery of specialized skills that are exhibited in fierce competition and can be judged by external standards. Coakley proposes that most sports can be defined as activities that demonstrate "a physical display of skill, competitively directed toward an end, and containing an organized element of rules and structures" (quoted in Klein 1993:42). Aerobics is disregarded as feminine, sexually provocative, and "dance-y"—quite distinct from and inferior to the domain of male sport.

Definitions of sport that exclude aerobics, figure skating, and even bodybuilding (suggesting that there are "male" sports that are not considered masculine) are flawed both factually and ideologically. The notion that dance is somehow inferior to sport is contradicted in both Japan and the United States, where dance is analogous to high culture and therefore esteemed in its own right. More important, I challenge current characterizations of sport by proposing a more inclusive definition, which emphasizes athleticism over competition. Klein agrees that conventional definitions do not account for the uniqueness of bodybuilding: "As suspect as its past may be, bodybuilding has evolved into a unique activity that combines a variety of cultural forms into something that purists have difficulty categorizing. Bodybuilding can offer us an alternative to traditional athletic events by fusing physical development through training with artistic expression, eroticism, and spectacle" (1993:44). Aerobics offers a similar combination of athleticism, creativity, sensuality, and even competition.

But even if we accept this definition of sport as a rule-based and competitive display of skill, I assert that competition is indeed an integral part of aerobics in Japan. From the members who compete at amateur contests held in the local clubs to the professional athletes who participate in national and international competitions, the thrill of performance and the zeal to win attract many to compete. The training of athletes, the ranking of competitors, the national media coverage of the aerobics events, and even the success of Japanese international competitors complicate the relationship between the acceptance of aerobics as a sport and the denigration of aerobics as dance or merely a hobby.

Maniacs: Competition and the Sport of Aerobics

Starting in the mid-1980s and increasing by the early 1990s, national and international competitions were held in Japan in greater numbers, and aerobics was beginning to be defined as a sport. The "sexy dance" days of the early 1980s began to be replaced by a stronger, more positive athletic image. This de-linking of aerobics and dance had significant ideological repercussions in the way aerobics was funded, regarded, and consumed. As explained, the sexy aerobics of the 1980s had been excluded from conventional definitions of sport that centered on competition rather than athleticism. Since the early 1980s, the narrow definition of sport has not changed to include a broader range of athletic activities; rather, aerobics has had to conform.

The first national aerobics competition, the Dole Cup, was hosted in 1984 and over 1,500 participants from five prefectures competed. The CEO of the International Aerobics Association and director of the Dole Cup explained the mood surrounding this first competition in Japan: "Because it was at a time when aerobics was not considered to be a sport by anyone in the business world, the thinking of most people was that aerobics should not be competitive. In addition, because until then, there had been no individuals who had competed in any way, the participants didn't understand the criteria for evaluation, which also made it difficult. But if we peek under the lid, the participants were of all ages, from elementary school to over sixty-year-old housewives. It was the first time, but the mood was, 'no matter how, I will win,' or 'at least, I'll have fun,' or 'I will sweat a lot.' This type of open mind . . . has continued even now" (quoted in "Fitness Now and Then" 1991:13). Despite the neglect or disdain of popular opinion, aerobics competitions proved that the participants had the skill and the drive not only to perform but also to compete. Aerobics began to encroach on the masculine definition of sport.

Extensive media coverage of aerobics competitions stirred up an increased interest in fitness, exercise, and aerobics itself (Figure 7). One instructor credits the broadcast of the Suzuki Cup aerobics competition with being the catalyst for her decision to become an aerobics instructor: "I have done aerobics for seven years now, since I was 17. I remember that I first became interested in aerobics when I was in high school. I was watching the Suzuki Cup on TV and saw Nomura Kenju, who was chosen as world champion. Well, the TV made a mistake and printed that he had only been doing aerobics for three months, instead of three years. I was amazed—three months?! I thought if he can do it, I can do it too. I decided to become an instructor even before I became a member. It was lucky the TV made a mistake, you know? [laughs]."

Aerobics began to be regarded more seriously worldwide, and there was even talk of aerobics becoming an Olympic sport. The ideological split between aerobics as dance and aerobics as sport divided programs and members. Some preferred the fancy, jazz dance–inspired choreography; others suggested returning to the basics, with sculpting and fat-burning taking precedence over the more snazzy moves. This division still characterizes clubs, programs, and instructors. Many of the more devout aerobics enthusiasts prefer complicated dance choreography over simplified moves, stressing that advanced participants must be able to execute routines with coordination and dance technique as well as with stamina and overall athleticism.

Anxious to distinguish themselves from the typical fitness club member who is reluctant to exert herself and to challenge mainstream reservations about the athleticism required to excel at aerobics, the self-identified exercise enthusiasts are quick to point out the dedication and skill required. Working at two clubs six days a week, I soon began to recognize a core of members who came almost daily, sometimes exercising for three to four hours at a stretch. Taking multiple aerobics classes in a row and winding up the workout with a jog on the treadmill, these women (and they were almost exclusively all women) clearly stood apart from the stereotype of the "fair weather" member described in the introduction.

Although they were few in number, the sheer amount of time they spent in the club and their overall visibility, combined with their un-

7. Participants execute one of the mandatory jumps in the 1996 Suzuki Japan Cup aerobics competition.

8. An amateur aerobics competition held at a local fitness club.

rivaled enthusiasm and skill, made these members some of the most easily recognizable. These exercise enthusiasts referred to themselves and were labeled by fitness journals and club staff, as *freaks* or *maniacs* (in katakana). As a small percentage of the total membership, the maniacs, swathed in sweat shirts and even Saran wrap to produce excessive sweating and lose pounds, could be considered compulsive exercisers for their single-minded quest for weight loss. But, for the most part, the maniacs were truly addicted to aerobics, demonstrating repeatedly their great love for the sport. Some even chose to compete in amateur aerobics competitions held at local fitness clubs (Figure 8).

Evident from the grins on their faces, the ease with which they executed the complicated routines, and their uninhibited tendency to stand front and center in the studio, the aerobics freaks were, in the words of one, "a fool [*baka*] for aerobics." Some of the women expressed a desire to apply their enthusiasm toward a future career as an instructor, taking advantage of the basic skills training course offered by Downtown Fitness as the first step for future instructors. Others expressed a life-long love of dance or explained that they simply enjoyed sweating and the pure physicality of exercise that "clears the mind." One aerobics devotee, who wistfully watched an intense aerobics class from the sidelines, commented, "I usually take advanced classes, but since I have been sick recently, I didn't have the strength to take the class. I'm so jealous because all my friends are taking it and I want to do it! Before I got sick, I was coming to the club every day, and even now, I still try to come every day. I took a beginner class earlier, but it wasn't as much fun. It was boring, so it was more tiring for my mind. In the advanced classes, the running makes you tired, but it's more fun. At first, I joined the club to lose weight and improve my health, but now I think aerobics is really fun. I can't wait to be able to do the advanced class again."

For the office ladies, whose tedious job responsibilities often "tire the mind," exercise is a welcome physical and mental release from the sedentary and mind-dulling office grind. To be able to shed the office uniform and don a sexy leotard and sweat out the stress and frustration experienced at work is liberating and, in the case of the aerobics maniacs, addictive. As evidenced by the exercise enthusiasts and the increasing number of aerobics competitions, the reputation of aerobics as frivolous, sexy, and trendy may be changing, but, for the time being, it has been unable to completely shed associations with its early history. I return to this tension over empowerment versus conformity in Chapter 3, when I examine the leotard and its meta-messages for sexuality and discipline.

Conclusions

I have situated the recent aerobics boom in the historical context of changes in sporting metaphors, participation, and status in Japan. The popularity of aerobics in the past twenty years gives us insight into processes of globalization, militarization, consumption, and feminism. The rapid and widespread popularity of aerobics in the 1980s was made possible by a confluence of historical transformations, in which constructions of sport shifted from expressions of patriotism and national solidarity to those of individuality and lifestyle directed particularly onto the female body. Seeing how sport has been interpreted, transformed, and manipulated in the past gives us insight into how sport is defined and experienced in the present.

I turn now to a discussion of the presentation and interpretation of these contemporary and contradictory ideologies of work and leisure, masculinity and femininity, and production and consumption within the walls of the fitness clubs themselves. In the next chapter, I explore the way the spatial layout of the Japanese fitness club reflects and organizes bodies according to cultural ideologies of leisure, gender, status, and hygiene. I argue that the architecture of the club is tied to power inequities that serve to regulate and manage bodies according to late-capitalist ideals of efficiency, productivity, and hygiene. I emphasize however, that these ideals often present certain contradictions when juxtaposed against long-standing cultural standards of effort, health, and beauty in Japan.

The Discipline of Space

Japanese fitness clubs, above all else, are constructed simulta- 2
neously as sites of discipline and spaces of luxury. The architectural layout reflects the club's dual emphasis and is inseparable
from larger cultural ideologies of leisure, gender, class, and hygiene.
These symbolic constructions map onto the architectural space of the
fitness club that, in turn, structures social relationships accordingly. As
Featherstone notes, changes in consumer habits and capitalist developments have been accompanied by changes in leisure spaces, "with much
greater opportunities for surveillance and display" (1991:173). In this
chapter, I illustrate[how disciplined bodies are created and contained
through the enclosure and exposure within space, the partitioning of
rooms, and the attention to cleanliness.]

By drawing on the work of Foucault (1979) and Eichberg (1998), I
show how the fitness club bears a structural resemblance to the panopticon, a space that organizes and is organized by relationships of discipline, surveillance, and normalization.[1] The panopticon, as described
by Foucault, is a prison tower designed "to induce in the inmate a state
of conscious and permanent visibility that assures the automatic functioning of power" (1979:201).[2] Power, then, is decentralized, dispersed,
and difficult to identify. The "inmates" are uncertain when and even if
they are being watched and, consequently, guard themselves.[3] Foucault
illustrates how architecture and power are interrelated and how "discipline proceeds from the distribution of individuals in space" (141). In
his discussion of docile bodies and the panopticon, Foucault outlines
the specific spatial techniques used to create decentralized power.

The organization of space in the Japanese fitness club is designed to be functional, compartmentalized, streamlined, and regulated. Eichberg likens the discipline of space in the modernist sports club to that of one-dimensional time (1998:151). He explains that space tends to be "panoptical, dominated by a straight line, monofunctional, divided into different lanes or zones, similar to a container or box of right angles, standardized, and expansive (domesticating outdoor activities)" (151). The clubs in Japan typically conform to these rational specifications. This style of architecture is well-suited to the late-capitalist ideological construction of bodies as efficient, productive, and managed. I apply Foucault's spatial categories of enclosure, compulsory visibility, and partitioning to illustrate how ideals of class, gender, leisure, and hygiene are constructed in the Japanese fitness club. The ways bodies are contained, displayed, and separated as well as the ways individuals organize and segregate themselves have direct consequences for social relationships and the distribution of power. Although the focus of this chapter is on the spatial ordering of the people within the club, subsequent chapters highlight the ways club members and staff contribute to the construction and, indeed, transformation of this structural organization.

Enclosed Space

In an essay entitled "The Enclosure of the Body," Eichberg (1998) explores the historical push-pull between advocates of exercise in enclosed spaces and those who recommend exercise outdoors ("Green Wave") as representative of timely perspectives on health, class, gender, and hygiene. He explains that enclosed exercise facilities flourished among twelfth-century knights and again among the European aristocracy in the seventeenth and eighteenth centuries as a way to exclude lower classes and children. These periods of strict control over space and the body alternated with the "Green Waves" in the early 1800s and 1900s. Calling for a return to nature and advocating the health benefits of exercise in open spaces, these reactionist movements were accompanied by a shift from indoor to outdoor swimming, the introduction of "grass sports," and an overall liberation in sports dress, particularly for women. Eichberg convincingly illustrates that the demarcation of an appropriate space for sport, either indoors in a rectangular gymnasium or outdoors in the elements, is far from "natural," but rather a product of historical and social construction.

What do we make of the move toward enclosed fitness clubs in Japan? Historically, all forms of body training have incorporated exercise outdoors as a means to teach the body to withstand cold, wind, and other forms of discomfort. Based on the premises of *seishin kyouiku*, or spiritual education, endurance (*gaman*) and effort (*doryoku*) are considered intrinsic to personal growth. Seishin kyouiku, which in direct translation means spiritual education, bears little resemblance to the notion of spiritual education offered in Sunday schools in the West. In Japan, the concept refers to the rigorous mental and physical discipline required to achieve spiritual growth and a responsible relationship between the individual and society. Rohlen (1996) has traced the historical transformations of seishin kyouiku from that taught through the tea ceremony and military training of the Tokugawa era to that co-opted by corporations and schools in the postwar period. In its contemporary form, spiritual education strives to build character through acts of emotional, mental, and physical hardship.

Institutions as diverse as martial arts studios, pyschotherapy clinics, and corporations have used endurance walks, meditation, and cold water baths as ways to socialize their students, patients, and employees to take responsibility for their own and others' actions, to cultivate loyalty and positive attitudes, and to generate strong spirits. Some preschools even encourage students to go barefoot or to wear only T-shirts in cold weather as a way to build character (Peak 1991:19, 35). Peak explains: "Japanese folk theories of health hold that developing resistance to the cold and stimulating the skin by contact with the natural elements develops resistance to disease and strength of character" (19). It makes sense that the fitness club, an institution dedicated to training bodies, would also exploit the outdoors to build character, stamina, and discipline.

But, despite the so-called jogging boom in Japan in the 1980s, exercise outdoors—not in the interest of spiritual enlightenment but merely for the sake of fitness—has not caught on as a national pastime. The pollution, crowded streets, and general aversion to sweating in public make jogging on a treadmill, as tedious as it sounds, all the more appealing. One female instructor, who worked at the club in Chiba, tried to explain why running is so unpopular in Japan:

In America, fitness awareness and running outdoors came first, while fitness clubs came later. In Japan, it was just the opposite. You never see someone our age running outside, only high school students in clubs or older people walking early in the morning. If someone our age was running, everyone would stare at them strangely. In all the American movies, you see the stars running. Like what's her name, Stone, Sharon Stone going for a 10-kilometer run before work. The Japanese feel that exercise equals pain [kurushii], and therefore they don't want to do it. A lot of the members say that they hate exercise when they first join, because they have never done it before, because it's so painful. . . . Once they enter the club, they realize that it is fun.

With tanning beds, air conditioning, artificial lighting, and indoor driving ranges, pools, and tennis courts, these windowless clubs eliminate all evidence of nature and the outdoors. The clubs even include restaurants, beauty salons, and retail shops, which do away with any need to venture outdoors during an extended stay. Despite this structural elimination of nature, the advertising campaigns of several health club chains rely on a sporty, healthy, outdoors image.[4] An analysis of the advertising campaign of a popular fitness club chain run during the second half of 1996 and the beginning of 1997 illustrates this profound contradiction between the enclosed architecture and the outdoorsy image.

Japanese advertising aims to create a mood and sell a fantasy rather than market the particular merits of an individual product (Creighton 1995:139). Creighton explains that Japanese cultural values that emphasize humility and cooperation play out in the advertising world, where overt competition and unabashed boasting must be avoided even when selling a product. Instead, advertising companies strive to create a mood or image, and this particular campaign creates a wholesome and sporty feeling. The advertising poster is divided into four panels and the same Japanese male model is featured in each photograph, engaged in three different sports (see Figure 9). The model featured is a tarento (star) who was popular in the mid-1980s but in recent years has become somewhat of a "has-been." By using a television star who was popular almost a decade ago, this club deliberately pitches the campaign to an older age group. The matching of product to persona is a tactic employed by Japanese advertising agencies as a means to project a certain image or to assign the product to a certain segment of the population. In The Japanese Market Culture, Fields explains that "the use of a per-

9. This 1997 advertising campaign emphasizes the beauty of the outdoors delivered in the sterility of the fitness club.

sonality in Japanese advertising is often the means to clearly identify a product in a social structure. A product which is purchased for social reasons, therefore, tends to use personalities heavily. . . . In this structured society, where one's status within it is fairly well-defined, the use of a personal stereotype is the quickest way to communicate which product one is 'expected' to consume" (1989:32–33).

One of the staff members at the club concurred: "Do you know [name of model] on the poster ad? Well, about eight years ago, when I was in high school, he was a very famous model, sort of like the star of SMAP,[5] you know? But now, [he] is not so popular anymore. If he were still as popular now as he was eight years ago, the posters in the train station would probably have been ripped down by fans. This just shows that [the club] is not trying to target a young audience, because they really don't care about [the model] at all. [This club's] image is more for older people, age 20 and older." Although no longer the sensation he once was, the model is nonetheless dimpled, tanned, and attractive. His clean-cut good looks are appealing but also approachable. Significantly, he is Japanese, so, in contrast to the foreign models used in the ads of other clubs, he is someone with whom a potential member can identify. Because of this tarento's current "has-been" status, the member admires him yet is not made to feel inferior.

The four photographs depict the variety of activities available at this particular club: squash, basketball, and most important, swimming in the refreshing and spacious pool, which is a primary attraction of this fitness club chain. The posters are done in bright blues and crisp whites, conjuring up feelings of nature and purity. Reading the poster from left to right, the first image features a close-up of the model in the pool. Emerging from the pool, he is young, tan, and smiling. The turquoise water ripples behind him and beads on his shoulders and hair. He looks relaxed, happy, and refreshed. In the next frame, he stands, squash racquet in hand, against the stark white walls of the court. Dressed in crisp black and white, he is tensed for a competitive game of squash. In the third photograph, the model is back in the pool, but this time, he is arching playfully backwards with mouth open and the printed words above his head: "It feels good in your body." The fourth and final frame depicts the model dribbling a basketball on the shiny, varnished court. Along the bottom of the four panels reads the caption: "You will change. Everyday, you will change." The photographs alternate between images of relaxation and those of competitive sportiness. The club projects an image of athleticism and good health, promising the engaging intensity of sports coupled with the ample opportunity to unwind. Radner observes a similar juxtaposition of relaxation and discipline in the Jane Fonda workout video: "Thus, the workout gives its practitioner a carefully orchestrated balance of constraint and release, of pain and pleasure—which Fonda calls 'your pleasure in your own discipline'" (1995:156). Relying on facilities over flash, sport over body image, and process over result, these advertisements center on photographs of the gym itself and on the types of activities available.

Because the clubs seal off sport from the outdoors, they promise the charm and associated good health of exercising in nature without the dirt, insects, crowds, and inclement weather of the outdoors. Given this desire for outside pleasures delivered in the sterility of inside spaces, it is not surprising that indoor golf simulators, pools, and tanning beds are becoming increasingly popular with the fitness club crowd. Wrapped in private, sterile, and elite packaging, the fitness clubs distinctly exploit the Japanese public's late-capitalist desire for catered service, quality leisure, improved health, and beauty and body perfection.

Exposed Space

Like the panopticon, supervision and surveillance are incorporated into the layout of the club. For members, looking fit is just as important as feeling fit, and Japanese fitness clubs are designed to encourage looking. Foucault explains: "In discipline, it is the subjects who have to be seen. Their visibility assures the hold of the power that is exercised over them. It is the fact of being constantly seen, of being able always to be seen, that maintains the disciplined individual in his subjection" (1979:187). Although most Japanese clubs are completely windowless, and some even subterranean, the placement of glass and mirrors throughout the gym, lined with comfortable benches or exercise equipment, invites self-monitoring and the scrutiny of others. Windows and glass also visually open up the narrow spaces in the downtown clubs, where expensive real estate makes space a premium. In fact, many of the clubs build up rather than out to take advantage of the narrow corridors of real estate available. Despite the undeniable modern feel of chrome and glass in the club, it is interesting to note that traditional Japanese *shoji* screens have played a similar role in extending small spaces and introducing a certain flexibility to the floor plan. Video cameras are placed around the club, channeling images of club members sweating on treadmills, swimming, or doing aerobics to strategically displayed monitors around the gym. In some clubs, monitors are also placed immediately outside the club, intended to invite the gaze of the passerby on the street.

Squash courts are enclosed by glass, driving ranges are lined with benches for spectators, and balconies overlook gymnasiums and basketball courts. The cafés and restaurants of the clubs are designed to look out onto the club pool or weight room. Aerobics studios are either open-air or framed with floor-to-ceiling windows, and exercise bikes and treadmills are positioned along the sidelines for easy observation. During particularly crowded or unusual dance classes, members jockey for bikes with the best view. One male member, while riding a stationary bicycle and admiring the women in the aerobics class, commented to his friend appreciatively, "Pretty good view, huh? It's like watching a movie."

Performance is a key part of aerobics in Japan and the United States, but Japanese instructors seem particularly conscious of this fact. Unlike the stamina and strength required for U.S. advanced aerobics classes, the Japanese aerobicizer requires, above all else, a flawless memory and skilled coordination. The instructor teaches an extremely long and very complicated routine and then stops cueing abruptly and turns to face the class to watch the performance in silence. The class is expected to remember the routine and perform it without cues. Never has the front row versus the back row position in an aerobics class been so important, or so marked. The front row performers are the stars, the enthusiasts in skin-baring and coordinated leotards. The gendered nature of this fitness club gaze becomes particularly tangible when we examine the overt sexiness of the leotards sported by many women in the club. In the following chapter, I explore the tension between the "male gaze" that objectifies the female aerobicizers and the undeniable power that these women gain by shedding their office uniforms and donning sexy leotards.

The few male aerobicizers tend to congregate in the front of the room or in the very rear. The middle row is made up of the masses—the ones who generally can follow the routine but don't have the confidence to vault into the front row. The back row consists of the newcomers, the self-conscious, and the T-shirted. However, sometimes the back of the room can actually be front stage. At Downtown Fitness, the back wall is made of glass and therefore showcases the back row. Some of the better dancers recognize this and adjust accordingly; others do not seem to realize that by seeking refuge in the back, they are actually subjecting themselves to the critical and admiring audience in the weight room.

The video cameras, glass, and mirrors positioned around the club, whether intended for the surveillance and managed safety of the club members, the novelty of modern technology, or the voyeuristic gaze, all set the stage for member performance,[6] audience scrutiny, and the discipline of self-monitoring. Surveillance is both blatant, as in the case of the video cameras, and invisible, when masked as performance and audience appreciation. With the exception of the locker rooms and private staff space, which are separated from the rest of the club by solid doors, the rooms flow into one another without the intrusion of walls and doors. The weight room, aerobics studio, café, and reception area are open to each other and present all bodies on display and render all activities public and subject to supervision.

Divided Space

Front versus back, public versus private, and outside versus inside are spatial dichotomies that have been used by many anthropologists to characterize the relationship between space and social relationships in Japan (e.g., Ohnuki-Tierney 1984; Rohlen 1983; Rosenberger 1992). Indeed, Foucault notes that the aim of partitioning or assigning individuals their own place is to institute control and mastery (1979:143). The layout of the fitness club conforms to this division of public and private or client and employee space. Club members are never permitted into the staff room or management offices of the club; the heavy door to the staff room is marked private and swings shut automatically, marking the room off-limits to members and visitors.

Goffman describes the importance of the door separating the back stage from the front stage: "Very commonly the back region of a performance is located at one end of the place where the performance is presented, being cut off from it by a partition and guarded passageway. By having the front and back regions adjacent in this way, a performer out in front can receive backstage assistance while the performance is in progress and can interrupt his performance momentarily for brief periods of relaxation. In general, of course, the back region will be the place where the performer can reliably expect that no member of the audience will intrude" (1959:113). The staff room provides a space in which instructors can relax, discuss opinions of the members and the overall organization of the club, and also smoke, snack, and exhibit otherwise inconsistent, "unfit" behavior. Although still subject to the critical view of the club manager and chief, instructors tend to be more boisterous and less inhibited behind the swinging door of the staff room. Access to the relatively unguarded and less inhibited behavior and relationships that took place in back-stage regions, meetings, and after-hours parties was crucial to my fieldwork and was initially difficult to secure.

The back region not only serves as a sanctuary away from the demands of the members but also functions as a haven in which instructors can act in ways that may actively contradict their "service demeanor." As I explore in Chapter 5, Japanese aerobics instructors who preach the benefits of exercise on the club floor and smoke and drink when offstage are neither resistant nor simply acting out two sides of "context-based" personhood. Rather, the inconsistencies of onstage and offstage behavior are indicative of the instructors' underlying frustration with gender inequities in the club. Here, I examine the architecture and design of the private and public spaces themselves (as opposed to the behavior characteristic of that space) and the partitioning of the fitness club for use by employees versus clients.

Hendry's discussion of "spatial wrapping" is useful for conceptualizing the use of public and private space in Japanese architecture. Distinct from North American fitness clubs, where the offices of managers and instructors are accessible to the public, with walls made of glass and doors intentially left ajar, the offices of Japanese managers are located in the basement or the dead center of the building, "wrapped" behind several layers of counters, doors, and windowless walls. Hendry (1993) explains how the use of space determines who will be able to penetrate the building and how far in they will be able to go. In her discussion of public buildings, she notes, "The heart of local politics, the debating chamber of the town or city council, is likely to be much further within, perhaps a room with no outside aspect at all. To wield power within a particular construction, one needs to know how to penetrate the various layers of wrapping" (106). To enter the inner recesses of the fitness club requires insider status or clout afforded only to high-ranking visitors. As Hendry explains, "Wrapping reflects degrees of distance and formality and the hierarchical structure of the people using the space" (99).

Goffman's definition of the back region or backstage accurately depicts the covert behavior and happenings that take place out of members' view in the staff room of the gym:

> Here grades of ceremonial equipment, such as different types of liquor or clothes, can be hidden so that the audience will not be able to see the treatment accorded them in comparison with the treatment that could have been accorded them. Here devices such as the telephone are sequestered so that they can be used "privately." Here costumes and other parts of personal front may be adjusted and scrutinized for flaws. Here the team can run through its performance, checking for offending expressions when no audience is present to be affronted by them; here poor members of the team, who are expressively inept, can be schooled or dropped from the performance. Here the performer can relax; he can drop his front, forgo speaking his lines, and step out of character. (1959:112)

With six desks crammed into a tiny space, there is scarcely enough room for the overflowing bookshelves and bins of extra dumbbells,

10. The club employees share a single, multipurpose room that is marked off-limits to the members.

let alone the kitchenette, staff bathroom, and male and female locker rooms (Figure 10). This single room must serve the daily needs of a rotating twenty-person staff and is a constant frenzy of activity. Instructors rush in and out to change from bathing suit to workout gear to club uniform and back again, while others sit at the cluttered desks, coloring large posters, drafting schedules and pay sheets, or making phone calls. At any given moment, a staff member can be seen eating at the end of the table, be it a quick riceball lunch choked down between classes or a light snack from the ever-present assortment of homemade snacks or *omiyage* (souvenirs) brought in by grateful members.

Togetherness and intimacy are both encouraged and unavoidable in the cramped back room. Markedly distinct from the privacy and spaciousness cultivated in the public spaces of the fitness club, the staff work, eat, and brush their teeth in full view of colleagues and superiors. Several scholars have noted that in Japanese homes, the same open living space has the capacity to be converted to the multiple uses of napping, dining, television watching, and socializing (e.g., Hendry 1993; Greenbie 1988). Emblematic of Foucault's "functional sites," these back rooms are engineered to serve multiple uses to increase their practicality (1979:143–145). This single, centralized work space, with desks facing one another, is by no means unique to the fitness club. Rohlen (1974, 1975) and others have explored the intentional intimacy of the office layout in the Japanese company, designed to foster a united spirit, de-centralize authority, and instill a sense of self-management. An unoccu-pied instructor is unable to sit idly for long without being assigned a new task or, at the very least, feeling extremely self-conscious under the constant, watchful supervision of the boss and fellow staff. Even back-stage, the "compulsory visibility" of Foucault's panopticon functions perfectly.

The mayhem and clutter of the private staff room contrast dramati-cally with the spic-and-span cleanliness of the public facilities, from the brightly lit entryway to the luxurious member locker rooms. In fact, for some private fitness clubs, it is these well-equipped locker rooms that are the showcase of the club. Roomy, card-operated "American" lockers, floor mats that are changed every two hours, tanning beds, whirlpools, and saunas ensure that private fitness clubs stand apart from less expensive, prefecture-run public gyms with their drab, con-crete floors and institutional shower stalls. A separate and, more im-portant, private and elite space in which to exercise sets the fitness club apart from the competition and enables the discipline of bodies within.

Just as the layout of the club separates clients and staff, sex segre-gation also tends to map out spatially. Unlike the "meat market" feel of many U.S. clubs, Japanese fitness clubs are not conducive to picking up members of the opposite sex. Despite the display of both male and female bodies in revealing workout wear, the atmosphere seems sterile and nonflirtatious.[7] Although aerobics classes are primarily made up of women, the weight room in the Japanese club is marked by their ab-sence. Even in the United States, where the weight room tends to be a male-dominated domain, a certain percentage of women use the ma-chines and the free weights. In Japan, however, there are seldom more than two or three women in the weight room at any time, and they usually enter in pairs. In my year of field research, I never observed a Japanese woman bench-pressing the free weight bar, nor did I see a woman using any machines other than the chest press or leg machines. Despite the gym staff's aggressive push to create muscle training pro-grams for women and their scare tactics about increasing fat percent-ages, women are reluctant to "bulk up."[8]

Even for women who would like to bulk up, entering the all-male weight room can be very intimidating. When using the Nautilus equipment or free weights, the staff recommends three sets of twelve to fifteen repetitions for each exercise. Given the time-consuming number of repetitions and the need to rest the muscles for several minutes between sets, it is common practice in the United States to alternate with people waiting in line, more commonly known as "working in" between sets. Klein describes the etiquette of American bodybuilders that discourages monopolizing the equipment (1993:89). Bodybuilders may use intimidation tactics to "encourage" other, smaller members to finish their workout quickly: "Should one of the larger men approach weights that a smaller person was using, a subtle kind of commandeering took place. The larger man would assert his territoriality by asking in a businesslike or, at times, gruff, tone, 'How many more sets are you doing?' He might also ask to work in with the smaller person, and pile on so much more weight that switching the weight off each time becomes too much trouble, and too intimidating to the smaller man or woman (who would have to acknowledge that he or she could not lift the heavier weights in the act of switching)" (89–90).

Although I did not observe the tactics of intimidation described by Klein at the Japanese clubs, the size, strength, and aggressiveness of foreign members at the Roppongi branch of Downtown Fitness did discourage many Japanese members from approaching the free weights and bench press area when in use by the foreign men. In Japan, not only do members not work in, but they also rest on the equipment in between sets, thereby preventing others from using it. After six o'clock, the lines can sometimes run ten people deep, a phenomenon that might better be referred to as "wait lifting." Occasionally, women would peek into the weight room, observe the lines, and quickly retreat.

The partitioning of space in the club organizes the members and staff according to sex and class, both mirroring and sharpening inequities. The staff room not only provides privacy from clients, but also physically separates the relatively uneducated, young, female instructors from their wealthier clientele. This division of space reflects the hierarchical system in the club. Power and control are achieved through separation and containment. At the same time, the sifting of bodies according to sex correlates to larger institutional and ideological constructions. The fact that women limit their activities to the aerobics studio and men to the weight room should not be read simply as two different but equally enjoyable and beneficial activities. Rather, the nature of these spaces tells us a great deal about power and equality in society. Separate is never equal. When women are excluded or exclude themselves from building muscles, choosing instead to craft their bodies in more socially acceptable forms, the division of space can be seen as a form of control and intimidation. ⌐

Numerous scholars have discussed the association of women with the home in both Japan and the United States (e.g., Lebra 1984; Vogel 1978). Perhaps the most obvious correlation can be seen in the word for "wife" in Japanese, *okusan,* which translates literally as "Mrs. Interior." As Cherry points out, "Oku means not just interior, but the depths far within a building. The suffixes -san and -sama are not gender specific, but broad enough to mean Mr., and Mrs., or even Ms. However, okusan can never be used to denote a Mr. Interior, no matter how much time he spends in the deepest recesses of his home. As the language makes clear, that is traditionally considered the woman's place" (1987:66). Similarly, although the situation is slowly changing, junior colleges in Japan are populated almost exclusively by women, whereas the most prestigious universities and white-collar corporations tend to offer most of their slots to men. The institutional separation of the sexes contributes to their symbolic hierarchy. Gender and class roles are assigned and reflected through the partitioning of space.

Leisure Space

Given the potent value attached to endurance and gritting one's teeth in the office, at home, and even in the fitness club, it is surprising that most Japanese members would shy away from exertion, discomfort, and effort only at the club. But it is precisely because fitness clubs are considered neither work nor home but rather a third space in which social norms are loosened and new roles are created that effort becomes somehow intolerable. For a substantial fee, the member buys space, time, and a new lifestyle apart from the self-effacing humbling required at the office, the obligatory drinking parties, or the endless laundry, shopping, and cleaning that awaits at home. The Western notion of home as the safe haven opposed to and removed from the stresses of work does not hold true in Japan. For many Japanese men and women, the home can also be a source of pressure and responsibility; activities that take place outside the home and away from work often prove to be the most relaxing and enjoyable. In the private and removed space of the fitness club, the service staff prioritizes relaxation, personal enjoyment, and self-indulgence, keeping pain, effort, and exertion to a minimum. It is not that Japanese members are unable to endure the effort and discomfort of an hour-and-a-half-long aerobics class, but rather that many are unwilling.

Although young women receive the brunt of criticism for their failure to stick it out in the club, it is important to note that both men and women quit at steady rates. Some cite specific reasons that range from straightforward personal obstacles, such as job transfers or upcoming exams and graduation, to specific complaints with the club, such as the cost, location, or class offerings. But for many members, exercise is simply not what they expected. One of the instructors suggested that, for many, exercise is simply another obligation in a litany of household and office responsibilities: "Japanese men have always worked long hours, and now they have more free time and so they just want to lie around the house. But their wives are nagging [*urusai*], always asking what they are doing, so they seek hobbies outside the home. But until now, they haven't had any hobbies, so they think they will try the fitness club or golf. It is not a voluntary choice [*jihatsuteki*] but rather an obligation. They feel the need to exercise as they lead very sedentary lives, but don't get the results at the club because they do the exercise without proper form and direction." Members may have the initial impetus, curiosity, and desire to join the club, but when faced with the hard work, hours required, and disappointing inability to achieve instant gratification, many become discouraged and quit. These half-hearted members far outnumber the maniacs described in Chapter 1.

But are work and leisure mutually exclusive in contemporary Japan? The work of Anne Allison (1994) on hostess clubs in Japan suggests otherwise. Work and leisure are merged in the liminal space of the hostess club, where businessmen in the guise of socializing apply themselves to the hard work of drinking. Drinking, or *nomunikeshon*,[9] is a popular pastime in Japan, and, as Allison explores in her work, alcohol serves to lower inhibitions and blur hierarchical tensions in the office. Here the boundaries that separate work and leisure are fluid and ill defined. Ben-Ari (1998) explores a comparable merging of work and leisure on the golf courses of Singapore, where expatriate Japanese strengthen business relationships with colleagues and clients over rounds of golf. One would expect the fitness club to be characterized as a similar space, where the labor of exercise is coupled with the leisure of being away from the stresses of office and home.

Given the official talk concerning the failing health of the Japanese workforce and the stamina required to be successful at the office, the work of Foucault (1980, 1995) and Douglas (1966, 1970) might lead us to presume that the managers of the corporate world would prioritize fitness. Indeed, the fitness club boom of the 1980s coincided with increased efforts by the state to improve the health of the nation and to maintain a strong, active, and independent population throughout the "silver" years. The tremendous success of Japan's postwar economy was built on the unflagging efforts of a physically fit workforce. As the recent recession continues to erode economic security, the strength, stamina, and independence of laboring bodies becomes even more important. Corporate managers and government officials recognize that by maintaining a high standard of health and fitness not only for company employees but also for the elderly and their caregiving children, the health of the economy is assured as well.

Yet, instead of backing fitness clubs, enormous sums of corporate money are funneled into hostess bars, pubs, and strip clubs. At these popular late-night spots, the economic rewards of company socializing outweigh the pain of hangovers, sleepless nights, and apple-polishing. Because fitness clubs cater to the individual or family, they offer no such opportunity to climb the corporate ladder. As Havens notes, after-hours entertainment provides "salaried employees with socially sanctioned time out from the pressures of corporate performance by temporarily creating an alternative form of community in a favorite coffee shop, bar, or restaurant where middle-class workers could lampoon, without rejecting, the values of the workaday social system" (1994:205). An hour on the treadmill, though healthier than bar-hopping with the boss, may prove to be detrimental to career advancement. In the end, the strenuous exercise required to keep healthy and fit simply fashions the fitness club as yet another workplace, but with none of the economic and social payoffs. The fitness club, then, presents a contradictory space, where the work of exercise cannot be reconciled with the leisure of service.

Clean Space

Spatial Pollution

I have illustrated the ways these commercial clubs are designed to demarcate a removed space for leisure, and now turn to a related discussion of the elaborate preservation of hygiene and privacy. According to Eichberg (1998), high standards of hygiene are both expected and suited to the space of the late-capitalist fitness club. He emphasizes: "There are also relations existing between the straight line of this social hygienic view and the straight line of hygienic sports space: clean and clear to survey, panoptical; the order of the gymnasium, *of the fitness centre* and of the school" (123; emphasis added). This attention to cleanliness in the Japanese club also reflects the exaggerated emic distinctions around hygiene unique to Japan.

Club rules are quite strict, particularly with regard to issues of sanitation. Makeup and jewelry are prohibited in the pools, and members are required to shower and wade through a highly chlorinated shallow pool before entering the lap or diving pool. This cleansing pool is believed to purify the dirty or contaminated lower half of the body before members are allowed into the publicly shared pool.[10] Consistent with the cultural predilection for removing shoes when entering homes and buildings, it is not surprising that outdoor shoes are not permitted in the gym in areas other than the club lobby and corridors leading to the locker rooms. Ohnuki-Tierney explains: "The outside, or more specifically, outside one's home but still within the cultural sphere, and the below, as represented by footgear, feet, floor, and ground are dirty. 'Outside' and 'below' are where germs and pollution, especially 'people dirt' are located" (1984:27). To ensure high levels of sanitation and cleanliness, at some clubs the staff is required to arrive one to two hours early and stay for an hour after closing to mop, scrub, and straighten up. The spotlessness of most clubs is proof of the staff's commitment and effort.

Keeping the fitness club facilities clean is a time-consuming, labor-intensive task that often is the sole responsibility of the club staff.[11] The managers oversee the cleaning but will help out with the dirty work when a shift is understaffed or time is limited. Chiba Club requires the staff to clean the club twice daily, an hour before the club opens and an hour after it closes. As staff shifts generally run four to eight hours, the same staff member never cleans twice in one day. I was alternatively responsible for morning duty, which requires staff to report a few minutes

11. In characteristic attention to hygiene at the club, these instructors carefully roll up the mats that cover the pool to prevent an overly humid room that contributes to the growth of mold and mildew.

before 9 A.M. to prepare the club for the 10 A.M. opening, and evening cleanup. Evening cleaning begins at 9:30 P.M., when the last few members are finishing up, and takes about an hour. As most staff sign up for the same schedule weekly, we would clean in the same groups of four.

Morning cleanup begins promptly at nine o'clock. The bleary-eyed and grumpy staff tend to stumble into the staff room with seconds to spare, rushing to change into a grubby T-shirt brought from home, the club uniform shorts, and flip-flops. They immediately file into the humid pool room to begin the daily task of rolling up the ten quilted plastic mats that cover the surface of the lap pool, keeping the evaporation of chlorine to a minimum (Figure 11). Not unlike rolling up an enormous and cumbersome poster, the center of the mat has the irritating tendency to slip out the side so that the entire roll becomes skewed. The only way to remedy this mishap is to unfurl the mat to the point of imbalance or to attempt to shove the center back into the roll. The mats are heavy with pool water, dripping and unwieldy; the ease and pace that the mats can be rolled and stacked serves to separate the neophyte trainees from the more experienced staff. One employee who had been working at the club for two years could finish three mats to my every one, and her rolls were tight, neat, and perfectly aligned on either side. I remember my relief when a new trainee came to morning cleanup and she had even more difficulty with the mats than I did. Naoko, a long-time employee, looked over at the trainee struggling with the mat and said with a smirk, "Are you doing okay?"

After all the mats are rolled and dragged to the storage room and the pool lane ropes secured, the towels and staff T-shirts, which had been laundered the night before and laid out to dry in the humid and warm pool area, are collected and brought into the staff room to be folded later. The staff then gather buckets, mops, and rags to clean the aerobics studio and squash courts. The management ruled detergent and cleaning soap unnecessary (or, as many of the instructors speculated, too expensive), so we were forced to rely on elbow grease and damp rags to polish the mirrors and glass of the aerobics studio, swab off the sit-up mats, and scrub off the scuff marks from the squash court walls.

Despite the early hour, nearly everyone preferred morning duty to the mess and nuisance of cleanup after hours. The time-consuming and smelly job of scouring mold off the shower stalls, saunas, bathrooms, and pool-side tiles was reserved for the evening crew. Using an old toothbrush to scrub away the mold on the tile grout is tedious at any hour, but particularly so after a full day's work. After hours, many of the staff opted for comfort over modesty and donned swimming suits to hose down bathrooms and mop the saunas in the muggy heat.

New staff members soon learned that to escape reproach requires not only enthusiasm and effort, but the all-important skill of pacing one's own cleanup speed to exactly match that of the other staff. A worker that is too slow and thorough holds up the others and does not do his or her fair share of the labor, whereas the speedy cleaner not only makes the others look bad but winds up finishing too early with nothing to do. To avoid standing around idly, the quicker workers invent new and somewhat useless jobs: dusting off the basketballs and realigning the stick pins in the bulletin board. They may even resort to redusting and repolishing windows and mirrors minutes after the job has been completed by someone else. Goffman dubs this phenomenon "make-work": "It is understood in many establishments that not only will workers be required to produce a certain amount after a certain length of time, but also that they will be ready, when called upon, to give the impression that they are working hard at the moment" (1959:109).

Not only do the fitness club staff perform in front of their superiors and club members, but they also engage in make-work in front of their peers. Arai suggests that in the monastic tradition, this "work period (*samu*) offers numerous possibilities for expressing resentment and feelings of alienation. You can work extremely quickly and make the others around you look lazy. Or you can work on easier tasks just slowly enough to not draw attention to yourself, but force your cohorts to do more of the harder work" (1999:93). At the same time, Foucault might refer to this make-work as a function of disciplinary time, when the staff labor under the constant gaze of supervision and ultimately internalize this surveillance. Is it any wonder that the clubs in Japan are so spotless?

The exaggerated attention to cleanliness and the rituals of purification performed to ensure a high standard of sanitation and a good public reputation are not unique to the fitness club. For many of the club staff, this thorough club cleanup may conjure up memories of their school days, where students are required to mop, dust, and sponge down the school building daily (Rohlen 1983). As explored in the movie *Dream Girls,* first-year actresses in the Takarazuka Revue [12] are responsible for the daily scrub-down of the practice rooms and theater. Cleaning serves as a form of seishin kyouiku, where neophytes learn how to discipline their mind and body through the repetition of daily chores. Precision cleaning figures prominently in the daily lives of Zen Buddhist nuns, who aspire to emulate Buddha in their diligence, efficiency and attention to detail. Arai notes that, for the nuns, "cleaning is perhaps the aspect of Zen monastic life that comes closest to achieving the ideals of the teachings on a regular basis. During a good part of the time in the monastery, enlightenment *is* cleaning" (1999:92). This emphasis on cleaning suggests that the fitness club may be marked as a spiritual space, but do the fitness club staff experience feelings of spiritual purification as a result of their efforts to eliminate dirt?

The club staff did not express any particular feelings of mind and body synthesis or spiritual cleanliness as a result of the long hours spent scrubbing and swabbing. If anything, they felt irritated at the time demanded of them in these tedious tasks, but chalked up the work as simply part of the job. Although most did not voluntarily vocalize complaints about the endless cleaning, many responded with a shrug and a curt "What can you do?" (*shikatta ga nai*) when I occasionally gave voice to my reluctance to clean. They expressed envy over the instructors at Downtown Fitness, who were relieved of cleaning duties by the employment of a full-time janitorial staff. Even when asked directly why we were not given strong cleaning formulas and mildew killers, most speculated that the management did not want to spend the money on cleaning aids and did not reflect on any larger philosophical implications. For the Buddhist nuns, cleaning without the aid of strong cleansers forces one to rely on one's own energy and diligence, where the act of scrubbing rather than the result of a clean floor reflects a purified spirit. Ironically, the absence of strong cleansers, though culturally understandable, actually renders the space less hygienic than expectations set by the late-capitalist service industry. Here, late-capitalist demands for sterility confront long-standing rituals of purification.

Many instructors did not complain simply because they admitted that they had been socialized to clean and reminisced about high school days dusting and mopping. They took for granted that they would be responsible for the upkeep of their place of employment. At the same time, the majority of the female staff took pride in their ability to clean quickly and efficiently, and expressed surprise when I didn't wring out the rags in the same way they did. One woman remarked a bit meanly, "What, you don't have to clean in America?" For these 20-something, unmarried or newlywed women, cleaning became an expression of diligence, virtue, and domestic affinity, in much the same way that cooking and serving tea and food to their managers and fellow staff did.

Bodily Pollution

Wearing special slippers in the bathroom and wading through highly chlorinated water to cleanse the *kitanai* (dirty) lower half of the body before entering the pool are preventive measures to kill bacteria, preserve sanitation, and protect the health of the members. But these acts also serve as symbolic rituals that, as Ohnuki-Tierney (1984) has explored, distinguish between *kirei* (clean; pure; beautiful) and *kitanai* (dirty; contaminated; ugly). A direct translation of the terms to English is impossible, as these words are used in a variety of cultural contexts, from the literal description of a filthy room in need of dusting to the more symbolic representation of contamination by outsiders or strangers. As Douglas explains, "Dirt is essentially disorder. . . . Eliminating it is not a negative movement, but a positive effort to organize the environment" (1966:2). In particular, the staff goes to great lengths to remove every droplet of sweat from the floors and equipment. But the members are also expected to contribute to the upkeep of the gym. All clubs provide hand towels, conveniently suspended from each machine, so that the members can rub off any sweat that may have collected during their workout.

But is sweat considered unclean? The discourse surrounding sweat is contradictory and, in the words of Douglas, represents both danger and power (1966:95–114). On the one hand, failure to wipe down the equipment after using it is one of the greatest social gaffes in the Japanese fitness club. Not only does the perfunctory wipe-down signal that the machine is now available to those who may be waiting, but more important, neglecting to wipe away real or imaginary sweat exhibits a blatant lack of consideration for fellow members, for whom contact with the sweat of another, particularly that of a stranger, is distasteful. As Ohnuki-Tierney explains, in Japan, "germs are contracted in crowds or in locations where other people have been, contrasting them with one's clean self. Outside is equated with dirt and germs because that is where the dirt of others is seen to be most concentrated. Ultimately, dirt consists of the excretion of others" (1984:22). In this sense, sweat is classified as polluted, dirty, and dangerous. Members and staff make a concerted effort to preserve the sterile and strikingly hygienic surroundings, free from the stench of bodies and evidence of effort, drudgery, or pain.

The constant battle against dirt and sweat distinguishes the luxurious and elite club from less exclusive, state-funded exercise facilities, home exercise equipment, and outdoor workouts. Attentive service, spotless surroundings, and, above all, a united effort by staff and managers to market exercise as an enjoyable and leisurely pursuit become symbolized in the elimination of sweat and dirt. The spacious fitness club serves as a welcome refuge from the daily commutes on crowded trains, cramped apartments, and long lines at the supermarket. Members pay for the individualized pampering of a private fitness club, in which contact with another member's sweat would be a sharp reminder that he or she is not alone. As Douglas aptly explains, "In short, our pollution behavior is the reaction which condemns any object or idea likely to confuse or contradict cherished classifications" (1966:37). Private versus public, leisure versus work, and inside versus outside are symbolized in the clean surroundings of the private fitness club.

On the other hand, one's own sweat is considered a welcome byproduct of exertion, a symbol of weight loss and stress release, and a natural body secretion.[13] George Fields, an advertising executive who has analyzed the Japanese market, has examined why deodorants, antiperspirants, and even perfumes have not caught on in Japan. Ironically, although strong body odor is considered "unnatural" and the result of illness, possibly requiring medical attention rather than cosmetic remedies, sweat is thought to be "natural" and its suppression harmful. To cure body odor, one would visit a pharmacist and buy a product that is "therapeutic rather than preventive, the opposite to the use of deodorants" (Fields 1983:105).

The daily, weekly, or even monthly ritual of exercise purges the body of impurities and pollutants by ridding it of unwanted fat and stress. In this way, sweat-inducing exercise in the late 1990s may be a way to exercise power over the daily social and economic pressures of company cutbacks, personal burdens of caring for aging parents, and the difficulty of meeting and marrying an appropriate spouse. In Japan, the central aim of exercise is to sweat as a personal release from stress, as proof to others of one's effort, and as a tangible first step toward achieving the perfect body. Sweat, as opposed to physical exhaustion or pulse elevation, is proof of a successful workout.[14] In fact, sweating in the sauna is preferable to sweating in the weight room.

Conclusions

I have described how the spatial layout of the gym orders social relations, prescribes behavior, and, most important, distinguishes the club as a site of discipline and control on the one hand, and privilege and service on the other. The fitness club, in its attempts to cater to both late-capitalist desires and long-standing cultural norms, embodies certain contradictions. On the one hand, the exposed, divided, enclosed, and hygienic spaces exaggerate and create power inequities of class and gender. Men and women, staff and members, and instructors and managers tailor their performances to the particular spaces of the fitness club. The way that space flows and is divided up by walls, windows, and mirrors and labeled private or public, male or female, clean or dirty has direct consequences for the symbolic organization of the bodies inside.

At the same time, the fitness club affords certain spaces where power inequities can be manipulated or transformed. From the cigarette-smoking aerobics instructors in the staff room to the reluctant exercisers in the sauna to the belly-baring aerobicizers in the studio, it becomes apparent that certain spaces in the club allow room for agency and compromise. In the next chapter, I conclude my discussion of the structural and institutionalized disciplinary techniques employed by and imposed on club managers, staff, and members, before turning to tales of resistance, co-optation, and the negotiation of power within the club.

The Discipline of Bodies

In this chapter, I extend the analysis of gender, power, labor, and leisure beyond the physical walls of the fitness club to the specific disciplinary practices of the bodies within. The management of bodies in Japanese fitness clubs is as institutionalized and unremarkable as it is distinct. Regular body measurements, precision cleaning, uniforms, standardized movements, adherence to timetables, recorded confessions, and criticism of others characterize the fitness club and bear a striking resemblance to both the monastic practices central to other institutions in Asia (e.g., Arai 1999; Reynolds 1980) and the militaristic production of "docile bodies" observed cross-culturally and historically in prisons, hospitals, and schools (Foucault 1979; Goffman 1961). The body, and indeed the relationship between the mind and body, becomes regulated in time, space, and habits according to the prevalent historical and social needs. Discipline ensures that cultural practices become habitually and unconsciously encoded in the body through everyday activities.

In Japan, aerobics instructors and club members are held to an unrealistic ideal that is intended to shape them from the inside out. Bodies are measured, outfitted, and programmed not only to appear but also to move in very particular ways. This ideological emphasis on outward conformity creates a climate where definitions of beauty, health, and productivity overlap. As explicit consumer-driven spaces, the fitness clubs and training schools conflate beauty with health and health with productivity in such a way that a body that is not "fit" for exercise becomes unfit by any measure. Being unfit, then, is synonymous with being unattractive, unhealthy, and unproductive by ideological, social, and economic standards. Discipline over appearances and actions does indeed translate into control over beauty ideals, sexuality, and gender roles. I demonstrate the ways members and instructors are controlled, but also the ways they exercise self-control and lack of control. The most invisible and hence most effective forms of control are those that are embodied and self-imposed.

By defining healthy as thin, attractive, and, most important, self-reliant, the clubs are positioned to produce women who continue to do the majority of the housework, to shoulder the care for the elderly and children, and to take on the necessary but undervalued officework required of a part-time workforce. But, as I have emphasized, the lack of effort exhibited by most club members contrasts dramatically with the institutionalized structure of discipline in the club. Members quit the club at alarming rates, and although some actively embrace the rhetoric of building strong bodies to better execute responsibilities in the home and workplace, the majority choose winding down over becoming winded. For members, the fitness club, in fact, provides a space where they can shed the constraints and expectations imposed on them in offices and homes. Many members pay the high fees for club membership simply because clubs afford a unique opportunity for enjoyment and relaxation.

As I have suggested, the emphasis on discipline in the clubs resonates with research conducted in Japan on *seishin kyouiku* (spiritual education) in company training courses (Rohlen 1996; Kondo 1990), psychotherapy techniques (Reynolds 1980), education (Rohlen 1980, 1983; Fukuzawa 1996), and Zen and martial arts training (Arai 1999; Donohue 1991). The central characteristics of seishin training, such as precision cleaning and self-reflection observed in the aerobics instructor training schools and fitness clubs, seem to prescribe a mind-body synthesis at the ideological level, but this synthesis is never actualized in practice. The clubs fail to make explicit the links between training the body and training the spirit. Thus, one might suppose that the clubs, in the end, have simply imported the Western notion of a mind-body dualism along with StairMasters, American music, and aerobics styles.

The uniforms, time schedules, and synchronized movements demanded of the staff and members overlap with Foucault's description of the micropolitics of control and an emphasis on detail and minutiae. In this Western paradigm, the mind is alienated from the body, resulting in both a theoretical and practical division. To be truly disciplined, the mind must assume complete control over the erring body. Laziness and fat can be banished if only one puts one's mind to it. The fitness club, as a Western import in a Japanese context, presents a unique space in which to observe the intersections between and contradictions in the relationship between mind and body in both theory and practice. In this chapter, I illustrate how the fitness club is neither exclusively influenced by the boundaryless continuum model suggested by scholars of Japanese philosophy nor the antagonistic dualism found in the West, but rather, like many late-twentieth-century institutions in Japan, contains elements of both.

The training demanded in the fitness club draws on many characteristics of seishin kyouiku and is consistent with other institutions in Japan. Rohlen (1996) argues that unlike in the West, where marginalized institutions are most often associated with heavy-handed acts of control, discipline in Japan is not restricted to prisons, hospitals, and the military. Rather, this type of corporal and mental training has become embedded in mainstream social institutions such as elementary schools, corporations, and fitness clubs. As Rohlen and others have demonstrated, a spiritual education incorporates hardship and difficulty as integral parts of education. Like martial arts training, fitness clubs demand working through pain and discomfort to achieve a sense of accomplishment. Seishin teachings encourage self-reflection (*hansei*) to develop the strength necessary for self-improvement. The fitness club, like other institutions in Japan, requires its employees and participants to record their thoughts and activities in daily journals or workout files to be read by managers and staff. The content of the journal entries and files at the clubs and in other institutions focuses on addressing weaknesses and finding appropriate paths to correction. In spiritual training, unity and conformity take precedence over individuality and independent thought. Hence, competition is discouraged as disruptive to group unity, and students are taught to emulate the teacher's instruction and group standard. In this way, training schools and fitness clubs enforce conformity in appearance, actions, and even thoughts in an attempt to produce a standardized corps of fit employees and clients.

By focusing exclusively on structure and socialization, there is a certain danger in furthering the well-worn stereotypes of "practice makes perfect" or "the Japanese as conformists," so popular in certain considerations of Japanese culture. This type of culture essentialism or *Nihonjinron* sets up rigid comparisons between Japan and the West, obscures historical and regional differences, and downplays individuality. The resultant stereotypes, which tend to conjure up an image of the prototypical high school student memorizing columns of dates in anticipation of a college entrance exam, deny creativity and thrive on conformity. Another image called to mind is that of Japanese baseball players fielding endless ground balls or racing back and forth between bases, which certain authors have used to suggest that Japanese baseball places more energy and emphasis on practice than on the actual games.[1]

Although there is no question that seishin kyouiku does produce a certain degree of standardization in the appearance, movements, and rhetoric of the instructors and members, I demonstrate that the ways these messages are received, accepted, resisted, and negotiated on the ground complicates the stereotypes of a passive and conformist society. The decided lack of discipline displayed by members and even instructors indicates that the messages about discipline, fortitude of spirit, and moral fiber are not being passed on or consumed in the clubs. The fitness club, attempting to combine both imagined "American" and "Japanese" influences, projects inconsistent messages about productivity, health, and leisure. This inconsistency results in a clientele that does not want to exercise but desires results and a cadre of employees who preach healthy behavior on the club floor while engaging in unhealthy practices behind closed doors.

Sizing Up: The Conflation of Beauty and Health

The emphasis on conformity begins with the attention and effort given to measuring and producing a standardized body. Although fitness clubs and training schools in the United States undeniably quantify the human body, Japanese clubs and schools take it further. Instructor training schools standardize bodies to a remarkable degree. I was given permission to attend the initial audition and several of the lectures and practice lessons at one well-known training school. Becoming an aerobics instructor in Japan takes dedication, hard work, athleticism, and deep pockets to endure the three- to six-month training in the schools that are affiliated with most of the private fitness clubs. Outrageously expensive, most of the courses cost anywhere from 250,000 yen ($2,080) at the lesser known clubs to 420,000 yen ($3,500) at some of the bigger chains. The schools struggle between balancing selectivity to

maintain a high reputation and profitability by accepting as many applicants as possible. Courses are offered two to three times a year, and the
class schedule is grueling, with two-and-a-half-hour classes held weekly
on Thursday, Saturday, and Sunday.

Despite the recession, applications to the instructor training schools
are steadily increasing. One journalist notes, "So popular is this career
option that many applicants underestimate the competition" ("Jumping" 1996:18). At the time of my fieldwork in 1996, there were approximately 5 applicants competing for each of the 10,000 full-time
and part-time instructor positions in the industry (18). Unlike in the
United States, where instructor certification is nationally administered
by several competing organizations (AFAA and IDEA Health and Fitness
Association being the two largest), national certification in Japan is not
required by most clubs.[2] Rather, the training of instructors in Japan
is privatized, decentralized, and managed by independent fitness clubs
and chains. All of the well-known fitness club chains and most of the
smaller aerobics studios offer training schools that vary in cost, reputation, and curriculum. Graduation from a club-affiliated training school
does not guarantee employment by that club or any other, but untrained
instructors have a very difficult time securing a job without some li-
censed evidence of basic training in physiology and choreography. Only
those instructors who have gone through the rigors of memorization
and exercise required for graduation from most training schools are assumed to have the stamina, dedication, and knowledge that the club
hiring personnel require.

Although training programs are decentralized, national certification
exams do exist in Japan, and the ADI (Aerobics Dance Instructor) certification exam, sponsored by JAFA in affiliation with the Health, Labor,
and Welfare Ministry, is one of the most well-regarded.[3] The ADI exam
was first held in 1987; at that time, seventy-two people sat for the test.
One Downtown Fitness instructor described her experience taking the
exam two years after it was first administered, in 1989:

When I sat for the test seven years ago, I was really surprised at the
quality of people sitting for the exam. I thought to myself: "Whoa, these
women don't look like what I think instructors should look like." Some
of them were really fat, and I thought if they look like this in clothes, I
wonder how they will look in leotards. One woman was wearing ballet
slippers, I remember. Ballet slippers?! She must have been an instructor

that just volunteers at a local community center and has never been appropriately trained. I didn't know where any of these instructors were teaching, but I was a little disappointed that these were the type of people that were my fellow instructors. Of course, there are also those instructors who take the instructor training courses, pay all the money and study properly, but this type . . . they are probably only one tenth of the total instructors. Of course, that was a long time ago. I don't know how it is now, but I think it is the same.

In addition to the Health, Labor, and Welfare Ministry, the Ministry of Education is also responsible for the national regulation of aerobics as a sport, administering distinct certification exams and programs. The rivalry between the two ministries is stiff, and many club managers and fitness authorities predict that the separately administered exams may disappear altogether or merge to become one. Although most instructors and upper-level management are unsure about the distinctions between and hierarchy of the national programs and the private schools, all agreed that the courses do not improve chances for employment or compensation but, rather, are strictly for "self-improvement."

Competition for the general certification courses is quite fierce everywhere, but particularly so at the most well-regarded clubs (see, e.g., "Jumping" 1996). One woman confessed after the audition, "I was so nervous that my legs were shaking. I was much more tired in this class than a regular class, probably because I was nervous. I didn't look at the clock, because it made me too nervous. Most of the women were excellent, like professional aerobics instructors already!" As this woman observes, an instructor-to-be must demonstrate a high degree of skill and technique even before being admitted to the training schools. Three to six months later, the graduates emerge with clean technique, enthusiasm, precision, and an undeniable uniformity, which is reinforced by management in the fitness clubs.

To gain entrance to these competitive training schools, applicants send a full body photograph and résumé of experience to the main office. The central manager explained, "Based on the photograph and résumé we decide whether or not to invite you to try out. If an applicant is fat, we will absolutely reject her. 'Big is bad.' [*Debu wa dame da.*] If we look at the picture of the woman in workout clothes and if her body shape is not good, we will reject her. The members will look at the instructor and think 'Even if I do exercise, I will look like that?!' And they will not want to participate." The training schools discriminate against older and heavier instructors, using photographs as a means of gauging technique, skill, and future success. The shape of the body is seen as indicative of the ability of the instructor. Beauty is then synonymous with fitness, health, and the capacity to teach and inspire. Much like the money poured into flashy advertising campaigns, state-of-the-art equipment, and high-energy music that characterize the club, the physique of the instructor is inseparable from the image of fitness and is intrinsic to the success of the club.

The audition process weeds the applicant pool to a relatively homogeneous group: thin, young, and attractive; precise in execution of moves; and enthusiastic. These basic qualities are then honed at the training schools, where sloppy moves and sloppy appearance are eliminated and technique is standardized. Once admitted, the students are photographed for alignment, put on a diet according to weight and fat percentages, and essentially molded into a single physical model. Older instructors, who were teaching well before the introduction of training schools, are cynical about the modern cookie-cutter type of instructor who is being churned out of training schools. They dub them 'kintaro,' a type of old-fashioned Japanese candy, in which each piece of candy is identical to the others.[4]

The attention to body measurement and appearance is carried over in the fitness clubs. Because the instructor is expected to be the polished product of daily exercise and careful dieting, subjected to the tape-measuring eyes of members, management, and fellow staff, many staff members become overly concerned with body proportions and self-presentation. The chief of fitness at one club cold-called staff members for impromptu fat test readings, and if the results were the least bit high, he ridiculed the staff member in front of club members and other staff. Although the members are warned that total body fat percentage for women must not drop below 20, female staff are held to much stricter standards and chastised by the chief that, "as instructors, you have to look your best and must keep your fat percentage at 18 or lower." The managers use the humiliation of public exposure to control the appearance of their employees and to inspire members to pursue similar ideals of health, beauty, and fitness.

Just as the instructors must bear up under the micropolitics of body control, so must the members. When a member joins a club, he or she is subjected to a series of body measurements. The staff counselor uses a tape measure to record circumferences and lengths at different points along the limbs and at the hips, bust, and waist. Height, weight, blood pressure, and the all-important fat percentage are measured and marked. These numbers are then compared to a standardized chart and the discrepancies duly noted. At one fitness club, I assisted another instructor in teaching a diet class that required monthly weigh-ins—when fat percentages were checked and body parts measured—as a means to judge individual success and failure. Equally anticipated and dreaded, these monthly check-ups sparked the most competition among members of the class. So intense was the mood that the diet instructor confided that she sometimes fudged the data to avoid the disappointment or anger of the members. She whispered conspiratorially, "Sometimes there is a huge increase from the month before, and I don't want the members to be shocked—'Oh my God' [in katakana]—so I tighten the tape measure or just write down the same measurement from the month before." Changing the data to show improvement also protects her own reputation and keeps her from blame, as she is ultimately held responsible for the success or failure of the program. When members first join the club, the fitness counselor generally will not inform them of their initial measurements unless asked directly, thereby serving both practical and ideological purposes. On the one hand, if the member is indeed thin and fit, there may be little incentive to continue with the program; if heavier than expected, the member may become so discouraged that he or she may quit the club immediately. Also, by withholding privileged information, the instructor has surrounded herself with an air of authority that distances her from members.

The instructors wield special instruments and calibrators, rely on blood pressure machines, tape measures, and scales, and invoke the objective word of science and the authority of Western sport research to prop up their rhetoric.[5] The emphasis on numbers, gauges, and scales is an attempt to quantify and objectify the human body. By citing muscle group names and describing both the etiology and treatment of various diseases, instructors attempt to affiliate themselves with the medical profession. Banet-Weiser (1999) discusses a similar use of numbers to judge contestants in beauty pageants in the United States. The use of numerical scoring in today's contests has its origins in the hundred-point body breakdown evaluations of Miss America pageants in the 1920s. Women in the earlier contests were evaluated on the basis of individual scores on eyes, hair, construction of head, torso, and so on (55–56). The authority of the judges rests on their ability to be "objective" in their objectification of the female contestants.

The final authority is science. Although Martin (1987) and others have exposed the biases of medicine and science, the mystique of an objective scientific authority is still intact. The fitness club, by aligning itself with the health and medical establishment, seeks credibility by association. Because clubs historically have not been taken seriously, managers seek to improve their image. The fitness club of the 1990s aimed to position itself at the center of debates on preventive health care, with club managers even lobbying for financial support from the government on these grounds. Some public bath houses and hot spring resorts, by emphasizing the healing powers of medicated baths, have petitioned for and received government funding in recent years, setting a precedent for fitness clubs to follow. But, as of 1997, fitness clubs have been denied funding because of their private management, exclusive membership, and perceived weaker links to medicine.[6]

By promoting the notion that an excessively thin body is actually a more healthy body, fitness clubs and training schools use discourse on health and fitness to mask a far more insidious and coercive message about women and their bodies. Ostensibly designed to provide facilities and educational programs to encourage a healthier lifestyle, fitness centers also subtly indoctrinate instructors and thus members into seeing the female body in a particular and limited way. It makes economic sense for the club to emphasize fat percentages and measurements as a way to induce insecurity and thus to maintain consistently high membership numbers. The instructors warn even the thinnest members that people who *look* thin often store unhealthy fat beneath the skin. A thin frame may still be flabby, and the only way to test for lurking fat is to be measured by a fitness professional. According to fitness club rhetoric, fad diets and diet goods may produce superficial weight loss, but they do not produce the important fat loss. Only consistent exercise and regular attendance at the fitness club can achieve the desired result. Expressed concern about the health of instructors and members becomes the justification for managing appearance. The tape measure thus serves to measure not only size but also health, progress, dedication, sexuality, and self-worth.

The anger that an instructor or member feels when the tape measure belies the effort he or she has given to diet and exercise reveals a certain distance between the body and the self. The body has the capacity to cooperate with or betray the self. This distance is distinct from the integration observed in other Japanese institutions and bears a resemblance to that observed in the West. It is likely that the fitness club, as a Western import, has also imported notions of a body alienated from the self. But it is important to bear in mind that, as I argue elsewhere, local aesthetic salons and diet industries in Japan also capitalize on antagonism between mind and body and an ability to separate out certain body parts for correction (Ginsberg 2000).

By focusing on quantifiable physical changes, the training schools and clubs equate a pleasing appearance with good health and then make explicit the links among beauty, health, and productivity. The official rhetoric of the training program emphasizes health and the importance of exercise in maintaining an energetic lifestyle. Although the program does concede that having fun and looking good is undoubtedly an essential part of exercise, the thrust is preserving an active lifestyle for oneself and others. At the introductory lecture for one well-known training school, the instructor explained, "Exercise, like other necessary activities for humans, such as eating, sleeping, and recreation, is necessary. You all already know that exercise is good for you, right? You all love aerobics, right? But you also have to worry about the health of your family and friends and get them to exercise. Health is not simply the absence of disease and sickness. Health is the physical, spiritual, and social training of the body. It is not only our own training, but as aerobics instructors, we must have the ability to give advice to others who want to train." The training lectures, while imparting basic information about anatomy and physiology, also contain an underlying discourse about the importance of exercise for a healthy body and, by extension, a healthy nation. Aerobics instructors are expected to be models of physical fitness and strength, but more important, as instructors, they are asked to assume responsibility for the health of immediate family, friends, and Japan as a whole. The state of their physical body must reflect this dedication to good health. The training teacher, in her introductory lecture, warned instructors-to-be that "in Japan, where everything has become so convenient and handy with portable telephones, cars, and convenience stores, people are becoming fat and blood pressure is increasing. When my mother was young, she used to have to carry blocks of ice far distances before there were refrigerators, and she is still healthy at age 85 from all the activity."

Couched in statistics and anecdotes about the deteriorating health of Japan as a nation, students are warned that to improve the health of Japan, instructors must begin by coaching family and friends to adopt a healthier lifestyle. The management recognizes the potential role that fitness clubs can play in fashioning the bodies that can handle the burdens of an increasingly aging society and the corporate demands of a flagging economy, but do not emphasize these effects of exercise on the club floor. Although management may recognize the potential to link fitness to corporate and state needs, they are unable to exploit these connections in the weight room and aerobics studio.

Time to Tan

The measuring, training, and sculpting of the body cannot be separated from the adornment or ornamentation of the body. As anthropologists have explored in prestate, premarket economies (see Brain 1979; O'Hanlon 1989) and late-capitalist societies alike, the body simultaneously serves as an adornment and as an object to be adorned. As a classic anthropological theme, the decoration of the body or the alteration of the natural human appearance, whether by scarification or Spandex, fasting or bodybuilding, must be read for its symbolic, communicative, and aesthetic meanings (see Wilson 1985; Kidwell and Steele 1989). Aerobics, like almost all other organized activities in Japan, requires a uniform that extends even to the preferred brand of sneakers (Nike) and the color of one's skin. Although very few members extend their concern over the appropriate costume to an obsession with skin color, every aerobics instructor flaunts a deep, dark tan as a signature of his or her profession.

In a decade where 25 protection sunblock and a wide-brimmed hat have replaced baby oil and tanning beds in the United States, the deeply tanned and leathery skin of the "healthy" Japanese aerobics instructor seems incongruous and off-putting. A deep, dark suntan—the result of hours on a tanning bed—is intrinsic to the look, even the uniform, of the aerobics instructor. The majority consider the time spent on the tanning bed relaxing and enjoyable, but many also feel compelled to constantly keep up their tan as part of "the look" prescribed by fitness journals and fashion magazines. The cover model of the November 1997 issue of *Fit-*

12. With her sporty haircut, tanned skin, and trendy leotard, this model featured on the cover of a popular fitness magazine epitomizes the coveted look of an aerobics instructor.

ness Journal illustrates the stereotypical image of an aerobics instructor in Japan. She is tan with a sporty short haircut, skinny with underdeveloped upper body strength, and wearing the trendiest new type of leotard (Figure 12). As one club manager explained, "The image of aerobics instructors is, in a word, tan. Tan connotes a healthy glow, active, and physical." Tanned skin is also rumored to show off muscle definition better, by highlighting shadows and bulges. Bodybuilders in Japan and the United States frequent tanning salons and coat their bodies with dark oil before competing to exaggerate definition.

Members and instructors were curious about my expressed aversion to tanning and the obvious untanned skin of aerobics instructors visiting from abroad. One instructor-in-training commented, "The foreign instructors don't seem to tan much. They are all so white. Is tanning not popular?" When I explained the dangers of skin cancer, she replied, "Well, yes, I'm concerned. When you tan, you lose moisture and your hands get very dry and wrinkled like an old woman. But the rays of the tanning machine are different from the sun. There are two types of rays, and the dangerous rays aren't used."[7] Although this woman expresses "concern" about the dangers of sun tanning, her worries center on a loss of beauty, that is, dry, unattractive, aging skin, rather than the more serious and life-threatening health concern of skin cancer. For a young woman of 24, the dangers of losing her job and her looks are more pressing than concerns about losing her life. She ends her comment with a "lesser of two evils" rationalization, that tanning bed rays are somehow less dangerous than the sun, which duplicates the arguments made by instructors to justify smoking some types of cigarettes over others.

How is this deeply tanned skin to be interpreted? Historically, in Asia as well as Europe and the United States, pale skin has been a marker of the upper class, those who had the material means to avoid working long hours in the hot sun. As early as the Heian period (A.D. 794–1195), a plump, white face with narrow eyes and shaved eyebrows and a small, delicate mouth with blackened teeth was part of the ideal for the aristocratic class. Both men and women applied a thick layer of white powder to their face to symbolize their privileged status, spared of any form of outdoor labor.[8] White skin continues to be part of the contemporary beauty ideal and an indicator of class. In recent decades, however, in the United States, Europe, and, to an increasing degree, Asia, tanned skin has come to distinguish the privileged few with both the time and money to cultivate a leisurely tan outdoors, preferably overseas.

The tanned skin of the aerobics instructor thus seems to comment on both class status and generational differences. Tanning is becoming increasingly popular with young women who are not on the elite trajectory. In the past year or so, these girls, called *Ganguro* (gang girl) and *Yamamba* (evil spirit; ghost), like the aerobics instructors, tan their skin to a very dark color to contrast with blond-dyed hair and white eye makeup. Although even some of the more mainstream young people in Japan have emulated the likes of Amuro Namie, a television star (*tarento*) who popularized tanned skin and bleached hair, for the most part pale white skin is still synonymous with feminine beauty. Most beauty supply stores and department store cosmetic counters, such as Shiseido, sell skin-whitening lotions, and self-tanning products have yet to catch on.

Although a light overall glow is indicative of leisure even in Japan, a deep and intentionally cultivated tan is a marker of something entirely different. Associated with the labor of the body and a lack of material wealth and educational credentials, the tanned skin of the aerobics instructor has come to mark her as one who labors with her body. Yet, because the tanning is intentional and artificial, it requires both time and money to keep up. Tanning beds cost 500 yen (about $4.15) for fifteen minutes and the requisite "aerobics" tan demands regular upkeep. Many instructors tan for half an hour to an hour daily to cultivate their look. In this way, the tan could be symbolic of both leisure and financial success.

The instructors enjoy standing out and intentionally brand their bodies as distinct. They feel they look healthier and more alive than the businessmen and secretaries who frequent their clubs. Tanning is a way to distinguish themselves from their white-collar clients and upper-level club managers, who have neither the time nor the inclination to devote hours to intense exercising, let alone tanning. But it is paradoxical. The instructors long to distinguish themselves, but the way they have chosen also brands them as inferior. As I explore in the next chapter, aerobics instructors, who labor with their bodies, indeed, their sexualized bodies, already experience a certain level of discrimination in Japan. Their deeply tanned skin visually sets them apart from their wealthier clients and confirms gender, class, and generational stereotypes.

Uniform Sexuality

Both members and instructors pay close attention to the flavor and style of the class before outfitting themselves. Instructors and even members often change leotards between classes to fit the type of class taught. One member confided, "The instructor must always look cool. People judge the quality of the aerobics teacher by her outfits. It is very important to look good." Aerobics instructors and club members assume a costume and, indeed, a persona that is not unlike the young Japanese rappers who dress in street wear or the Beatles imitators in their bowl haircuts.

The professional bodybuilders in California also adopt a certain uniform, in which the body is shaved, tanned, and oiled to play up muscle striation and tone. Ripped tank-tops and baggy pants round out the costume designed to show just the right amount of muscle (Klein 1993:247–248). Certain aerobics classes, such as hip-hop, can be characterized not only by type of music and dance moves, but also by the dress of the class (Figure 13). The retail boutique at most fitness clubs have a special rack of "funk" street clothes in varying combinations of

13. These club members demonstrate a hip-hop aerobics routine, wearing cornrows, baggy pants, and Bulls jerseys.

black, white, and gray. At one hip-hop class downtown, out of twenty participants only one woman wore a bright pink leotard, which stood out in the sea of muted colors. Baseball caps, basketball jerseys, black high-top sneakers, oversized T-shirts with brand names emblazoned across the front, and baggy, mid-calf-length pants round out the costume. The members describe this type of clothing as "gang wear"; one member even joked that she was once asked if she was a gang member when outfitted in her full regalia.

Workout clothing styles tend to change annually; for instance, in 1995 and 1996, the sexy yet terribly uncomfortable thong leotard, or *T-back* as it is called in Japanese, was the workout style of choice (see "Dressing Well for Exercise" 1997). But as one female member commented wryly, "If I wore a T-back, it wouldn't be a T-back anymore, but just a piece of thread because the flesh of my backside would close around the leotard and you wouldn't be able to see it. I wouldn't be able to do aerobics, because I would have to keep stopping to adjust my leotard. I would look like an elephant with a thin tail between two huge cheeks. Of course, the T-backs are very popular with the men. When an aerobics teacher wears one and faces away from the class, all the men start hooting and staring straight at her backside."

In 1997 and 1998, the biking shorts coupled with a sports bra for women or a tank-top for men replaced the thong and seemed to be a step in the right direction. However, the tiny shorts had the annoying and embarrassing tendency to ride up during the course of the class, and as a result, both women and men were tugging down the shorts every few minutes. Solid colors of white, black, red, yellow, and blue, with minimum detailing, were worn by the most style-conscious members; thong leotards, animal prints, and pastels clearly marked members who were a year or two behind. Not surprisingly, those with the most confidence in their body, appearance, and/or dance skills tended to wear the most revealing outfits. At the fitness clubs in the suburban and more rural areas, many women in their early thirties and older wore flesh-colored tights under biking shorts for the sake of modesty.

Aerobics has been criticized as complementing rather than challenging unequal gender roles. Feminists have argued that the leotard defines women by their body and equates women's sport with sexuality (see Lenskyj 1986; Shaw 1994). T-back leotards and short shorts exaggerate legs and buttocks and their uncomfortable fit requires constant attention, and sports bras, which do perform a utilitarian function when worn as undergarments, showcase breasts when worn alone. S. Willis (1991) asserts that the sexy leotard contradicts the potential emancipatory effects of sport for women. The aerobics uniform glamorizes and trivializes the sport by overemphasizing the look and engendering rivalry and competition over empowerment. Hargreaves agrees: "The focus of publicity is on appearance (the athletic-looking body), fashion (the trendy-looking image) and physique (the sexy-looking shape); rather than on movement (the active-looking woman). The idea of exercise is blurred with sexuality" (1994:160). But the sexual nature of the leotard is by no means lost on the women who wear them and can also be interpreted as a source of power and an expression of freedom.

The overt sexiness of the leotard offers a radical form of resistance to gender roles. Donning a racy and revealing leotard has the potential to transform the wearer from housewife or office worker into a sexy, confident performer, just as bulking up or slimming down through exercise and diet can produce similar results. In fact, the leotard, so distinct from office uniforms and housecoats, is credited by many fitness authorities in Japan with being a major contributing factor in attracting the initial hordes of women to aerobics (Kawahara 1995:43–44). Yumiko Yamaoka, the director of the first Japanese aerobics instructor training program and one of the early pioneers of aerobics in Japan, explains the appeal of the leotard:

> Now it has become usual for women to wear leotards, but at that time [1982], they longed to wear the leotards . . . the leotard brought about big changes for women. It was thought that when they wore the leotard when they went to the aerobics studios, that they could be different from their everyday selves. I think that many women wanted to be ballerinas when they were little. No matter what age you are, the feeling of wanting to become something gorgeous doesn't change, you know. The leotard carries you into that feeling. When you wear a leotard you are transformed into a different person and you are freed from yourself as you begin to sweat. . . . For women who seldom had the chance to move their bodies to the rhythm of the music, this was an opportunity for fun and beautiful exercise. Of course, it wouldn't be wrong to say that the leotard was a big attraction. (1996:14)

Aerobics provided a form of escape from the tedium and day-to-dayness of uninspired and unappreciated office jobs or the stress of caring for children and elderly parents. The sexy and flashy leotards, so unlike the drab office uniform or housedress, were the costumes that transformed the women into someone else. Leotards function as "life-style clothing," that is, "repertories of signs that transcend their functional utility and define their wearers in particular images and associations" (Chaney 1996:108).

Given the transgressive nature of the sexy leotard, it is not surprising that instructors who appear too sexy in the club are criticized by conservative members and even other staff. When an aerobics instructor wore a white lace thong leotard with strategically placed opaque white insets over the breasts, I noticed a male member in his mid-thirties shaking his head disapprovingly and commenting to one of the male staff, who agreed that the leotard looked like lingerie. In this instance, the female aerobics instructor was exhibiting confidence in her body and her sexuality and was using the aerobics studio as a stage on which to perform. Confident sexuality is clearly distinct from the passive sexuality imposed on instructors in the after-hours parties and is viewed as threatening. The leotard and the flesh-colored tights worn by older women simultaneously exaggerate and constrain female sexuality, not unlike the loaded meanings of corsets, girdles, and brassieres.

With an emphasis on beauty, body, and aesthetics, aerobics and the leotard do seem to conform to traditional notions of sexualized femininity. But the exoticness and blatant sexiness of aerobics also provide women with an opportunity to resist the prevalent feminine stereotype of the demure, passive, and sexually inexperienced ideal. The *burikko,* or pretend-child—cute, innocent and naïve—was one of the most accepted feminine ideals of the 1980s and 1990s (McVeigh 1996; Kinsella 1995; White 1995). The self-confidence and sexual freedom exhibited by these women is simultaneously rebellious and standardized or, in the words of Kelly, "co-opted, contested and complicit" (1993:216). Although aerobics' provocative uniforms and sensuous moves actively challenge the feminine ideal, rebellion plays out only in certain accepted costumes like the leotard and only within certain circumscribed spaces of the fitness club or disco.

The sexiness of the leotard appeals to the same young women who in recent years began baring their bodies at popular dance clubs, like Juliana's Tokyo, which opened in Roppongi in 1991 and has since closed only to be replaced by another dance club, Velfarre. Labeled *body-con* by the media in the early 1990s, this expression is based on the phonetic spelling of "body-conscious" in English. It refers to the young women, typically office ladies, who exchange their conservative working uniforms for revealing shirts and microminiskirts to be worn for after-hours disco-hopping. As one journalist colorfully describes, "Most nights of the week a couple of hundred young women, clad in backless, sideless and see-through creations, pay to become the stage show. On one podium tonight, a dancer sports a gold G-string, stiletto heels, nipple tassels, and little else. Glitter bras and leather bikinis jostle with feather boas. A large hole has been cut in a blue vinyl mini-dress to expose a firm, naked bottom. The dancers, seemingly oblivious to the staring men who crowd the club's large bar area, are fixated on their own reflections in the looking-glass walls. . . . Tomorrow at nine, however, this modern Cinderella will be back at the supermarket checkout, in a uniform of grey serge" (Robinson 1995).

The women typically dance in large groups on makeshift disco stages. The body-con continues to be regarded as a "new breed of woman," independent and uninhibited, proud of her body, and assured in her sexuality. The *esute* (aesthetics) salons in the early 1990s capitalized on this new image of the independent woman. Free, fun-loving, and rebellious was the message of an advertising jingle from a 1991 campaign of one of the largest and most popular aesthetic salons in Japan: "OL's have got it made: Get the work done and forget overtime! Sneak out behind the boss' back and run off to aerobics, *karaoke,* or an aesthetic salon! Isn't it great to be a woman? Come on OL's, let's go for it!" (quoted in Watanabe 1993:A1). Aerobics studios, esute salons, and nightclubs provide the space and the outlet for a defiant expression of confidence, freedom, and sexuality through the moving, shaping, or undressing of the body. ⌐The body becomes a medium by which to resist gender roles and chafe against social constraints.⌐ Brownell describes the similar use of colorful clothing worn by older Chinese women who disco-dance as a way of "breaking a taboo by adopting the trappings of youth" (1995:281).

But scholars like Sumiko Iwao suggest that the seemingly liberated body-con is expressing an "artificial" freedom: "In reality, they're caught between traditional collectivism and individualism. They're still not really free from group pressure. They go in groups, and the costumes are almost a kind of uniform" (quoted in Robinson 1995). She proposes that the self-confidence and sexual freedom exhibited by the women is ephemeral and inconsequential, predicting that these same women will later find themselves in a traditional marriage and caregiving role, mirroring those of their mother and grandmother. Empowerment and constraint are not mutually exclusive. Rather, in the removed space of the fitness club or the nightclub, women are simultaneously rebellious and compliant. Although the effects of the unprecedented exuberance and exhibitionism of these young women may not be unique, long-standing, or even particularly influential, in the words of James Scott, significance lies in "everyday" resistance where "neither outright collective defiance nor rebellion is likely or possible" (1985:27).

Although working out can be conceived as a way to empower the body (and self) through the agency of self-discipline, Radner points out, "Insofar as the workout functions in a world in which beauty is defined ultimately in terms of a marketplace that has yet to 're-think' cultural standards, 'working out' will always be geared towards the reproduction of these standards. Otherwise it would not be a source of public empowerment and control. This is the paradox of the feminine culture of the body" (1995:173). Chaney also notes the contradiction of fashion, which promises individuality while demanding conformity: "Being in fashion both provides a badge of inclusion and incorporation confirming your social identity as at the same time, allowing individuals to differentiate themselves from others" (1996:49–50).

Uniforms standardize appearance, assign identity, and erase individuality. They are one of the most effective and obvious ways to discipline bodies and control self-expression. Prisons, schools, and the military rely on uniforms as a form of control. McVeigh discusses the ubiquity of uniforms in Japan as a deliberate project of the state designed to discipline and control minds and bodies. He explains that "donning a uniform does not *reflect* the wearer's commitment to social norms; rather, the very act of donning a uniform *produces and reproduces* on a daily basis the subjective substructure of norms demanded by politico-economic structures" (1997:208). On the one hand, the leotard positions the female body for consumption by the male gaze, sexualizing the wearer and, indeed, the sport of aerobics. But on the other hand, the sexiness of the leotard simultaneously liberates sexuality, body consciousness, and self-expression, just as it constrains.

I have demonstrated how the act of measuring and outfitting women's bodies in the fitness club reflects and resists larger definitions of health, class, productivity, beauty, and sexuality. I turn now to a discussion of the ways stylistic movements are coordinated in the training schools and later in the clubs. Does enforced synchronicity play on societal constructions of effort, endurance, and pain?

Coordinated Actions: Feeling through Form

Training schools dedicate an enormous amount of time to the synchronization of movements. For many instructors-in-training, the practical lessons are far more grueling than sitting passively for anatomy lessons. As one student explained after the first practical, "It was only walking, but it was really tiring. Plus, we kept doing pliés and squats over and over, the same movement, and we all got really sweaty." The students, if nothing else, certainly built cardio stamina through the twice weekly practical lesson. For two and a half hours every Saturday and Sunday, students are required to perform full-out in incredibly intense workouts under the scrutiny of critical instructors. And they are "encouraged" to build strength, stamina, and flexibility on the days when they are not at school.

Although U.S. courses teach a core curriculum of cueing, anatomy, kinesiology, and strength training, the workshops spend remarkably little time teaching choreography and execution of basic moves. The

Japanese training course, on the other hand, is designed to standardize the instructors from the bottom up, erasing differences and flaws. No moves, not even marching, are taken for granted, and nothing is beyond scrutiny. The angle of arms, the tilt of the head, and the distance between feet and legs are all subject to intense critique. There is a right way and a wrong way to execute each move, and the instructors' eyes are trained to pick up every flaw. The instructors teach in pairs, one explaining how the moves should be done down to the distance between the fingers and the angle of turnout of the feet, and the other demonstrating the move correctly, and then incorrectly.

The moves are exact, and there is no room for improvisation or creative license. It is assumed that the movements taught in the schools have been fine-tuned to work muscles most efficiently, and therefore any individual modification, no matter how insignificant, threatens to disrupt the benefits and effectiveness of the move. For example, one instructor stressed, "The 'step hop' is a hop, not a jump, and it is always accompanied by a clap, with arms bent at ninety degrees at the elbow." Those students whose arms were not held in the clap for a second long enough, whose legs were too wide, or who didn't have the correct bounce in their step were scrutinized by the instructors and made to practice until they conformed. Drilling a single member over and over again on a single move may seem like hazing, but, in fact, the instructors were most attentive to the less polished members and often stayed after class to help them improve.

One woman was having some trouble with the jumping jack, as her knees and ankles were not in a straight line. The instructor stayed with her for a good ten minutes as the class moved on without her. Under the hawk's eye of the instructor, it was no surprise that she had trouble catching on, and the more she struggled, the more the instructor criticized. The students train to blend in rather than stand out, and individuality, at this level, is discouraged. The more the students begin to conform, to where even the slightest imperfections are identified and corrected, the more easily the smallest flaws stand out, until even I could notice an angle or a position that was a bit off. It is as if the students are rehearsing for a group performance of the Rockettes instead of building the basic skills to branch off alone as individual instructors.

The training schools operate under the guiding principle that by executing a move enough times, it will be ingrained or memorized corporally. Zarilli has described what he terms "in-body disciplines of Asian meditational, martial, and performing arts," in which "the daily repetition of physical exercises and/or performance techniques encodes the techniques in the body" (1990:131). Employing techniques of rote memorization and rigorous training, the instructors drill certain concepts and moves into the students' minds and bodies. As one student explained, "We did squats for an hour and a half. We were not allowed to get a drink of water even. I was so thirsty that my throat hurt, but that wasn't part of their goal. They just wanted us to exercise and didn't give us any breaks. They wanted our bodies to learn the movements without thinking. My legs were soooo sore the next day, I almost fell down the stairs. It felt like I didn't have any legs at all. Actually, I didn't want to go back on Sunday, and I was so nervous and uneasy that my stomach hurt. Tomorrow is Friday, and it's almost Saturday so I'll begin to feel *blue* [in katakana] again." Repeating squats for hours on end may seem an unnecessarily grueling exercise, but it is intentionally designed to teach students to internalize the correct form so that the squat can be performed automatically. Much like the precision demanded of soldiers and prisoners as described by Foucault and reminiscent of a martial arts exercise that requires the repeated punching of a rope-wrapped plank with one's bare knuckles, the pain of aerobics training is intrinsic to the path of proper learning and development.

The rigorous exercises at the training schools draw on two character-building principles consistent with seishin education used by other Japanese institutions: "feeling created through form" and "hardship shapes character." In this way, the mind and the body are progressively integrated through the repetition and imitation of a formalized *kata*, or fixed set of physical moves designed to induce spiritual enlightenment. The training course rhetoric is markedly similar to the underlying discourse of corporate ethics retreats (Kondo 1990), the training for office ladies (McVeigh 1995), and martial arts instruction (Donohue 1991). McVeigh's description of stewardess training manuals for Japan Airlines bears a keen resemblance to the standardization of body movements in the aerobics instructor training schools. The manual includes a checklist for the prescribed way for a stewardess to walk, including such questions as: "Your head doesn't swing from left to right, does it?" and "Do your heels and toes hit the ground at the same time?" (46). Proper body movements are expected to produce appropriate and corresponding attitudes of docility and demureness in the stewardesses and an emphasis on synchronicity has the capacity to inspire group cooperation and spirit.

It is not simply that instructors impose their synchronized routines on the members: their clients insist on it. One member explained that although one of the most popular instructors was nice and friendly, she didn't like her because "she always makes at least five mistakes per class. I don't know why, but she always does. The rest of the class will do the routine correctly, but the instructor will make a mistake and turn around and apologize again and again. I hate that!" The aerobics instructors agree; one explains, "The Japanese are very picky and complain about small things, like if a staff doesn't do the appropriate cues, a member will complain." Another instructor confirmed that although "Chiba is relaxed and quiet, where people laugh nicely if you make a mistake, [Downtown Fitness] is scary. I feel bad for the instructor who makes a mistake there, because the members get very angry and complain." Repetition is essential to training the aerobics instructor. But I would emphasize that, although originality is initially squelched at instructor training schools, the instructors learn basic skills and techniques that enable them later to employ remarkable creativity in crafting individual routines. The training schools lay the groundwork that indeed standardizes instructors to a certain degree, but the truly successful and popular instructors go beyond the basics, introducing complexity and originality to their choreography.

By cultivating an ability to synchronize movements on the aerobics floor and to endure endless repetition, the training schools might be able to produce employees and members who will be dedicated in other capacities. But this point is never made explicit. Physical endurance is never equated with mental endurance, and synchronicity remains unmarked, serving merely as a concession to members who have a limited amount of free time and who desire workouts that are both effective and entertaining. By managing the delivery of exercise down to the proper execution of a jumping jack, managers ensure that their clients receive the expected service of a good workout. Body discipline at the fitness club is most evident in this synchronization of movements, emphasis on effort and pain, and Zen-derived notion that feeling follows form. But in the end, the heavy-handed control of behavior in the training school and, to a lesser degree, in the club has the opposite intended effect, deterring clients rather than attracting them.

Self-Critique

I have illustrated the ways disciplinary techniques have been imposed on instructors and, to a lesser degree, members through strict control over appearance and actions. But as Foucault, Bourdieu, and others point out, control is most effective when it is self-imposed. In this section, I describe how the fitness club imposes self-regulation through self-reflection and critique of others. Aerobics instructors are required to write a club diary entry after the completion of each lesson, explaining their impressions of the class. The diary is kept in the staff room and is reviewed periodically by the chief of fitness and the club manager. The instructors must have each entry stamped by one of the full-time employees at the club before they leave for the day. The entries range from a brief, two-line sentence, such as "The class went well today, but I messed up once. I will try harder," to longer and more thoughtful paragraphs. One such detailed entry was written by an instructor at Chiba Club after teaching a beginner aerobics class:

> *Type of Class: Beginner (Number of men: 2, Number of women: 11)*
> *Total: 13*
>
> Today I had two people who had never taken my class before. . . . I asked the beginner people after the lesson how the class went and they said that it was very fun, but I feel a bit uneasy about whether or not they meant it. But in the end, I think that they will come again next week. . . . Another person left the class just as it started, but I was unfortunately unable to follow up. (Shoot!) [*Shimatta!*] I will be careful not to let this type of thing happen again. The content of the class was very simple, but I felt very energetic. My throat felt a bit sore so I felt that I wasn't able to perform 100%, and it seemed to me that my class wasn't that exciting today. I will be more careful about my taking care of my throat, and next week I will try very hard.[9]

Similarly, club members are expected to record their blood pressure and weight, the number of repetitions and sets executed, and exercise goals in designated individual charts every time they use the facilities. Members share questions and concerns and even divulge details about alcohol intake and other vices. The files are checked periodically by the instructors to monitor progress, to offer personal attention and motivation, and, perhaps most significant, to assert a form of control over the members. Instructors write little notes in the margins of the file: "Go for the perfect body" or "Try harder." In this way, instructors prescribe a body type and fitness goal for an individual member that is desirable yet always just out of reach. Designed to ensure the club's own success and to keep the members returning, instructors' comments are careful to balance optimism and encouragement with subtle criticism to prevent members from ever achieving complete success. Even if weight goals are reached, the staff cautions members that maintenance is crucial and that a few skipped weeks will result in inevitable backsliding.

Fukuzawa (1996) describes a similar use of self-reflective diaries and essays (*hanseibun*) in Japanese middle schools. Students write daily on feelings, events, homework assignments, and an overall review of the day's accomplishments. Teachers collect notebooks throughout the semester to gauge academic progress and psychological health and to stave off problems. The sharing of the notebooks with teachers and fellow classmates leaves the individual open to the criticism and help of others. Fukuzawa asserts, "Discipline consisted of gathering information on the details of students' lives, feelings, and attitudes, then persuading students to adopt the prescribed pattern embodied in the numerous routines of the school" (305).

Hansei, or reflection, serves as a means of social control through the imposition of self-critique and is common to many institutions in both Japan and China. Brownell observes a similar attention to "thought control" through the distribution of self-evaluation forms among the Chinese Olympic athletes (1995:165). She notes that certain key phrases are expected and that the style is both formal and formulaic. Symptomatic of the Maoist period, when state control of minds and actions was particularly virulent, self-critique has since been rejected in the reform period. As Foucault notes, "A 'power of writing' was constituted as an essential part in the mechanisms of discipline" (1979:189). The use of these essays forces students, Olympic athletes, and aerobics instructors to think constructively about their own actions and feelings and those of their peers.

The diaries add another layer of control, so that not only appearance and actions but also thoughts and feelings may be held to a certain standard of normalization. Hansei allows managers to better discipline the instructors and instructors to better control the members, illustrating what Bourdieu describes as "a self-control that predisposes them to control others" (quoted in Brownell 1995: 178). It is a small step from jotting down notes about how to improve one's own teaching style and exercise regime to penning notes of "encouragement" in the margins of members' exercise charts or voicing criticism of weight gain to one's peers and clients.

Fat Talk

Your eyes seem smaller, has your face gotten fatter?
— *An instructor to a member who hadn't been in for a while*

You shouldn't wear those pants, they make your butt look big.
— *One instructor to another*

Do you ever weight train? You have no muscles. You look like a woman. — *A female instructor asked of a male instructor when he took off his shirt to change into his uniform*

It is quite usual to hear comments such as these in the fitness club, where instructors, members, friends, and acquaintances feel free to comment on one's physique or overall appearance.[10] This commentary can take the form of a compliment, as in the staff's evaluation of coworkers discussed above, or a critical observation of weight gain or acne. In the United States, even the most innocent or well-meaning comment on weight gain is considered not only a cruel insult, but a subject taboo to all but perhaps family members and one's closest friends.[11] But in Japan, compliments and criticism about the body are not only common, they are generally taken in stride. Friends typically greet one another after a long absence by commenting on weight gained or lost. This greeting is both a way of inquiring about health or lifestyle and a simple observation on how a friend has changed in the time that has elapsed. In Japan, where being thin is the ideal, suggesting that a person has gained weight is almost never a compliment. But there are situations when commenting on a few extra pounds may be intended as a statement on a friend's good health or steady job, when he or she is satisfied and prosperous and food can be enjoyed with gusto. Several of my American friends and colleagues who have spent time in Japan have observed that Japanese friends and even casual acquaintances feel comfortable commenting on any weight gained or lost during their course of stay in Japan. Westerners are initially taken aback by this, but in this instance, Japanese friends may simply be expressing concern over how their foreign friend is adapting to the food and lifestyle in Japan.

As Brownell (1995) points out, fat talk, or more generally body talk, in China is acceptable because physical appearance constitutes merely one part of the self; therefore, comments on the body are not taken as direct personal attacks but as expressions of concern about the well-being of the person. She suggests that body talk in China is indicative of the more "fluid boundaries" between bodies in East Asia versus the more fixed body boundaries characteristic of the United States. Connected to historically grounded assumptions in classic Chinese medicine, "the human body was perceived as intimately connected with the world around it: the body and the environment mutually influenced each other, each being permeated with essences that circulated throughout the cosmos" (241). When the boundaries between mind and body and between body and cosmos are blurred, the notion of a communal body emerges. And it is this communal body in China that creates a space for body talk without fear of insult.

Interestingly, Becker observed that Fijians exhibit a similar referral to body size and shape in the form of greetings, jokes, insults, and concern, particularly in the case of children and guests: "The Fijian body reflects the achievements of its caregivers. A body is the responsibility of the micro-community that feeds and cares for it; consequently, crafting its form is the province of the community rather than the self" (1995:57). Similarly, Sobo has observed that in Jamaica weight loss "signals social neglect" (1997:259). Remarks on weight gain or loss become an expression of community concern and pride in the adequacy of caregiving. In Japan, certainly in the case of guests and children, the fitness, health, and overall appearance of the body can be taken as a measure of the care received. Although body size is "a matter of social, not personal, concern" in Fiji, Becker explains that the individual is generally complacent about his or her body image and seldom alters his or her body to achieve the cultural ideal (1). In Japan, however, individuals invest tremendous money, time, sweat, and worry into attaining the "perfect body." And it is in this context of active personal effort that the Japanese individual may express or recognize an alternative motive, be it idle observation or more pointed criticism, for such blatant remarks on body size and shape.

In certain contexts, comments on weight gain or loss can be intended as well-meaning expressions of concern, but, more often than not, they are simply observations intended as neither insults nor compliments. Ohnuki-Tierney notes that inquiring about and describing one's health is quite common in Japan and is characteristic of both men and women of all ages and socioeconomic backgrounds (1984:57). To note one's size, appearance, and well-being may be a way to inquire about one's state of health or *jibyou,* which Ohnuki-Tierney defines as "an illness one carries throughout life and suffers at some times more acutely than others" (53). From stiff shoulders to a weak stomach or high blood pressure, the current status of one's "personal illness" is a common topic of conversation and may manifest itself as weight gain or loss.

In this sense, inquiry about jibyou may be bereft of deeper meanings of criticism, malice, or even concern. Just as a Westerner may comment on a friend's haircut, observing weight changes is "something you notice right away. You can easily see if someone looks fatter or thinner than the last time you saw them," explained one of my coworkers at the club. As there is less of a taboo on criticizing a person's size, stature, or appearance, these observations, critical or complimentary, can be neutral and value-free. But in other instances, these comments are more judgmental, as this coworker explained, "If someone says 'You've gained weight,' it is never a compliment. . . . It is simply stating a fact, which is said more easily in Japan than in America, but it still isn't a compliment. It is not meant to be insulting, just not complimentary. Friends may say it as a joke, but there is always truth in a joke, right? That is, the friend who says it probably really feels that he wants the other to get thinner." In Japan, many expect a good friend to tell the truth about one's appearance, even if it is difficult to hear. As one male instructor explained, "Superficial friends lie and say that you are not fat, even if you are, but good friends will tell you the truth."

Instructors are not only openly critical of one another, but often warn members if they are getting chubby or need to lose weight. One instructor admonished a male member that his large belly was proof that he was drinking too much beer, and another instructor urged a woman to lose weight before her upcoming wedding so that she would "look beautiful in the photographs." The instructors are expressing concern, which is designed to motivate members into action and to provide support for members who may not know how to begin an exercise regime. The job of the instructor is to be a fitness and nutrition counselor for the members, dispensing advice and offering direction. At the same time, a critical staff member may be trying to ensure his or her own necessity and that of the club. If a member is made to feel inadequate and less than perfect, he or she may be more likely to take advantage of the club facilities and programs.

At the same time, expressed concern over weight gain may be a veiled barb, intended to hurt, insult, or, at the very least, provoke change.[12] Boyfriends and girlfriends, close friends, acquaintances, and even parents offer unsolicited criticism and advice in the guise of concern but often with little regard for how the comments will be received. One young woman mentioned countless times about how a close female friend may be lucky to be skinny, but that this didn't make up for the fact that she was flat-chested. When the three of us went to a department store together, the young woman held up a padded bra and called her thin friend over to say that the bra was made for her. The friend laughed good-naturedly but looked very uncomfortable.

Another female college student at a Chiba university explained that men readily dissect the body of the woman they are dating: "Most guys say about the girls they are dating: 'Even if she is fat, I don't mind.' All of my ex-boyfriends said this, but when I did get plump, they would say: 'You got fat, didn't you?' On the surface, they would say to me: 'I don't mind.' But in reality, they would complain: 'You got fat!' They also said, when we ate together, that they liked girls who ate a lot, but in reality, you know, when I did eat a lot, they would exclaim: 'Ehhh, you're going to eat all that?! You're not going to be able to fit into your jeans.' But Japanese men usually don't think it's rude to say those things, they think it's fine." Fat talk, open criticism, and innocent observation serve as forms of social control, measuring the weight, health, and overall appearance of an individual against the group ideal. Deviation from the ideological standard is cause for comment directed at improvement. Much like the self-monitoring characteristic of Foucault's panopticon, instructors and members manage themselves. Fat talk directs criticism outward rather than within, as in the case of the self-reflective essays (hanseibun).

Conclusions

Whether in the interest of producing healthy workers, increasing efficiency and productivity, controlling sexuality, or instilling rivalry and competition among women, the fitness clubs and training schools attempt to structure appearance, actions, and thoughts around ideological norms. This standardization, while striking when viewed in isolation, becomes hegemonic and culturally rationalized because of a consistency with other forms of education and sports training in Japan. The techniques of the fitness club resonate with local institutional prescriptions for the rationality of science, feminine modesty, and a strict social hierarchy based on age, credentials, and gender.

Despite the heavy-handed controls on appearance, behavior, and demeanor of both members and staff at the fitness club, conformity is not always a given. As I illustrate in the remaining three chapters, female instructors and club members at times conform to feminine stereotypes and roles, and at other times actively resist these expectations. In the next chapter, I turn to a discussion of the aerobics instructors, who are acutely aware of the hierarchical structure of the service industry and express frustration with gender- and age-based inequities. Although they may parrot the rhetoric of health and fitness when working, after hours and backstage many of the female aerobics instructors drink and smoke as a way to challenge patriarchal constraints.

Cigarettes and Aerobics

Frustrations with Gender Inequities in the Club

With sweat beading on her forehead and still breathless, the Japanese aerobics instructor slips behind the swinging door of the staff room, collapses into a chair, and gratefully lights up a cigarette. To most Americans, this image seems, if not contradictory and self-defeatist, at least ironic. How do we reconcile the "healthy" aerobics instructor indulging in such blatantly "unhealthy" behavior? In this chapter, I examine the multiple ways that Japanese aerobics instructors craft themselves, from couching their expertise in nonthreatening and culturally recognizable feminine forms on the fitness club floor to engaging in the unhealthy and traditionally masculine behavior of smoking and drinking after hours or in the privacy of the staff room. At first glance, this oppositional onstage and offstage behavior is consistent with the literature on personhood in Japan, as an expression of multiple and fragmented selves. But, on closer analysis, it becomes a way of acting out frustrations with both upper-level male managers and demanding club members.

As young, relatively uneducated female employees in notoriously patriarchal corporate Japan, these women must conform to expected feminine roles in the workplace. But, because they are structurally situated in the service industry as "free agents" and are not affiliated with any one club, aerobics instructors have a unique freedom to challenge these gender biases. Co-opting male speech and behavior becomes a way to act out frustrations with both upper-level male managers and demanding club members and to disrupt gender boundaries and grasp power in a male-dominated industry. The Japanese fitness club affords a unique space in which to examine how gender biases influence employee-employer and worker-client relationships in a late-capitalist service industry.

Situational Selves and Resistant Agents

To understand the contradictory behavior of the Japanese aerobics instructor, I draw on both the anthropological literature of the shifting and relational self in Japan and feminist and cross-cultural literature on the body and resistance. The majority of studies on selfhood in Japan, while extensive in their explication of the fragmented and context-based notion of personhood, do less in terms of explaining the relationship of power, dominance, and hierarchy in this determination of the situational self. With the exception of Rosenberger's (1992) compilation on the self, there have been few studies that explore not only how the self in Japan is constructed differently according to context, but also how these constructions are informed by relationships of power and hierarchy. By considering the literature on resistance, particularly the work of Scott (1985, 1990), Ortner (1995), and Gal (1995), in conjunction with that on notions of selfhood in Japan, I illustrate how the dyadic relationship between onstage and offstage is often a product of power-laden contexts. Considered in this light, the cigarette-smoking, beer-drinking aerobics instructor begins to make cultural sense.

In light of the vast anthropological literature on the shifting, relational self in Japan (e.g., Doi 1973; Rosenberger 1992; Lebra 1992), the question becomes whether the opposition between onstage and offstage behavior should indeed be considered contradictory. Scholars have convincingly illustrated that selfhood in Japan is constructed situationally: spontaneous and intimate behavior characterizes private relationships, and formality and distance characterize public relationships. Dyadic terms in Japanese, such as *omote* (front and public) and *ura* (back and private), *soto* (outside) and *uchi* (inside), and *tatemae* (surface; superficial) and *honne* (interior; true feelings), have been used to suggest what Doi (1973) terms the "twofold consciousness" of the Japanese. Bachnik (1992) summarizes how these terms play out in various spheres of Japanese society, from company organizations (Kondo 1990) to family organization (Hamabata 1990; Bachnik 1992) and school organization (Tobin 1992b; Peak 1991; Ben-Ari 1994), and from health and illness (Ohnuki-Tierney 1984) to marriage (Edwards 1989) and religion (Hardacre 1986). If we consider the cigarette-smoking aerobics instructor in terms of these structural analyses of the context-based and fragmented self, her behavior seems less contradictory and more reflexive of shifting levels of intimacy and distance, spontaneity and formality.

The fact that instructors assume a public persona while on the gym floor that requires strict adherence to club policy and a parrotlike mimicry of exercise rhetoric is not surprising. Aerobics instructors realize that to ensure that their clients lose weight and improve cardiovascular health as well as receive the level of entertainment and service expected, they must not only preach the benefits of exercise but must also physically embody the effects. From clean and well-fitting uniforms to a thin physique, instructors publicly demonstrate adherence to club policy. Their body becomes an extension of their uniform and a part of the club's advertisement for success. Aerobics teachers and club staff publicly regulate both their words and behavior, for if observed indulging in "unfit" actions on the club floor, they may lose members' confidence.

Given the strict monitoring of onstage behavior, it follows that instructors choose to relax away from the prying eyes of the clients. It becomes possible to reveal one's *honne*, or true self, where smoking and drinking alcohol can be indulged without inhibition, fear of reprimand, or loss of employment. Although Doi's (1973) work has been criticized for reproducing an essentialist view of culture, in which certain traits and behaviors are characterized as uniquely Japanese, his notion of a twofold consciousness seems to offer a plausible explanation for the seemingly contradictory behavior and actions in Japan.

Smoking backstage makes cultural sense when viewed as a means of "letting down one's hair" in the comfort of friends and colleagues. A North American instructor may feel reluctant to engage in unsanctioned behavior in front of upper-level managers, but in Japan, where all company employees, including managers, are considered part of the "in" or *uchi* group, smoking in front of one's boss could be interpreted as an expression of intimacy. Similar to the drinking parties described by Allison (1994), which level relationships in the corporate hierarchy, this *ura* (back) culture at the club gives a human quality, or *ningenkankei*, to the hierarchical structure of work. In light of the literature on the fragmented self, that healthy instructors engage in unhealthy behavior is not contradictory so much as an expression of the context-based self.

But does this tell the whole story? Certainly, studies on the situational self in Japan are useful for making sense of oppositional backstage and frontstage behavior, but this explanation seems to eliminate the roles that power and gender play in the crafting of selves. As Kondo notes, most studies of selfhood "tend to emphasize static, essentialized, global traits disconnected from power relations in the society" (1990:41). She encourages the study of self in grounded contexts, particularly in the domain of work, where one "cannot ignore struggles over the meanings of power, hierarchy, and discipline" (41). To get at this issue of power, it would be tempting to apply Scott's (1990) analysis of public and hidden transcripts to reconcile symbolic acquiescence and onstage presentations of self with contradictory behavior and offstage resistance. He explains that actions displayed on the public stage often mirror or mimic ways that the dominant class prefers things to appear, whereas backstage actions that take place "beyond direct observation by powerholders . . . confirm, contradict, or inflect what appears in the public transcript" (4). For these young, relatively uneducated female aerobics instructors, smoking behind closed doors certainly contradicts their public rhetoric of good health, but is it resistance?

Sherry Ortner (1995) and Susan Gal (1995) have launched devastating critiques of the "ethnographically thin" literature of everyday resistance. They claim that studies such as Scott's fail to take into account the ambivalence of local politics, the artificial starkness of public and hidden transcripts, the inevitable conflict of intentions, and the dangerous notion of a natural self that can be expressed only in private. The aerobics instructors, while undeniably dissatisfied, do not smoke collectively as a way to change the status quo, buck the system, or express some form of a true self free from hegemonic domination. They are neither collaborative nor intentionally subversive.

Employment practices in the fitness clubs, and in Japanese corporations at large, prevent solidarity among female office employees, eliminating any possibility for collective action. Ogasawara, in her work on female clerical workers in Japan, concludes that differences in age, educational background, and status among the women undermine any sense of unity, while an "overt emphasis on early retirement for OLs also weaken[s] their solidarity" (1998:68). I demonstrate that although aerobics instructors are markedly homogeneous in age, educational background, and gender, a fact that would seem to cultivate a common bond, it is the cyclical rotation of employees and their lack of affiliation with any one club that ultimately undercut any potential for collective resistance. Quite simply, aerobics instructors do not organize because they do not form long-standing relationships with other instructors, are not employed long enough to care to change the system, and, for the most part, express overall enthusiasm for their job despite a consistent dissatisfaction with low pay and prestige.

Although the instructors do not engage in overt resistance, it would be a mistake to characterize their lack of organized protest as proof of compliance or contentment with gender-based hierarchies in the company. I assert that the remarkable consistency of the instructors' contradictory and oftentimes self-destructive behavior performed through the medium of their bodies is an expression of dissatisfaction with power inequities at the club. By co-opting traditionally male behavior, smoking and drinking, these young women are attempting to transcend or at least play with gender stereotypes.

Class consciousness, in the Marxist sense, is not particularly well-developed in Japan, as illustrated by the famous "90 percent middle class" results of a government-administered census. When respondents were asked to select from categories that marked them as lower, middle, or upper class, the vast majority self-identified as middle class. These results are likely to be a reflection of the powerful equalizing ideology that discourages and downplays economic and social difference, rather than a reflection of true income discrepancies. Nevertheless, although there are undeniable class differences in Japan, these inequities are experienced in more discrete institutional contexts. Gender, seniority, and academic credentialing subsume class difference and determine power and prestige along a hierarchical continuum in corporate environments and the service industry in Japan.

The complicated position of the instructors as formally uneducated yet possessing specialized knowledge, young yet imbued with authority, and female yet strong and fit has dramatic consequences for the way they simultaneously project and are projected as "docile bodies" and experts. Playing on Scott's (1985) "everyday forms of resistance," an analysis of hypocritical onstage and offstage instructor behavior becomes a way of viewing what I term "everyday forms of frustration." Because most instructors quit after five to seven years, either voluntarily or as a result of "encouragement," they have little to lose.

Engaging in subversive behavior away from and often directly in front of the prying eyes of bosses and clients should be interpreted as a way of expressing frustration with the glass ceiling in corporate Japan. In particular, aerobics instructors, unlike most female corporate employees, use the masculine self-referent for "I," tell bawdy jokes, use loud voices and expansive gestures, and smoke cigarettes and drink beer (two vices that continue to be associated with masculinity in Japan) as dramatic ways to challenge gender- and age-based stereotypes. Young women who openly smoke and drink in front of clients and managers, where gender stereotypes sanction such behavior and fitness club rules strictly forbid such indulgences, are engaging in highly loaded acts. These dramatic displays of agency are not isolated events, but pervasive and consistent ways to achieve recognition in a gendered and hierarchical industry (Bourdieu 1977).

But much like the case of the anorexic, the young woman who appears to exert control over her physical self but ultimately conforms to society's standards of thinness (Bordo 1997), these acts of agency in the fitness club are self-defeatist if normative definitions of health are accepted. Smoking a cigarette and drinking to excess, while accepted masculine behavior, are considered by the mainstream to be not only unfeminine but also unhealthy. Therefore, aerobics instructors, in their attempts to act defiantly and to blur corporate hierarchies, inevitably damage their own health and reproduce suffocating standards of feminine modesty and beauty. Similar to the plight of the lads in Paul Willis's (1977) study, whose rebellious acting-out in school ensures the reproduction of their lowly position in the class hierarchy, the aerobics instructors' acts of indulgence serve to reproduce inequities. I next examine the everyday acts of frustration of the aerobics instructors as an expression of dissatisfaction with inequality in the Japanese service industry.

Gender Bias in the Service Industry

It's really too bad, but aerobics instructors are not well looked-upon by society at large. Although compared to before, when they just thought of aerobics instructors as sexy women wearing leotards, with their long legs, it is better now, but still not that good. Because instructors get paid by the lesson, it is not considered real work. Everyone thinks that aerobics teachers don't use their brains, that they only move their bodies. . . . It's too bad, but it is probably thought of at the same level as an *izakaya* [pub] employee. . . . The people on *Necktie Road* think that people who use their bodies are all the same.

—An aerobics instructor

In Japan, a society that associates age with experience, rewards academic achievement, and unapologetically discriminates on the basis of sex, the primarily young, high school–educated, female aerobics instructors are in triple jeopardy. Age, sex, and academic credentialing boundaries separate the staff from both the members, who have the economic means and leisure time to join a costly health club, and the almost exclusively older male fitness club managers, who deliberately erect impenetrable glass ceilings. Several forces are at work to denigrate the social position of female aerobics instructors in Japan.

Although men do teach aerobics in Japan, they are outnumbered seven to one by female instructors. For both men and women, teaching aerobics is a relatively brief career. The men who do instruct are quickly promoted into managerial positions after five years of club experience, but many of the veteran female teachers are "encouraged" to quit after only several years of service. At the fitness clubs, and in Japan more generally, youth equals attractiveness and strength, and although experience is valued by clubs, attractiveness appears to take precedence. One male instructor's callous remarks reflect the hostile environment for older female aerobics instructors at the club: "Young women [instructors] don't weight lift, because they don't need to. Things start to fall in their thirties, and they want to look young, so many start to lift after age 30. Also, aerobics begins to become boring. Many women quit teaching aerobics in their thirties, because they either get married and have a baby, become bored, or are not encouraged to stay. The club has an image to protect, and they don't want a lot of old women [*obaasan*] running around teaching." His intentionally derogatory use of the phrase "old women" to describe instructors over the age of 30 reflects the overall hypocrisy of the fitness club, which pledges to preserve health and an active lifestyle for members well into their silver years but devalues the experience and merits of female instructors and staff over the age of 30.

The common employment pattern for Japanese women, who peak in their early twenties, quit to marry or have children, and return to the workforce later on, has been characterized as an M curve (Brinton 1993). The M curve reflects the statistical peaks and valleys of female employment and describes many industries where women's labor is devalued and undercompensated. It should come as no surprise, then, that managerial positions at both central and local levels are held, almost without exception, by men.[1] National statistics on large Japanese corporations indicate that only 1 percent of managers are female and that 60 percent of these women are single (White 1993:66). Although some women are employed as full-time company workers (*shain*) and are given raises and promotions up to a point, the majority marry, quit, or change jobs before reaching any level of true authority and prestige. Those women who resist quitting face demotion, criticism, and pay cuts (Atsumi 1988).

Aerobics teachers hold a rather unique position in the white-collar corporation of the fitness club. Although some instructors are employed as shain, which provides them with job security, health insurance, and bonuses, most are characterized as *free* (katakana for "freelance") agents. Circulating from club to club, instructors are quite distinct from the stereotypical loyal company worker that one associates with most large, white-collar corporations in Japan.[2] Independent yet insecure, the aerobics instructor is often at the mercy of the market and the whims of her employers, and this may contribute to the lack of prestige and respect associated with her career choice as well as a lack of solidarity with her cohorts.

The majority of aerobics instructors are high school graduates, and those with college degrees tend to have graduated from one of the many *Taiiku Daigaku* (physical education) colleges in Japan.[3] Scholars of education concur that earning a degree from a prestigious four-year university virtually guarantees success in a well-regarded and well-paying career (e.g., Rohlen 1980, 1983; Brinton 1992), but two-year colleges in general and Taiiku Daigaku in particular neither prepare nor position their graduates for employment outside the fields of sport and dance. Consequently, most aerobics instructors' salaries are quite low by national standards and are determined by the size and prestige of the club and the experience and reputation of the instructor. Even the most well-known fitness club chains, including the two where I conducted research, attract top instructors with low starting salaries, offering only about 3,500 yen ($29) a class. The myth of meritocracy and the emphasis on academic credentialing in Japan ensures that aerobics instructors will be regarded by members, management, and society at large as flighty, sexy, and not entirely bright.

Physical labor in a societal climate that privileges the mind over the body automatically assigns instructors a low status, in which the body, in particular, the sexualized body is emphasized. The hierarchy of mind over body, in which the work of the mind is more highly regarded and, hence, more highly compensated than the work of the body, characterizes the workforce and national opinion in Japan.[4] Because fitness clubs are sites of leisure and entertainment, working at a club is dismissed as a cushy, sexy, and fun job. Aerobics instructors who work in studios and gymnasiums do not obtain the formal office training that their pink-collar contemporaries receive. One instructor explained, "We don't learn appropriate manners, such as the correct way to answer the telephone or how to exchange a business card. We just don't need to know this, but as a result, we are viewed as impolite and coarse."

The stigma against physical labor in general and the sex industry in particular leads one to question how the work of aerobics instructors is regarded as distinct or similar to the work of hostesses or strippers, in which sex appeal, attractiveness, and a fit and shapely physique determine the success of the employee. I asked an instructor if aerobics teachers are regarded in the same way as hostesses and she replied, "Well, yes, probably in the same sense that they both use their body. Of course, instructors are more healthy, because they don't have to drink, but still, it is the same idea of body strength." Aerobics instructors do drink quite a bit, in fact, and this is where the lines between the sex industry and the fitness club are blurred. As noted, aerobics has been sexualized since its import in the early 1980s, when the sexy U.S. television show *Aerobicize* ignited the fitness boom in Japan. The sexy image of the aerobicizer continues to be embodied in the costume of the leotard, which marks an instructor as a sexual body.

The hierarchy within the central office of the fitness club is not unlike that of other large, white-collar corporations in Japan. Anthropologists and corporate envoys alike have studied the managerial techniques of Japan's booming late-capitalist corporations. Studies conclude that the Japanese style of company management, based on decentralized authority and quality control checks and balances, is democratic, participatory, and nonauthoritarian (Rohlen 1975). However, whether the theory of decentralized management is actualized on the company floor of a typical white-collar corporation is up for debate. Management practice in the fitness club, however, is far removed from this conceptual model. Decidedly top-down, commands and new programs are initiated at the central office and then farmed out to the local branches. Communication between upper-level management and branch managers and between branch managers and staff tends to be inhibited and censured.

The instructors and club staff, who work on the floor with the members every day, are the best informed about how programs could be improved or changed. Yet these same staff members are the most reluctant to voice suggestions and complaints. One of the staff at the suburban club where I conducted research recognized that the spacious and well-equipped gymnasium is sorely underused and stands empty for most of the day. He mentioned off-handedly to me that the gym could be put to much better use by organizing ball games and activities for silver members during the day. When I asked why he had not directed this thoughtful proposal to the club manager, he replied resignedly, "In the Japanese system, you can't really suggest things because they won't be well received. Suppose they did implement such a program and people didn't come? It would be the responsibility of the person who thought of it. [Here], it is really top-down, and people at the bottom don't have much say. It is our experience that, whenever we tried to say something, it would be rejected so we just don't say anything. All of the new programs are initiated by the central office. Everyone is risk-averse, cowards." Aerobics instructors and staff feel frustrated and powerless when managers make authoritative and often unsuccessful mandates about club policy and classes without consulting the people who interact with the members on a daily basis.

At the same time, instructors are squeezed from below by members who expect the impossible: painless and effortless results of exercise and weight loss. Membership at a private fitness club chain in Japan is quite expensive. Most clubs require an initial registration fee averaging 30,000 yen (approximately $250), with monthly payments of 11,000 yen ($91). Time for leisure is limited in Japan, and the choices available are numerous and varied. Those who have both the means and the time to join an exclusive fitness club expect a high level of service. To learn to cater to their members' wishes, incoming staff are put through a semirigorous training program that involves memorizing the rules and system of the club, sampling a variety of classes and programs offered, practicing member counseling in front of a supervisor, and passing a series of written and oral tests.[5] As hiring is staggered throughout the year according to the fluctuating needs of the club and the marked turnover of employees, fitness clubs do not offer an annual unified training course to all incoming employees. Unlike the en masse training classes orchestrated at most large Japanese banks and companies in April, the fitness club training program is more individualized and flexible.

When I entered Chiba Club in August 1997, I was assigned to train along with one other part-time employee (*arubaito*) who was hired during the same month. The assistant chief was in charge of our instruction and scheduled hourly lessons two times a week. We were instructed to spend several hours a week on our own, attending aerobics, swimming, and squash classes, assisting the staff with desk work, memorizing how to use all of the machines in the weight room, and studying the facilities, layout, and programs offered by the club. As trainees, we were often caught between wanting to help out and make a good impression and, at the same time, not knowing what to do and hesitant to ask the busy staff. Many of the unscheduled hours of a trainee are spent lurking around the staff room and shuffling self-consciously through notebooks and papers until rescued by a simple photocopying errand.

Training for the arubaito position generally takes about two months to complete, and exams are given intermittently. The first exam, administered at the conclusion of orientation, is the Institution Familiarity Confirmation Test; it asks questions about the layout and basic programs of the club. The later tests delve into more specific questions on anatomy and physiology. The first test was the simplest and covered general questions ranging from the number of courses in the pool and the depth of the diving pool to the number of golf lessons offered each week and the cost of private squash or diving lessons. One question asked for the names of all of the staff to be written in the correct Japanese characters. Each correct name earned two points.[6]

The managers at Chiba Club place great importance not only on memorizing the names of fellow staff, a reasonable request, but also on making a substantial effort to call the roughly two thousand members by name. This mind-tasking job is an explicit attempt to build club community and to increase fitness consciousness and enjoyment. Calling members by name is designed to forge a level of intimacy and comfort between member and instructor, to personalize the exercise experience, and to motivate members to come on a more regular basis. Fashioning the club as a community center, where members can chat, exercise, and relax with friends, is particularly suited to the older clientele of Chiba Club. At the same time, members who have a tendency to drop out or exercise infrequently might be less inclined to miss a workout if they know that a staff member is taking note.

On the first day of training, the assistant chief emphasized the importance of chatting with the members. The ideal staff member should not only be able to answer specific questions about muscle groups, blood pressure, and conditioning but also must be approachable, friendly, and well-groomed. On his periodic trips up to the weight room, the chief would ask trainees how many members they had talked to in the past hour. If dissatisfied with the number, he would require the trainee to speak to at least fifteen different members in the next half hour. The assistant chief explained in one of our training sessions: "The fitness club is part of the service industry and the members must always come first. It is the staff's job to be bright, friendly, and smiling. You should not talk to other staff members when working, and should make an effort to talk to all of the members. Make sure to talk to everyone, not just the members that you know the best. At the same time, you must constantly be looking around to make sure other members do not need assistance. If a member looks like they don't know how to use a machine, go over to help."

The staff are required to engage all members in light-hearted, friendly chat, but are especially encouraged to target the members exercising on the treadmills, stationary bikes, and StairMasters. After working in a fitness club in the United States, where extended conversations with members in the midst of a strenuous workout would be unwelcome, to say the least, I was surprised to see staff members sidling up to talk with a member huffing and puffing on the treadmill or sweating on the bike.[7] But the instructors felt differently, as one explained: "Exercising on the bike is boring and difficult. Members are grateful to get their mind off the exercise." Unlike Americans, who invariably wear a Walkman or read a magazine to take their mind off the tedium of the cardio equipment, Japanese seldom engage in such distracting diversion and merely plod away at the exercise. Talking to an enthusiastic instructor may indeed take their mind off the boredom and encourage them to extend their exercise beyond the typical ten minutes.

The emphasis on "service with a smile" is consistent with employee training in other areas of service-oriented corporate culture in Japan. Several scholars have explored the ways new employees are instructed to internalize and embody a pleasing demeanor and appearance. McVeigh (1995) has examined the micromanagement of the female body at women's junior colleges in preparation for service employment in Japan. In his textual analysis of training manuals used for Japan Airlines stewardesses, he explores the way greetings, facial expressions, appearance, speech, and attitude are carefully controlled and perfected. From the pitch of a trainee's voice to the precise angle of her bow, the demeanor demanded by the airlines manual is consistent with the regime required for tour guides and ride operators at Tokyo Disneyland, elevator girls and sales clerks at department stores, and instructors and training staff at fitness clubs. Brannen quotes from the training course manual at Disneyland, which echoes the rhetoric of the fitness club: "First we practice the friendly smile. Second, we use only friendly and courteous phrases. Third, we are not stuffy" (1992:221). Such heavy-handed control over the appearance, conversational and teaching styles, and even facial expressions of the aerobics instructors is cause for profound frustration.

After a particularly curt reprimand from the club manager to stand up straight, remove her hands from her pockets, and smile, one instructor exaggeratedly grinned toothily and stood ramrod straight with her arms pinned to her side. When the manager returned to the back room, she saluted to his back, giving me a sideways wink. Other instructors complained about the chief of fitness behind his back, noting his resemblance to a snake and his obvious discrimination against the female staff. One woman wondered aloud how his wife could tolerate him. On Valentine's Day, when tradition calls for female employees to bring gifts of chocolate to their bosses, the instructors giggled over the discrepancy between the number of boxes given to the assistant chief versus the head chief. One of my friends whispered that although she gave the head chief a gift, she purposely gave him milk chocolate when she knew that he preferred white.

In one particularly telling incident, I took it upon myself to serve the head chief a cup of tea when I was the only female staff member in the back room, trying to fit in as well as I could. I mistakenly served the tea with the tea bag in the cup, thinking that he could remove it himself when it was steeped to his liking. When I gave him the cup, he frowned at the tea bag and said, "I guess you don't know how to make Japanese tea." Taking the bag from the boiling water, he held it out to me with a look of distaste. At that moment, another female instructor entered the staff room, gathered that the chief was irritated, and ran forward with her hands outstretched to take the dripping tea bag. I tried to warn her that it was very hot, but she didn't hear me and shrieked and threw the tea bag when it scalded her hands. The chief simply turned back to his work, without a word. Later, I apologized to the woman, who told me conspiratorially, "Please don't worry. The chief's a pain, isn't he? [*Shimpai shinaide kudasai. Chief wa mendo kusai, ne?*]." As these anecdotes suggest, although many of the instructors truly love teaching and doing aerobics, they are acutely aware of the day-to-day inequities of corporate employment.

Goffman's (1961) discussion of the relationship between a server and his or her client is useful for considering this bind between the "have it your way" philosophy of service and the unavoidable "have it our way" bottom line at the Japanese fitness club. The instructors must negotiate the often difficult line between delivering good service according to certain standards of health and fitness as determined by the club, and pleasing a client, who may refuse to execute what is determined to be "good for" him or her. In the case of the fitness club, quite similar to the medical service models described by Goffman, the members are literally placing themselves in the hands of club staff (326). Surrendering one's body to the manipulations and advice of an instructor requires a certain degree of trust and confidence that exceeds that required when servicing a material object, such as a car or watch. Powerful institutional sanctions encourage this unquestioning surrender of one's body to the expert hands of a doctor or health practitioner. This is especially true in Japan, where patients are expected to follow the doctor's orders without questioning or even receiving a full explanation of their illness. Doctors typically choose to withhold potentially unnerving diagnoses from patients, informing only family and loved ones of the severity of the illness.[8]

Aerobics instructors, by virtue of their sex, youth, education, and sexualized body labor, are afforded relatively little respect, status, or compensation in the service industry. Compared to the upwardly mobile career tracks of their male colleagues and superiors, the long-term job prospects for a young female aerobics instructor are depressingly limited. As I have illustrated, the hiring, compensation, and promotion processes of the corporate fitness club reproduce gender distinctions that breed dissatisfaction among the instructors. Yet, despite limited opportunities within the company hierarchy and society at large, aerobics instructors do have access to exclusive expert knowledge.

Trained to dispense specialized nutrition and exercise rhetoric, these women can be perceived as experts and in this way may disrupt societal and corporate power hierarchies. The instructors, like other health care professionals, have responsibility for the well-being of the "patients" in their care and therefore hold very real power over their clients. How do the members feel about placing their body in the hands of young and, in their mind, uneducated women? The female instructors recognize the reluctance of the clients and take special care to frame their fitness expertise in nonthreatening ways. Although their "free agent" status does permit instructors some space to resist traditional gender roles, they remain service employees who are required to please the customers. To appear simultaneously knowledgeable and deferential, female instructors deliberately construct themselves and are constructed in culturally familiar roles as mothers, daughters, and sexual objects.

Couching Authority: Mothers, Daughters, and Sexual Objects

As noted, membership at Chiba Club is composed almost exclusively of men and women in their late fifties and early to mid-sixties; hence, the club has the feel of a community center. The age difference between the young instructors and older clientele at Chiba Club makes for a unique and complex dynamic. The service industry is characterized by a power inequality between staff and client that is constantly shifting. Furman explores this inherent power hierarchy at a U.S. Midwestern beauty salon: "A customer, after all, is an employer of sorts, a beautician or manicurist an employee. These power inequalities surface on occasion" (1997:22). But, at Chiba Club, the instructors have the additional pressure of giving counsel to members thirty years older.

The staff has adopted a variety of ways to handle the age and gender differences and the complications of authority that ensue. Some instructors consciously or, more often, unconsciously infantalize the older members, adopting a maternal, concerned position. In a rehabilitation class attended primarily by women in their sixties, one instructor led the class in a game of jump rope, turning the rope with another staff member while the women skipped in and out. Although the activity seemed to be enjoyed by all, the members appeared vaguely embarrassed when I dropped in to watch. Another instructor at Chiba Club taught an aqua aerobics class in which the choreography was distinctly childish. Aqua aerobics, which attracts almost exclusively women in their late fifties and early sixties, generally features a variety of resistance exercises using kickboards and hand weights against the weight of the water. The choreography of this class, however, featured partner dances, not unlike the children's game London Bridge, where the women were expected to sashay under the outstretched arms of each other and participate in piggyback races, jumping on their partner's back when the music stopped. The instructor gave oversimplified cues in a sing-song, babyish voice. As she led the women around the pool, she assisted an older, slower woman by pushing on her back with exaggerated movements and calling out "*Yosh, yosh, yosh*" (onomatopoeic grunt of exertion).

By treating the members as children, instructors could seem to invert the age difference between instructor and member and the subsequent power hierarchy. I argue, however, that this does not happen. The instructors assume the culturally familiar caregiver role, which mimics the ways in which women are constructed and used by the state as caregivers of children and the elderly. In Japan, where old age homes as well as day care facilities continue to be stigmatized and underutilized and social security is not provided for the aging population, the responsibility of caring for both children and older or ill parents falls primarily to mothers, daughters, and daughters-in-law. Women who shirk their caregiving responsibilities are constructed as selfish, unhealthy, and even unpatriotic. This structural relationship is at once familiar and disempowering.

Consistent with a service role, the instructor cares for and indulges the member. A young woman imbued with the authority to lead classes of older men and women may be perceived as unusual at best and offensive at worst. Therefore, the instructor is crafted and crafts herself into the more familiar role of a selfless mother. Allison has observed a tantalizing similarity in her work on Japanese hostess clubs, in which hostesses are conceived of as mother substitutes who coddle and accept men unconditionally as a mother would, yet are not mothers because they are sexualized (1994:170). The cultural archetype of the indulgent mother, though certainly not unique to Japan, does seem to be exaggerated here. As I explore in Chapter 6, the selfless and other-oriented mother figure serves as the epitome of femininity in Japan and plays out in the dieting and food-refusal habits of young women. By adopting a culturally, indeed cross-culturally familiar maternal role, aerobics instructors displace their potential authority and expertise by treating club members as children.

Indulging and spoiling a child has a specific name in Japanese, *amayakasu,* and characterizes the idealized mother-child relationship. Several scholars have explored the pervasiveness of this concept of dependence in Japan, which is rooted in the mother-child relationship but subsequently bleeds into all interactions, from the home to the school to the company (e.g., Doi 1973; Peak 1991). Psychological dependence can be a source of comfort, but amayakasu also reproduces and inverts hierarchical relationships and social inequality. It is crucial to note that this caring relationship is informed by power. Doi has indicated that the indulger is responsible for the indulgee, and the caring relationship simply masks this social and psychological responsibility. It can be argued, then, that treating the club member as a child disguises the authority of the instructor under a veneer of ningenkankei, or human closeness. By indulging the member, the instructor disguises her expertise and ultimate responsibility for that member.

Rosenberger has asserted that the *amae* (indulgent) relationship gives temporary power to the social inferior or the indulgee (1992:69), who is in a position to express free will. In this case, the member has authority over the instructor and can act in willful or selfish ways. This freedom nicely suits the service industry, where clients pay for the luxury of indulgence. Members expect to be catered to and the structural model of a doting mother-child relationship is appealing in its familiarity. Rosenberger notes, however, that this is only a temporary shift of power, because "the *amae* relationship does not end with the receiving of indulgence. The person who enjoys the indulgence incurs a debt to the person who allows the indulgence" (69). Club instructors and members are engaged in complicated and continually shifting relationships of power. As I show, who is responsible for whom and who is the superior and who is the inferior depends on the situation and the roles assumed or created. In this maternal role, the instructor does not disturb the illusion of the client as elite and dominant.

In the club, as in other corporate environments (e.g., Kondo 1990; Hamabata 1990), familial relationships are mapped onto formal relationships as a way to mask inherent power relationships. Japanese corporations, in particular, draw on the metaphor of the company as family. The family model in Japan is, of course, patriarchal. By locating formal business relationships in familiar personal relationships and exaggerating ningenkankei, power can be disguised or symbolically inverted. In this corporation-as-family model, women are cast in nonthreatening roles as mothers and daughters. Kondo discusses this mapping in her analysis of a small Japanese confectionery shop, where young male and female employees seek advice and comfort from the older part-time "mother" workers.

In the fitness club, other female instructors go to the opposite extreme and assume a childlike, daughterly role by acting naïve and coquettish. Some confide about boyfriend or school worries and seek advice from concerned and doting club members. Many of the older female members adopt a maternal role in return, bringing home-baked goodies and *obentou* (boxed lunches) for the hard-working staff. Several of the housewives expressed concern over the fact that I was living alone and didn't know how to cook Japanese food, bringing me special snacks and lunches. One particularly generous woman even invited me over to her house for weekly cooking lessons, which not only enabled me to learn to prepare some simple dishes but also gave us the opportunity for leisurely conversations in the kitchen. She confided that with two grown sons and an overworked husband, she was often home alone. She admitted that she was lonely and considered me the daughter she never had.

In this case, the age difference between member and instructor is capitalized on and, again, the roles assumed map onto culturally recognizable family relationships of parent and child. The instructor is no longer the mother, but the daughter. Despite the potential for an instructor to instruct and for a "daughter" to be indulged, power is reinvested in the member. Childlike, socially naïve, and cute, the female instructor poses no threat to the status quo. Youth conjures up images of vulnerability, innocence, dependence, submissiveness, a lack of sophistication, and childish playfulness. A child is seldom regarded as an intellectual equal or a formidable opponent: the instructor's expert knowledge becomes more acceptable when delivered with a light giggle and a careless shrug of the shoulder. She may have physiological knowledge of muscle groups, but she doesn't have the practical know-how to fix herself dinner.

Playing cute or acting young is symptomatic of larger social trends in Japan. As noted, the 1980s witnessed the resurgence of the cult of cuteness, which revolved around naïveté, youth, and childlike prettiness embodied in the new crop of young singing stars or *aidoru* (idols). Each year or two, a new teen idol was recruited, groomed, and marketed to stardom, appearing on television and in music recordings and ads. This obsession with cute (*kawaii*) paraphernalia, style, and appearance became particularly popular among young women in the early 1980s and became part of the *burikko* (literally, "pretend child") image. By deliberately pretending to be young and childlike, the fitness instructor performs the part of the burikko and is therefore able to deliver her rhetoric without posing a threat to the staff/member hierarchy.

Still other instructors assume an almost flirtatious role with the members, complimenting them on their youthful appearance or recent weight loss. Dating between staff and member is strongly discouraged by club managers. At the same time, however, instructors are cautioned against rejecting a smitten member outright. The proper protocol is to offer to bring along another instructor. On several occasions, pairs of young female instructors were invited to join middle-aged male members for drinking parties at local pubs. When Mamiko, a coworker at Chiba Club, and I were invited to one of these so-called member parties, I naïvely believed that a relaxing evening of drinking and talking outside of the club would break down inhibitions and provide a unique opportunity to discuss exercise and the club. But the bawdy jokes, lascivious flirtations, and drunken songs of the party afforded little opportunity for serious inquiry.

Mamiko, a 20-year-old certified diving and aqua aerobics instructor with a cherubic face and cheery temperament, was a favorite among many of the members who enjoyed swimming and diving. To show their appreciation for her enthusiasm and skill, a group of ten middle-aged male members often invited Mamiko to their after-hours celebrations and urged her to bring along the new foreign instructor. On one occasion, we arrived about an hour and a half late and were greeted by catcalls and cheers when we made our appearance at the pub. Mamiko and I awkwardly sat at the table, exchanging glances and refusing offers of beer. She immediately dug into the food provided, laughing good-naturedly, while I attempted to follow suit. As in the hostess bars in Anne Allison's *Nightwork* (1994), Mamiko and I were expected to pour drinks, laugh appreciatively at jokes, and endure lewd remarks with good humor. As Allison explains, "All hostesses . . . quickly learned three skills that fall under the rubric of 'taking care of': servicing the cigarettes and drinks of the customers, servicing male egos with compliments and flattery, and servicing male authority by never contradicting what the man says" (177). Servicing members is required of staff on a daily basis in the club, where they are expected to "take care of" members, massaging aching backs and egos. But should the staff be expected to continue service outside the club in the name of fostering good staff-member relationships?

A friendly invitation designed to express appreciation and encourage close relationships is, in effect, a power-laden and highly gendered exercise that cements the hierarchical relationship between female employee and male club member. In this instance, as relationships between staff and member become more informal, the authority that the female staff has built up in the club is somehow diminished as she is reduced to the sexualized prop of a drinking party. For female staff, the imposed intimacy of after-hours socializing has the unfortunate consequence of increased distance and inequality. Favored male employees are also invited to parties with the middle aged male members, but rather than merely pouring the drinks like their female coworkers, the men are encouraged (pressured) to drink on pace with the club member revelers. Jokes are shared with the male staff rather than created at their expense. As a result of this drunken bonding, the male staff and members subsequently stand on more equal footing.

Whether through infantilization, an assumed naïveté, or flirtatious banter, the instructors couch their authority in socially recognizable roles that play with and exaggerate age and gender inequities. It is significant that despite the variety of roles that instructors assume, the power hierarchy is never disturbed. In all cases, the end result is the reproduction of inequalities, which place the paying club member firmly on top. On-the-job acquiescence is not necessarily conscious or deliberate, but a result of trial and error, where instructors have learned which public behavior is acceptable, palatable, and convincing and which is not. This public concession to the status quo in no way suggests false consciousness, as I illustrate in the next section, but indicates coping strategies designed to preserve instructors' self-respect and livelihood.

The instructors do not see the unequal power relationships with members and management as somehow inevitable and therefore legitimate, but they lack the solidarity and incentive to overtly buck the system. As Scott eloquently states, "Subordinate groups . . . may judge that the severity of possible reprisal makes open resistance foolhardy, their daily struggle for subsistence and the surveillance it entails may all but preclude open opposition, or they may have become cynical from past failures" (1990:86). Although the plight of the instructors is in no way as grave as that of the Malaysian peasants that Scott describes, the instructors have little recourse for change. As I have illustrated, they have not had much success in making suggestions to management, and it certainly does not require an active imagination to hypothesize what would happen if a young female instructor decided to take an authoritative and demanding tone with her older, wealthier clients or male superiors.

Instructors, though experts in nutrition and exercise, may find it easier to deliver advice on fitness and nutrition when cast in familiar feminine roles as the selfless mother, the cute ingenue, and the sexy coquette. On the one hand, the fitness club seems to present a unique space where young, relatively unschooled women can have access to specialized knowledge and prestige. It seems to be a step above the typical office lady responsibilities of copying, filing, and pouring tea. Most aerobics instructors rejoice in their unique free agent status, which grants them freedom from performing the banal tasks required of the permanent female employees. Although catering to fitness club members requires a certain amount of selflessness and subservience that undoubtedly takes its toll on the self-esteem and goodwill of the instructor, the liminal status of the aerobics instructor affords distinct opportunities to challenge the status quo. How are gender roles transgressed?

Smoking, Drinking, and Swearing

Smoking at most fitness clubs is a regular and accepted practice. It is not uncommon for both instructors and members to light up immediately following a workout to relax and cool down. Although smoking on the premises of one of the clubs where I conducted research was prohibited one year, many of the staff got around the no-smoking rule by stealing outdoors during breaks to smoke under the fire escape behind the gym. At after-hour parties or when meeting for coffee before shifts, there was a scramble for available ashtrays, as the staff, scarcely seated, whipped out designer-brand cigarette cases and coveted Zippo lighters. Although many of my friends among the staff longed to visit me in the United States, most expressed concern about the nonsmoking laws in restaurants and public areas, which receive a lot of hype in the Japanese press.

Similarly, after-hours socializing among the staff inevitably includes the consumption of large volumes of alcohol. These parties may be informal, impromptu gatherings of instructors at a restaurant or coffee shop, or the more official, required parties given by club management or hosted by club members. At these parties, where alcohol is poured freely and the air is cloudy with cigarette smoke, most observers would be amazed to learn the occupations of the revelers. In most cases, it was the female aerobics instructors who drank the most alcohol, becoming quickly red in the face and boisterous, while most of the club secretarial staff made a point of simply ordering juice. The alcohol serves to loosen tongues and lessen inhibitions so that staff and managers, in particular, are able to let down their guard.

Much of the appeal of alcohol lies in the sanctioned relaxation of social boundaries and the leveling of client/staff and management/instructor hierarchies. But, as described above, this social leveling often applies only to males. For women, although drunken revelry is considered amusing or, in some instances—when the instructor is particularly attractive—"cool," for the most part it is perceived as overly masculine and therefore unappealing. At one after-hours party, I asked one of the male staff what he thought of one aerobics instructor's heavy drinking. He responded, "Well, it's not very feminine [*onnarashii*], is it? She gets a bit carried away. But I guess she likes to relax during her time off. Exercise is hard work and alcohol helps us relax."

It is interesting to note that many of the female instructors who smoke and drink also use traditionally masculine language, referring to themselves as *boku* (a male self-referent) rather than *watashi* (the female or gender-neutral self-referent). These young women also tend to gesture expansively, speak in booming and gravelly voices even off the aerobics floor, and tell off-color jokes, and are much more expressive in body language and movements. Being an effective aerobics instructor requires a certain flamboyance, a high level of self-confidence, and a voice that carries. Greater license is afforded to the instructors than the typical office lady.

With their loud laugh, well-toned body, and aggressive behavior, aerobics instructors disrupt traditional expectations of femininity, as embodied in contained movements, a soft voice, and small appetite—all of which imply taking up as little space as possible (Bordo 1993). Lebra (1984) has noted the importance of restrained body movements for Japanese women, even while sleeping; a mother may even rearrange her sleeping daughter's arms and legs in a more contained, tidy manner. McVeigh (1995) describes the embodied process of "learning to be an office lady," noting that femininity is synonymous with docility, restraint, and humility. As noted, I overheard several conversations between club members and managers criticizing one particular aerobics instructor for consistently wearing "overly revealing" leotards, because she was perceived to be transgressing notions of feminine passivity and sexual moderation.

Although I would have beer with other instructors after hours, I stood out as one of the few nonsmokers and was constantly applauded for abstaining. Many of the instructors acknowledge that smoking causes cancer and lung disease but rationalize that the dangers of smoking are overrated. One staff member remarked half-seriously, "We smoke *because* we work in a fitness club. We don't want to be too healthy [*kenkou sugiru*]. Too much of anything isn't good, right? Unlike nonfitness people, my lungs are healthier from all of the exercise, so I can afford to smoke! Anyway, I'm smoking thin cigarettes. One millimeter instead of five millimeters. They have half as much tobacco, so they are twice as good for me, right?" she chuckled. Instructors admit feeling entitled to smoke because they spend their days exercising and improving their health. In a common office space where idle hands attract the unwelcome attention of the boss, instructors use the excuse of smoking as a way to escape outside for relief.

At the same time, many women in Japan and the United States dismiss the proven dangers of smoking because of a rumored relationship between smoking and weight loss. Smoking satisfies an oral craving without the calories of snacking and is believed to increase metabolism rates and calorie-burning efficiency. Many smokers then become afraid to give up smoking, given the almost inevitable weight gain that accompanies quitting. Also, young smokers may feel a certain invulnerability of youth or a need to fit in with friends, but they also possess an all-consuming desire to be skinny, which may overshadow common sense and health concerns. When couched in the rhetoric of concern over gaining weight, relief from daily stress, and as a reward for a job well done, the harmful effects of smoking can be excused or ignored. Scholars of personhood in Japan might argue that the instructors are simply indulging their *ura* (backstage) or situational self. The women smoke only during certain times, in certain spaces, and with certain people. Onstage, they strictly adhere to the rhetoric of good health, but once offstage, norms are relaxed and they feel comfortable smoking a cigarette with their friends and colleagues.

[Certainly, all of these explanations are true to a degree, but I argue that smoking, as well as binge drinking, should be seen as an expression of frustration and, more important, a desire to disrupt gender hierarchies.] It is no coincidence that smoking and drinking are considered characteristic of masculine corporate leisure. In Japanese hostess bars, the quintessential site of after-hours corporate entertainment, it is the women who serve the alcohol and light the cigarettes and the men who indulge. The full-time secretarial staff at the club, aware that smoking and drinking to excess are considered unfeminine, consequently refrain. Aerobics instructors, on the other hand, use smoking and drinking as a way to eliminate or at least challenge gender stereotypes that characterize the service industry.]

As one instructor confided, with a devilish smile and a backward glance over her shoulder, "The chief really hates it when we smoke. He says it's not healthy and looks bad to the members. Especially the old grandmother types [obaasan]." Another instructor concurred: "We can do what we want when we're on break, right? Besides, it's cool!" One of the upper-level managers told me that he was embarrassed for me to see all of the aerobics instructors kicking back with cans of Coke and cigarettes after teaching a class. He said to me in English, "I know that American instructors do what they say. The Japanese instructors say one thing and do the opposite. It's terrible. Do you hear their voices? [he imitated the raspy sound]. It's from cigarettes, you know!" He frowned disapprovingly. Significantly, the managers never made a comment about the male instructors and their smoking and drinking.

Several scholars have noted the correlation between class, race, and gender inequalities and the prevalence of smoking in Britain (e.g., Marsh and McKay 1994; Jacobson 1981, 1986). As Marsh and McKay note, "Put most simply: disadvantage doubles smoking" (77). These studies suggest that those with less education and lower income tend to smoke more and have greater difficulty quitting. It should come as no surprise, then, that Japanese aerobics instructors, who fall near the bottom of the age and gender hierarchy in the fitness club, co-opt stereotypically masculine behavior and turn to cigarettes and alcohol as means to express anger and frustration with occupational limitations.

It is surprising, however, that the occupation of these women as health experts does not provide them with an incentive to avoid smoking.

Jacobson has observed a similar inconsistency in British, Australian, and American hospitals, where nearly half of all female nurses ignore health risks and smoke, while the majority of male doctors and medical students do not (1981:50). According to Jacobson, doctors have responded to the knowledge of the dangers of smoking and the pressures to set a good example for their patients, but nurses have not. She attributes this discrepancy to the overwhelming inequalities faced in the hospital. Like the aerobics instructors, the hospital nurses work "under the double hierarchy of medical and nursing authority and, as the daily frustrations pile up, [they] resort, like other women, to cigarettes" (52). The inequities of gender and age are compounded in the service industry, where the aerobics instructors cater to others' needs and cope with low status, little autonomy, and high responsibility on the job.

Smoking provides a rush, a release, and a way of exerting control and expressing frustration in an often powerless social context. Feminists have explored the disturbing effects of advertising campaigns that link nicotine addiction to women's liberation (Bordo 1993; Jacobson 1981, 1986). The infamous Virginia Slims campaign "You've come a long way, baby" ties independence, autonomy, and strength to cigarettes. Smoking has become increasingly popular with women under 30 in Japan, as a fashion accessory and a symbol of modernity, progressiveness, and equality. By imitating traditionally masculine behavior and by consciously transgressing gender stereotypes that stigmatize female smokers and drinkers, the young aerobics instructors are attempting to gain recognition and power.

But, as is true for the anorexic who asserts power over her body through starvation, the results of smoking are inadvertently self-defeatist. Lighting up may provide the aerobics instructor with the immediate benefits of weight loss and stress relief, permissible rest breaks on the job, and a challenge to her boss's and clients' expectations, but in the end, it becomes an addiction over which she has little control. Alcohol, like nicotine, appears to offer freedom, independence, and a release from stress and inhibition, but produces yet another level of dependence. The aerobics instructors who deliberately contradict their own rhetoric about health, muscles, and nutrition are using their body as a canvas on which to project their dissatisfaction with strenuous, sexualized, and undervalued labor. Esteemed as experts on health and exercise and admired for their thin physique and "good style," fitness club employees are expected to practice what they preach.

By smoking and drinking, the instructors seem no more concerned with health and fitness than many of their contemporaries. It may be that for many, being an aerobics instructor or fitness staff is seen as just another job. As one young woman expressed, "It's enough already. I would be really happy if I got pregnant tomorrow so I could have an excuse to quit. I would feel bad quitting for no reason, and plus, we do need the money. But I really want to quit. I never see my husband because our schedules are so different—we even go to sleep at different times. I don't have time to do laundry, clean, or cook, and I can't wait to do this when I have kids. When I get pregnant, I want to do things for myself. I never have had any free time. I went right from graduation to working here. I want to paint or do the tea ceremony. That would be really nice."

Considered in this light, drinking and smoking for the aerobics instructors may have no greater implications than they would for OLs who take smoking breaks to escape the tedium of working in a telecommunications or automobile company. But because the instructors presumably know better and are held to higher standards of fitness and health, and because smoking and drinking continue to be associated with masculine corporate behavior, this nonnormative behavior should be interpreted as an expression of everyday frustration with low pay, little prestige, few benefits, little opportunity for advancement, and high demands on time and patience.

Conclusions

The fitness club presents a unique locale where young, high school–educated women have access to specialized knowledge unavailable to the majority of the population. But, as I have shown, gender and generational boundaries and stigmas against physical labor prevent authoritative delivery of this rhetoric. Club members and management do not tolerate directives and demands in a luxurious and client-oriented space. The aerobics instructors learn that to be successful at their work they must disguise their expertise in socially recognizable feminine roles. As mothers, daughters, and sexual objects, they are able to counsel the members without publicly threatening the status quo.

This careful self-monitoring and self-deprecation takes its toll on the patience and confidence of the instructors. Given the short tenure of employment of the majority of instructors and their lack of affiliation with any one club, they are unable to collectively resist inequality. But this structural liminality also affords individual instructors the freedom to challenge gender biases and to blur the boundaries that stand between them and their clients and managers. Sharing a drink or cigarette after hours with colleagues and superiors is one way to break down the hierarchical divisions implicit in the service industry. Co-opting masculine speech and gesture is another way to disrupt patriarchy. But are their efforts successful? On the one hand, these actions produce inadvertent results. Instead of providing a source of control, independence, and autonomy, these acts of self-indulgence produce yet another layer of dependence. Engaging in nonnormative activities that have only begun to be associated with sectors of upwardly mobile and "modern" women as a way to downplay hierarchical differences in the corporate environment simply reproduces age- and gender-based hierarchies when practiced by these young, relatively uneducated women of the Japanese service industry. The instructors come across as coarse, bawdy, and unrefined.

On the other hand, many members admire these women for their fit physique, cool persona, and indeed masculine presence. In fact, nearly every young female instructor has had the experience of fending off lecherous members and heart-sick admirers. Aerobics instructors are particularly susceptible to the unwanted attentions of adoring "groupies," both male and female. In the end, although the unique position of aerobics instructors as free agents in the service industry leaves them vulnerable to job insecurity, few benefits, and patriarchal control, it also offers them the freedom to challenge stereotypical feminine roles and behavior.

Young,

Proportionate,

Leggy, and Thin

The Ideal Female Body

In an attempt to conform to the pervasive standards of beauty that revolve around youth, good proportions, shapely legs, and, above all, bone-thin skinniness, one might expect young women to exercise, if not enthusiastically, at least diligently. Fitness clubs, without a doubt, urge members to exercise to improve their looks, but do so by emphasizing muscles over thinness, fat loss over weight loss, and cardio conditioning and strength training over improved appearance. Success at the fitness club equals failure according to cultural standards of beauty.

Working out at the fitness club does offer improved health and condition, but even with devoted effort and dedication, members are unable to approximate the beauty ideal. Consistent exercise may improve the condition of one's heart and even shave off extra pounds, but exercise alone cannot erase wrinkles, reshape hips and breasts, or add inches to legs. *Esute*, diet aids, and the like, on the other hand, promise the impossible—spot slimming and bony skinniness—and they promise it without hard work. In the expensive and service-oriented fitness club, most members hope to escape from the demands of office and home and come to expect entertainment, relaxation, and passive weight loss. The fitness club, then, presents a contradictory space, where the beauty ideal cannot be reconciled with standards of health.

Mind and Body

The tendency to isolate a single body part for improvement suggests an ability to distance the body from the mind. Although not surprising when considered in the Western construct of mind-body separation, this readiness to break apart the body, distancing one's self from one's "problem areas," runs contrary to traditional beliefs of a mind-body unity in Japanese philosophy. Much of the literature on the Western body explores the disjuncture, indeed the antagonistic alienation, of the self from the objectified and lived body. The self is characterized as separate from and often trapped in a traitorous body, which, through illness, weight, and age, has betrayed the timeless and healthy soul.

Chernin describes one North American woman who "would write down in her notebook, without being aware of the violence in what she wrote: 'I don't care how long it takes. One day I'm going to get my body to obey me. I'm going to make it lean and tight and hard. I'll succeed in this, even if it kills me'" (1981:24). Bruch quotes a 17-year-old girl who felt a marked separation of mind and body when dieting: "My body could do anything—it could walk forever and ever and not get tired. I separated my mind and my body. My mind was tricky but my body was honest. It knew exactly what to do, and I knew exactly what I could do. I felt very powerful on account of my body—my only weakness was my mind" (1997:217). The estrangement of the mind from the body in the United States has been explored in work on pregnancy and childbirth (e.g., Martin 1987), obesity (e.g., Chernin 1981), anorexia nervosa (e.g., Brumberg 1988; Bordo 1997), physical disabilities (e.g., Chapkis 1986), and old age (e.g., Foster 1994).

But is the antagonism between mind and body a universal problem? The few scholars who have addressed the cross-cultural implications of this question propose that most Asian philosophies do not recognize a sharp distinction between mind and body (Becker 1995; Kasulis 1993a, 1993b; Yuasa 1987). In both Fiji and Jamaica, for example, the body and the self are negotiated through the macrocontext of the collective, that is, the community (Becker 1995; Sobo 1997). Quite unlike the mind-body problem of the West, in which the self is bounded and fixed within and against the body, Becker explains that in Fiji, "the body and self do not share a mutually fixed or exclusive identity; their common substrate is the collective" (127). The body becomes the responsibility as well as the showcase of community, rather than individual, care. Sobo observes a similar "body-in-relation" phenomenon in Jamaica, where the shape of the body is recognized "as an index of aspects of the social network in which a person is (or is not) enmeshed and of those individual traits that affect that person's social connectedness, such as the ability and willingness to give" (257). Brownell (1995) has explored this notion of "fluid boundaries" between self and others in China, asserting that food and the act of feeding become a way to express ties among the individual, the family, and the nation. In these non-Western contexts, body and mind are intimately connected, but their relationship is neither fixed nor antagonistic.

Kasulis (1993b) also recognizes a distinct, more fluid relationship between mind and body in Japan, which he categorizes as an "internal," interdependent relationship rather than the "external," independent relationship that characterizes Western consciousness. He offers the following analogy to illustrate this distinction: "From a legal standpoint at least, we consider marriage an external relationship, for example. Divorce returns the relatents to their former legal independence. . . . From the standpoint of love, we might add, a married couple might see their marriage as an internal relationship. If they were separated, they might say, neither of them would be the same" (305). He proposes that in Japan the relationship between mind and body can be compared to this marriage of love, in which mind and body are interdependent and intertwined.

Quite unlike modern Western thought, Japanese philosophical and religious traditions, while acknowledging a difference between mind and body, view the relationship as an ongoing, progressive integration. Grounded in Buddhism, this philosophy of integration is actualized in the Japanese practice of training through *kata* or *katachi* (fixed postures of movements), in which the repetition and imitation of distinct and standardized movements is thought to bring about spiritual and mental enlightenment. As witnessed in the training for martial arts, the tea ceremony, and even aerobics instruction, learning is accomplished through doing. Although Kasulis's argument is quite persuasive from a theoretical perspective and indeed plays out in certain institutional contexts, I am not convinced that the rather unproblematic intertwined relationship between mind and body can be consistently applied to all social relationships. There are many times, even in Japan, when the body is conceived of, talked about, and regarded as distinct from the spirit, mind, and source of thoughts and feelings.

Historical Origins in the Twentieth Century

The unprecedented emphasis on physical beauty during the postwar period signals a dramatic shift in the feminine ideal. A brief examination of ideological trends in the construction of female beauty reveals the distinctiveness and derivativeness of the contemporary ideal. In this section, I briefly outline the historical evolution of female beauty ideals in the twentieth century, from the end of the Meiji period (1865–1911), through the Taisho (1912–1926) and militaristic era, concluding with a discussion of the postwar period. By situating the contemporary emphasis on thinness, youth, and good proportions within a larger historical context, I hope to illustrate the contingency and distinctiveness of the beauty ideal in contemporary Japan. Despite abundant historical scholarship on Japanese femininity and the socioeconomic position of women in Japan, thorough accounts of beauty have been markedly absent. In this brief history, I glean descriptions from a variety of sources in the fields of art history, literature, history, and anthropology. I trace the ideological construction of beauty over the past one hundred years and, by necessity, focus on ideological standardization of image as opposed to local difference. I consider the roles that age, class, region, globalization, and gender play in the construction of these images, but I emphasize production rather than consumption of ideology. In this section, I call particular attention to those aspects of the beauty ideals from centuries past that reappear in the late twentieth and early twenty-first century.

Westernization

The opening of Japan to foreign influence and subsequent nationalistic resistance characterized the Meiji period and had a dramatic influence on constructions of feminine beauty. Once the feudal government of the Tokugawa era was overthrown, the newly established government, in an effort to abide by Western standards of morality, codified notions of femininity both in the home and in the *mizu shobai* (floating world).[1] With the termination of the *sakoku* (seclusion) policy in 1868 and fearful of the disintegration of Japanese traditions in the face of Westernization, the Japanese state stressed national unity and loyalty. As Western influences infiltrated Japanese society, "the ideal Meiji woman of the 1870's, 1880's, and 1890's . . . served as a 'repository of the past,' standing for tradition when men were encouraged to change their way of politics and culture in all ways" (Silverberg 1991:264).

The paradigm of feminine virtue during the Meiji period transcended all classes, for each woman was expected to contribute equally and whole-heartedly to the modernization of Japan. A woman's desirability depended on her family's social status and her ability to effectively run a household. A healthy woman with sinewy limbs and a tireless vigor would be valued over a frail beauty with a fair complexion and long, cumbersome hair. The feminine ideal portrayed women as selfless, efficient workhorses, laboring for their family and their nation. *Ryosai kenbo*, the feminine paradigm for good wives and wise mothers, continued to hold sway, emphasizing labor and productivity over physical beauty. One Meiji woman described the relative unimportance of beauty: "We never had time in the morning to put on any makeup. The attitude then was that a girl who spent time in front of the mirror was no use to anyone, and certainly no farmer's daughter who did her hair up nicely and put on makeup would've found herself a husband. . . . Provided she didn't actually look downright filthy, her appearance didn't matter in the slightest. Anyway, all you had time to think about during the day was work, so you weren't expected to worry about how you looked" (quoted in Saga 1987:143). Regardless of natural beauty, women were expected to be tidy and careful in their appearance (Lebra 1984:43). This clean, neat appearance was consistent with the Meiji notion of feminine modesty.

The nationwide preoccupation with moral integrity even extended to the segregated floating world of the geisha. Despite increased government regulation of fees and boundaries, the geisha continued to epitomize beauty, charisma, and charm—the very qualities that were markedly absent from the ryosai kenbo ideal. Descriptions of geisha from the Meiji period and after emphasize her ephemeral beauty. The correlation between beauty and youth reappears in the postwar era, when the two become synonymous. The geisha of the early twentieth century have been described as "the fair sex, generally very young and good looking"; it was a time when "the closing pages of the geisha life [are] like a withering flower whose pretty color and fragrant scent have forever gone, nobody caring even to spare a glance to it and more so to touch it any more" (quoted in Longstreet and Longstreet 1970:58, 60).

Their made-up faces and ornate kimonos that harked back to the styles celebrated by the Heian aristocrats and their elaborate hairstyles symbolized the geisha's position in the floating world and distinguished them from the plainer wives and mothers. The voluminous kimonos gave way to a slimmer style that was best suited to a "tubular" body, with slim hips and small breasts that did not disturb the straight lines of the kimono. In fact, the *obi*, a wide piece of ornate fabric wrapped around the waist, was intentionally designed to minimize any discrepancy between hip and waist size. Contemporary emphasis on slimness and proportion recalls this period, when the shape of the kimono determined the idealized body.

The tension between tradition and modernization played out on the body of the geisha. Fair skin, jet black hair, and small lips and eyes continued to be part of the beauty ideal, recalling the standard of femininity set by the imperial court of the Heian period. But at the same time, even the Meiji geisha flirted with Western influences. The traditional Japanese coiffure was altered to incorporate Western trends. The bun was lowered and reduced in size to imitate a Western look, and permed curls added softness at the nape of the neck. With the onset of the modern age, the geisha initially tried to keep abreast of Western influences and trends in fashion, but after a brief period, they reverted back to a traditional style of kimono. As Dalby explains, after a brief period of Western imitation of fashion trends, "geisha ceased being fashion innovators and became curators of tradition" (1983:74). The geisha, whose function was recreational rather than productive, capitalized on their physical appearance. The Japanese state, however, de-emphasized beauty in the mother/wife ideal and played up productivity in an effort to expedite Japanese industrialization. The fitness club represents an ideal institution through which to revisit the influence of globalization and Westernization on standards of beauty and the body.

The Unconventional Modern Girl

In the years following the opening of Japan and leading to its militarization, advances in commercialization and the mass media provided the public arena in which to vent criticism of imposed gender ideology. Resistance to traditional standards of beauty reflected a larger dissatisfaction with dominant notions of femininity. Increased literacy of women and new employment opportunities for middle-class women sparked discontent with female inequality. The thrust toward industrialization dramatically increased the number of available jobs and necessitated middle-class female employment. Although lower-class women, propelled by economic necessity, historically constituted a large percentage of the agricultural and light industrial workforce, most middle-class women had worked in the home. The Japanese government did not openly discourage women from entering the workforce and, in fact, dictated that "feminine modesty was quite consistent with economic productivity" (Nolte and Hastings 1991:158). The state stressed childcare and home management above all else, discouraging outside obligations if these detracted from domestic efficiency. Although the number of middle-class women seeking paid employment was still quite low, the Taisho period witnessed a dramatic increase in the total number of working women.

Economic independence hastened discontent with traditional gender roles. The Takarazuka Revue, an all-female theater troupe founded in 1914, is a provocative example of this inversion of gender roles and beauty ideals within the constraints of the dominant Taisho ideology. Robertson (1991) explores the tension between the intentions of the founder, Kobayashi, to promote state-sanctioned notions of femininity and the subversive actions of the actors. Kobayashi asserted that the actors epitomized normative standards of beauty, "namely, a woman who looked Western but acted Japanese. . . . He proudly maintained that a Takarasienne, with her 'long' legs and 'straight white teeth,' better epitomized the Western (patriarchal) ideal of feminine beauty than did Euro-American women" (169). The *otokoyaku*, the female actors who played male roles, collectively resisted traditional standards of beauty with a radical decision in 1932 to cut off their long hair. Long, straight, black hair had been emblematic of femininity for hundreds of years; short hair, worn both onstage and off, symbolized a blatant break with convention.

The *moga*, or "modern girl," a media product of the early twentieth century, was created as a composite figure to embody the revolutionary and potentially dangerous new type of woman. The moga symbolized change and aggressively defied traditional codes of behavior and fashions of dress. The modern girl Silverberg notes, was "a glittering, decadent, middle-class consumer who, through her clothing, smoking, and drinking, flaunt[ed] tradition in the urban playgrounds of the late 1920's" (1991:239). The modern girl exuded sexuality both in her flirtatious actions and her sensual form of dress. Sexually aggressive and ferociously independent, this caricature of the modern woman did not conform to the traditional role of wife/mother or to the role of geisha, both of which catered to the needs of men. Resisting the dichotomy of the Meiji period, which assigned beauty and sexuality to one class of women, the moga transgressed the boundaries between the erotic geisha and the dutiful wife.

Although her political activism, intentional use of male speech, and overt sexuality set her apart, it was her appearance that most dramatically distinguished her from her contemporaries. Silverberg notes, "First and foremost, the Modern Girl was defined by her body and most specifically by her short hair and long, straight legs" (1991:242). The reference to long, straight legs as somehow modern, progressive, and foreign is a theme that appears throughout the twentieth century. As I will highlight, thin and shapely legs became emblematic of Westernization. For the moga, this emphasis on her body and appearance was also linked to her sexual independence, which stood in stark contrast to the socially constructed feminine role. A slim body with straight legs symbolized her break with the stocky, productive body favored by ryosai kenbo ideology. Her short hair, like the style sported by the women of the Takarazuka Revue, contradicted traditional notions of beauty and passive sexuality. The moga favored Western clothing, and when she did concede to wear the Japanese kimono, she wore her obi high to emphasize her buttocks. By consciously abandoning the intended function of the obi to disguise the curves of the body and invoke a tubular kimono form, the modern girl was rejecting more than fashion trends. I have taken up this theme of the ties among sexual liberation, body consciousness, and clothing in the discussion of the appeal of the leotard and the sexuality it represented in the 1980s.

In the fifteen years from the Manchurian Incident through the Second World War, the Japanese state curtailed all attempts at modernity and internationalism. Censoring popular culture and regulating gender roles according to the Neo-Confucian "good wife, wise mother" ideology, the state attempted to eliminate all evidence of Western influence. Women's magazines were subject to strict control, women were not permitted to wear men's clothing, and even permanent hair waves were prohibited (Silverberg 1991:266). Nationalistic sentiments again took the form of traditional kimono dress and a predilection for productivity over beauty. Social change and discord manifested in greater control over physical bodies. This tension between structural control and expressive agency as played out through the medium of the body is an important theme in the interpretation of contemporary ideals of beauty.

In this brief history of shifting beauty ideals in Japan, I have illustrated not only the specifics of the ideal across time, but also the role that the sociopolitical climate plays in the determination of feminine beauty. From the expensive kimonos worn by performers in the floating world to the Westernized and modernized moga of the Taisho period, the female body has been situated at the center of debates on class, morality, national loyalty, progress and modernization, gender roles, and sexual liberation. The pale skin and elaborate hairdos of the Tokugawa geisha indicated class, profession, and rank; the de-emphasis on physical beauty for "good wives and wise mothers" in the Tokugawa, Meiji, and prewar eras was symbolic of nationalistic tendencies and patriarchal dominance. In the Meiji and Taisho periods, the import of Western clothing and hairstyles and the celebration of Western features, from eyes to legs, symbolized the simultaneous desire for progress and the threat of a dissolving national identity.

I move now to a discussion of the construction of contemporary standards of beauty as both derivative and unique and explore the symbolism of these same tensions over issues of gender, patriarchy, globalization, and capitalist desires.

Contemporary Standards

To begin to pin down the shifting yet coherent standards of female beauty in contemporary Japan, I asked well over one hundred men and women, young and old, club members and nonmembers, and instructors and managers to define female beauty and the ideal woman's body in their own words. Answers ranged from the specific names of supermodels Kate Moss and Cindy Crawford to detailed prescriptions for perfection that break the body apart feature by feature and limb by limb, but most answers converged on four defining characteristics of female beauty: youth, good proportions, attractive legs, and thinness. In the following sections, I explore the first three features of ideological beauty; I save the lengthier discussion of thinness for the following chapter. The intersection of Western and Japanese ideology becomes manifest in the radically distinct notions of female beauty and the implicit contradictions over the relationship of mind and body. As I explore the beauty ideal in depth, I concentrate on how cultural notions of personhood, gender, and nationalism are projected onto and experienced through the body.

Youth

In Japan, to appear younger than one's chronological age is a crowning achievement. By the same token, accurately guessing the age of a new acquaintance or friend has become almost a ritual of salutation. People who guess correctly may impress others with their skill at reading fine lines and wrinkles, but an accurate or, even worse, an overestimated guess will offend all but the very young. On one telling TV show aired midday, two men attempted to line up thirty-four women according to their age, which ranged from 16 to 40. The true ages of the women were not disclosed until the end of the program, and the men good-naturedly berated a young-looking woman for tricking them into underestimating her age. Fitness clubs exploit the ties between exercise and a youthful vigor. But feeling young is quite different from looking young, and many of the members, especially at the downtown clubs, seemed to care more about looking youthful than about feeling energetic and healthy.

In Japan, as in the United States, looking old means looking unattractive. By strict cultural standards, the flawless skin and firm muscle tone that define attractiveness are thought to begin fading by age 28 or 29. By age 30, most women and some men have begun to actively defend against the onslaught of age. As one male instructor explained, "Thirty is a turning point, where women begin to work out more and more. For young women, beauty is natural and taken for granted, but at age 30, things begin to fall and a woman begins to lose her sex appeal." Associating flabbiness or chubbiness with old age is not uncommon, as indicated by this teenage member's complaint: "I'm so fat. My body is just like a middle-aged woman's." Even in a culture that praises youth, a healthy middle-aged body can continue to be a source of pride and high self-esteem. One 45-year-old woman explained that she always did her hair and put on makeup before coming to the gym because "it makes me feel better about myself, so I exercise harder."

In Japan, where sexiness is defined as young, firm, and thin, middle age and the accompanying scars of childbirth, gravity, and hard work are not considered sexy. One recent statistic even suggests that hair dye is selling as well as milk in Japan (Jordan 1997a). Miller describes esute

14. In this car advertisement, virginal youth is being used as a marketing tool. The copy across the top reads: "I am a 4WD virgin."

programs aimed at older women who are dissatisfied with the shape of their breasts and the topical pigment lightener called Virgin Pink, that is intended for application to nipples that have darkened with pregnancy or age (forthcoming:15). In one advertisement, a famous actress in a flirty white dress is being used to sell a car; the copy reads: "I am a 4WD [four-wheel drive] virgin" (Figure 14).

A married woman or a woman in her thirties is not expected or even allowed to define herself as sexy. One male instructor even had the audacity to suggest that middle-aged men should be permitted to have extramarital affairs because women "don't enjoy sex" after having children. Scholars, of course, disagree, as White explains: "Sexual satisfaction may or may not come with marriage, but it is not a pivotal determinant of marital success. By their forties, women whose husbands are frequently absent, who are posted away from home, or who habitually return home exhausted may have taken on lovers, or found other ways to give themselves sexual release. Only when an extramarital relationship gets in the way of family functioning is a woman persuaded to terminate it" (1992:70-71).

Marriage marks a crucial turning point in definitions of beauty and the importance of looking attractive. Men and women agree that Japanese men have different expectations for a wife than for a girlfriend. When asked to describe the ideal woman, Kyoko, a bubbly, outgoing 28-year-old who recently divorced her husband and now exercises at Downtown Fitness, explained: "Unlike American men who care about more than just looks and want their girlfriend to have a sense of humor and a good personality, Japanese men only care about what a woman looks like. What men want in a wife and what they want in a girlfriend is completely different. For a wife, they want a good cook and someone who is good at housework, but for a girlfriend, they want someone with good style, who they can show off on their arm. The ideal look is thin, with long hair. Since I cut my hair, I haven't been asked out on many dates. . . . Not that I was asked out on very many before [laughs]." A young man confirmed this point when he informed me, "I would like to enjoy myself with a beautiful woman, but I would marry an ugly woman." Recalling the division between wives/mothers and geisha/entertainers of Japan's earlier history, the emphasis on productivity for one category of women and beauty for another corresponds to patriarchal gender roles.

Youth conjures up images of vulnerability, innocence, dependence, submissiveness, a lack of sophistication, and childish playfulness. A child is seldom regarded as an intellectual equal or a formidable opponent. A feminine ideal that revolves around youth strips a woman of her intellectual, social, and sexual maturity. Japan has been characterized as a nation obsessed with cuteness (*kawaisa*). Cuteness has crept into nearly every aspect of Japanese popular culture, from the crowd of tittering high school students sporting ponytails and clutching Hello Kitty bags to the school girls in sailor suits featured in Japanese pornography. As Figure 15 illustrates, teens and even women in their twenties style their hair in swingy pigtails and braids. Youthfulness has come not only to describe the desired female look but also a certain idealized demeanor. By accentuating a woman's sexual innocence, lower intelligence, and social ineptitude, she poses little threat to the dominance and virility of aging men. At the same time, though, Kinsella (1995) has aptly observed that acting childish may also be interpreted as rebellion against gender roles. Several feminists have noted, however, that this rebellion must be enacted within dominant and normative terms and, in the end, simply serves to reproduce that which it aims to resist (Radner 1995; Bordo 1997).

なりたい」髪型、「似合う

どんどん変
きれいに
定番でいつも
新鮮

15. The cutesy hairstyle of this
model featured in a popular
women's magazine is an example
of the equation of youth and
female beauty in
contemporary Japan.

Good Proportions

Young women and men in their late teens and twenties consistently
define female beauty as young, thin, firm, and, most important, pro-
portional. Good proportions, or *balance* as it is referred to in Japanese, in which the upper and lower body fit together, is the key to a
nice body (a borrowed English term). Although large breasts, a narrow
waist, and slender legs are part-and-parcel of a nice body, breasts that
are too large or hips that are too narrow throw the balance off-kilter.
One well-known beauty salon even calculates a prescription for "correct" proportions according to a mathematical formula, mapping out
the client's measurements on a grid to show the specific body parts that
do not conform to the equation. The importance of a balanced body
is expressed by one 23-year-old female club member, who explained,
"The ideal body is firm and tight. The places that are supposed to stick
out, stick out, and the places that are supposed to nip in, nip in [*detteru tokoro ga detteru, shimetteru tokoro ga shimetteru*]. Unlike Western
women, Japanese women are thin but their stomach sticks out and their
legs are heavy. American women may be fatter but they are also taller,
so it balances out better. I have no breasts and my behind is way too

big. I would like to take some of the fat from my hips and transfer it to my breasts! Oh well, what can you do?"

Robertson recounts a similar emphasis on proportion in the national beauty contests of the 1930s: "What the Miss Japan judges meant by 'healthy-body beauty' was a quality found in a 'pure-blooded' Japanese female body free of disease and assorted flaws, and which met the classical Greek standards of shape and proportion (7.5–8 heads) in height" (1997:12). The use of Western standards in both the beauty contests of prewar Japan and in the fitness clubs today is intentional, prescriptive, and loaded. Just as the eugenics movement in Japan during the 1930s derived beauty standards from Western ideals, the imagined and idealized "American body" is often held up as the epitome of perfection against the lacking and ever inferior "Japanese body."

Downtown Fitness, located within walking distance of well-known bars, restaurants, and clubs that line the cosmopolitan streets of Roppongi, is the club of choice for many of the foreign dancers, models, and bar hostesses employed in the area. In fact, the Roppongi district is well-known for the concentration of foreigners living in and around the area, as well as for those swarming in for after-hours bar hopping and drinking. Downtown Fitness in Roppongi has nearly 40 percent foreigners at any one time, many of whom choose not to use the other facilities in the chain. The majority of the foreigners work in the investment banks, modeling agencies, and embassies located nearby or, most commonly, in the hostess bars and strip clubs that line the Roppongi streets. The foreigners hail from the United States, Australia, New Zealand, Canada, Israel, Europe, and Mexico. Many plan to stay in Japan for only a few months or a year at most, and the majority cannot speak Japanese and have very little interest in learning it.[2]

The foreign community obviously has had a profound effect on the way fitness and the ideal body are constructed in Japan, and the interactions between Japanese members and staff and foreign members proved to be quite insightful. Conducting research at this particular branch, where nearly half of the total membership is composed of foreigners, afforded a unique opportunity to observe how the "American body" is constructed, measured, viewed, and consumed in the fitness club. The strippers and hostesses, whose livelihood depends on creating the fantasy body, are some of Downtown Fitness's most consistent members. With a workday that begins at seven o'clock in the evening, these women spend their days cycling, lifting, and stepping to burn off the calorie-laden beer from the night before and to prime their body to maximize potential tips for later that night.

Downtown Fitness understands the appeal of the idealized American model and ran a very provocative and controversial campaign, featuring a series of black-and-white photographs of nude Caucasian models. In one poster, a bare-chested woman is photographed from the waist up. She is extremely skinny, fine-featured, and unsmiling, with her hair drawn back in a severe bun. She stands with an arched back and shoulders thrown back, jutting her bare breasts toward the camera and the viewer. The name of the fitness club is emblazoned across her bare breasts and reads in English: "Handsome Body [Downtown Fitness]." The use of English words further emphasizes the foreign flavor of the ad and, by extension, the club (see Stanlaw 1992; Fields 1989). The captions along the side of the poster read in Japanese: "I am wearing [Downtown Fitness]" and "Let's have fun becoming beautiful." In another version, a man, also Caucasian, is featured; he is shot in a similar fashion, nude from the waist up, with muscles rippling on his bare, flexed chest. Downtown Fitness also distributed desk calendars to their members, each month featuring a different black-and-white photograph of a disembodied nude arm, leg, buttocks, or chest of men and women.

It is significant to note that this model and the majority of other female models who are photographed half-dressed or nude in Japanese advertisements are Caucasian (this discussion does not include pornography). Certainly, North American women and, in most cases, Caucasian women are constructed as the body ideal in contemporary Japan. Supermodels such as Cindy Crawford and Claudia Schiffer and American movies and magazines all contribute to the dissemination of this particular body type. But more important, Creighton explains that nude images of foreigners are quite common in Japan, "where naked depictions of Japanese would be considered inappropriate . . . nude depictions of Japanese for everyday, mainstream products and businesses are not common, whereas nude depictions of *gaijin* [Caucasian foreigners] for these are not unusual" (1995:137). The explanation may be tautological. That is, the American body may be considered sexier and hence is portrayed in this sexualized manner, but, because of this portrayal, the American body has become synonymous with sex.

The sexy, attractive body seen in the advertisement resonates with the overall fitness goals of Downtown Fitness. A handout, tellingly printed in English, describes the variety of activities offered at the club, in which the same image of sexiness and beauty is reproduced: "Discover the [Downtown Fitness] that suits you best. With the refreshing feeling you get after having exercises [*sic*], and a strong, healthy and supple figure, you'll look gorgeous just as you are. The best brand-name clothing couldn't make you look better. For you to wear the look of a physically fit, healthy person, we have prepared a variety of programs under the brand name [Downtown Fitness]. Programs that will spice up your life. Our staff are waiting for you. Do not hesitate. Experiment with a variety of exercises at first, and you will discover the style of exercise and [Downtown Fitness] that suits you best."

In this excerpt, the club has defined fitness in a very specific way: strong, striking, physically fit, and foreign. The emphasis is on appearance, with good health, well-being, and exercise serving as the means to achieve good looks. The message is clear: exercising at Downtown Fitness will produce a beautiful body, idealized by the American model. Ideal female beauty is defined in this context as skinny and sexy, with breasts emphasized as the defining and central feature. This kind of voluptuous emaciation is not only impossible to achieve with exercise, it is also unhealthy.

The emaciated models and the hard-bodied and silicone-enhanced strippers mark just two of the distinct body types that have come to represent ideal beauty in the United States today, and are symbolic of the skewed Japanese perspective of what the typical American woman's body should (or does) look like. When a young Japanese woman encounters a tall, blond model or a buxom dancer in the fitness club, what is her reaction? Not surprisingly, given a national predilection for skinniness, most club members, both men and women, prefer the waifish, long-legged bodies of the models to the curvaceous figures of the strippers. In keeping with the desire for balance, women desire breasts that are *tekitou* (appropriate) in size to offset wide hips or heavy legs, but a woman with extremely large breasts that are out of proportion to the rest of her body is considered foolish (*baka*). One Japanese woman, pursuing her Ph.D. in clinical psychology, explained how she hated growing up with large breasts: "I always wear very baggy shirts because I am embarrassed. I don't want people to think that I am stupid. I wish

I was smaller." Although breast size has definitely become part of the beauty ideal in the past five to ten years, the fixation on breasts has not reached the level of worship that it has in the West.

This is not to say that the feminine ideal in Japan is more obtainable. Achieving perfectly balanced proportions is just as anatomically impossible as metamorphosing into the top-heavy Barbie-esque figure idealized in the United States. The emphasis on balance in Japan is largely responsible for the fad dieting and proliferation of miracle diet aids that have become so prevalent. To achieve perfect balance requires the ability to isolate certain parts of the body for selective dieting and shaping. Breasts, hips, stomachs, legs, and even faces that are perceived as disproportionately small or large must be kneaded, wrapped, stretched, or worked into the elusive but all-important tekitou size and shape. The diet aids feed on and induce insecurity, as perfection is always just out of reach. As Bartky asserts, "The very idea of 'spot reducing' is both scientifically unsound and cruel, for it raises expectations in women that can never be realized: The pattern in which fat is deposited or removed is known to be genetically determined" (1990:67). Bombarded with quick fixes outside the club, most members become dissatisfied inside the club, where staff denounce spot slimming and concentrate on full body health and low fat percentages over proportion and balance.

Although the concept of isolating one body part for slimming or toning up is not unique to Japan, it does seem to be exaggerated there. North Americans talk about "problem areas" and certainly take advantage of liposuction and breast implants, but concentrating on just one body part to the exclusion of others is not quite as extreme as in Japan.[3] In Japan, diet aids, popular magazines, and beauty salons in particular exploit this "divide and conquer" notion. Beauty aid supply shops and most department stores have special sections for quick weight-loss products, specializing in metabolism-altering diet pills, sweat-inducing wraps, and the infamously dangerous diet tea.

One of the more popular beauty supply chains is Matsumotokioshi, which has over fifty branches near train stations. The stores are generally small, but each nets close to $1 million a month. The shops are packed after five o'clock with office ladies and students (Figure 16). One fitness club manager exclaimed, "They are even more crowded than supermarkets after work!" Every shelf is filled with cosmetics and hair products. Nail polish and perfume line the stairs between floors, and the countertops are covered with tester makeup and mirrors. The diet

16. After work, the beauty supply stores are crowded with shoppers.

goods are all shelved together, most often at the entrance to the store. Ironically, at one of the larger chains, chocolates, cookies, and chips were displayed next to the diet aids in a not-so-subtle attempt to warn women that if they want to indulge, they also had better reduce.

Many of the quick-weight-loss products in Japan rely on the notions that sweat loss equals weight loss and that body parts can be slimmed independently. When the body sweats, it does lose water weight, which can be noted on the scale. But the scale records the results of dehydration, not calories or fat burned. The inducement of temporary weight loss has been capitalized on by the diet industry in Japan, and fitness clubs even take advantage of this. Accordingly, the *home sauna*, designed to recreate the effects of the steam or dry sauna at home, is one of the most popular weight-loss aids stocked. Made from a thick, rubbery fabric, the saunas are remarkably similar to the wet suits worn by surfers. Sold for about 3,400 yen (about $28.33) each, home saunas promise to take inches off the face, stomach, hips, calves, and thighs (Figure 17).

Advertisements for home saunas encourage the user to weigh herself before and after wearing to see the difference. They exploit the desire to lose weight easily and tirelessly, promising inches lost while relaxing or sleeping. Claims on the box of the leg sauna guarantee "(1) Sauna results of perspiration without effort; (2) Prevent the effects of fatigue as

The Ideal Female Body 159

well; (3) Prevent legs from swelling; (4) For the standing body, it tightens the calf and makes for a slim and beautiful leg line." Relying on the notion that water loss equals weight loss, many women buy clear or gray plastic tape to wrap around legs and arms with the idea that inches will be sweated off. As Figure 18 indicates, there is a particular way to wrap the leg to ensure the tightest fit and therefore the slimmest results. This Saran wrap–like plastic is sold for 2,800 yen (about $23.33)!

Similarly, the notion that weight loss can be targeted to individual body parts, such as the stomach, neck, or thighs, is particularly influential. *An-an*, a popular magazine aimed at women in their early twenties, devotes entire issues to weight loss, with articles such as "Modern Women's Number One Desire: The Reality of Wanting a Small Face" (1997) and "The Most Common Worry of Women about Their Bodies Are Their Legs, But Without a Doubt We Will Make Them Beautiful" (1997). As alluded to above, this "divide and conquer" strategy is employed by most of the diet aids sold in Japan. One fitness instructor strongly criticized *bubun* (body part) dieting, but tried to explain its appeal, albeit, with a misogynistic bent:

It isn't possible to diet for just one part of the body, but this is very popular in Japan. This type of *bubun* dieting fits in the space between healthy diets and women's desire to be thin. . . . Women who are really slim, but feel fat, buy these diet aids or do spot exercises. Of course, spot exercising is very important, but it must be combined with fat-burning exercise for at least twenty to thirty minutes. While spot exercises are picked up by magazines, fat-burning cardio exercise is not. Young Japanese women are bored by everything. They try running but say "I hate running." Especially young women, who have little free time because they are working, drinking, and dating, don't want to do an exercise that takes thirty minutes. They would rather do the spot exercises, which they can do in their homes and are not such a pain.

The enormous variety and short shelf-life of products and diets in Japan is made possible by "batch production," which allows short trial runs of highly specialized items. This type of marketing provides the economic framework to enable a high diet consciousness but relatively weak fitness consciousness. The desire to lose weight effortlessly and quickly has allowed a mind-boggling number of products and beauty aids to glut the market. To adequately describe and analyze the sheer variety of fad diets and quick-loss diet goods sold in Japan would re-

17. These thick girdle-like *home saunas* are designed for spot slimming, as promised in this advertisement that claims that these products can "even prevent one from eating too much and subtracts 3.5 cm from one's waist."

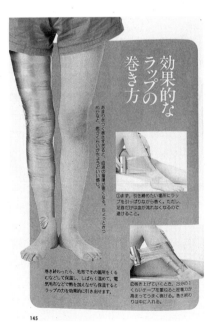

18. When wrapped correctly, this spot-slimming product promises slimmer legs.

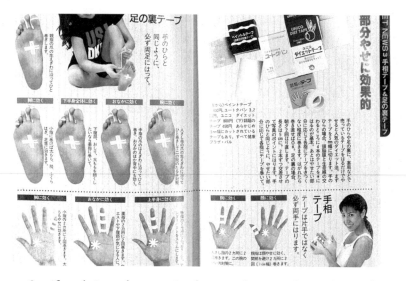

19. Specific techniques for wrapping fingers and toes are designed to produce slimmer waists, hips, and legs.

quire an entire chapter, or even a book. I will just touch on the most popular diet aids—those used by many of the fitness club members prior to and during their membership, as revealed during interviews. Because of the enormous range of products available, popular women's magazines publish rankings of the most popular diet aids to assist the consumer in her (and it is always a "her") selection. Based on test trials by staff and volunteers, the diet goods are ranked according to price, effectiveness, and ease of use. *Ray* magazine has published a small handbook entitled *Wonderful Diet Goods* (1996), which classifies the majority of available products into five categories: wraps, creams, pills, drinks, and products to be used in or after the bath.

The most common wraps include both the home saunas and plastic or metallic tape described above, and what is called *spiral tape*. Spiral tape is based on the premise that pressure points, when properly stimulated, will produce weight loss. Extrapolated from the underlying principles of acupuncture, thin pieces of tape are wrapped around certain areas of the fingers and toes to stimulate weight loss in corresponding body parts. For example, according to the method depicted in Figure 19, the tape is wound around the top, middle, and third knuckle of the ring finger to slim down the stomach.

Spiral tape was extremely popular two years prior to my fieldwork, and many of the members and staff wrapped their fingers before coming to the fitness club. One college student at a Chiba university admitted to using the tape: "The wrapping tape? I've done that a lot! My mother has done it even! My mother doesn't really move around much, so she doesn't have any way to get thin, so she often used the tape. But she didn't get thin, because she kept eating and didn't exercise when she wore the tape, so she didn't get thin at all!" Drawing on the same principles of pressure points, *diet slippers,* or miniature slippers, which end at the middle of the foot, thus forcing the heel to hang off the back of the shoe and transferring all of the weight forward, are said to stimulate pressure points in the ball of the foot. Cynical fitness instructors insinuated that both the spiral tape and diet slippers may work by the power of suggestion; that is, by making the wearer conscious of trying to lose weight, she may be less inclined to overeat or snack.

Most certified acupuncturists and chiropractors in Japan offer weight-loss programs based on the techniques and philosophy of acupuncture and bone and muscle manipulations (see Ohnuki-Tierney 1984, for a discussion of *kampou,* or traditional Japanese medicine of Chinese origin). I went to one such specialist and was told that by keeping tiny 1-millimeter-length pins in the wells of my ears for up to three weeks, I would lose up to 5 kilograms (11 pounds). Although the pins were not particularly painful, they did sting when I tried to talk on the phone or sleep on my side and I removed them after only three days. I didn't notice any difference in my weight or my appetite; in fact, when I asked a friend who accompanied me to the doctor whether she had experienced anything, she replied, "I think I am eating even more! I think it stimulated my appetite instead."

Cellulite cream is also exceptionally popular in Japan. Lotions, creams, and oils that are applied to the skin are thought to penetrate to deeper tissues to alter or eliminate stored fat. Some experts disagree, as this professor of surgery at the State University of New York Health Science Center in Brooklyn maintains: "These are extraordinary claims . . . nothing you put on your skin will break down fat cells—or any cells for that matter. Neither will increasing circulation through massage" (quoted in Tung 1997:79). The Asian market, particularly Japanese women, are reputed to be responsible for nearly one quarter to one half of all sales of Christian Dior Svelte Cellulite cream, which sells for $45 per eight-ounce bottle in the United States and nearly double that in Japan: "Asian women were scooping it up by the armload—even after they had bought up all available supplies in their local stores. . . . On the West Coast alone, forty percent of Svelte's sales were from visiting Asian women. What makes these statistics especially mystifying is that very few Asian women *have* cellulite . . . they thought Svelte was a slimming cream and used it not just on their thighs, but all over their bodies" (74). Japanese tourists to Hawai'i and the mainland are asked by friends to stock up and later distribute the elusive Svelte cream, which disappears from cosmetic counters in Japan almost as soon as it is displayed. (Relatedly, I toted back spiral tape and home saunas for my American friends who were intrigued by the chance for a new quick fix.)

It may be assumed that the fitness club has imported Western notions of the body along with the Nautilus equipment and aerobics classes. There is no denying that the antagonistic relationship between mind and body is exploited in the American notion of fitness, where Nautilus equipment and "buns and abs" classes invite the isolation of certain body parts for strengthening. Yet, as seen in this brief analysis of the weight-loss industry in Japan, even diet products that derive much of their credibility from explicit ties to "Eastern" medicine and acupuncture capitalize on body part fixation. The stomach, breasts, and legs, viewed as interrelated through a system of nerves and pressure points, are individually subjected to manipulation and domination through wrapping, sweating, and kneading. To understand the relationship between mind and body in Japan, one must be open to contradictory practices and contextually dependent distinctions. Neither mind-body synthesis nor mind-body dualism consistently explains the myriad social and institutional relationships. Rather than pinning a larger model of synthesis or dualism on Japan, it is more useful to consider how and, more important, why certain situations lend themselves to certain constructions of mind and body or mind versus body.

Shapely Legs

In Japan, far more important than the size of one's breasts are the shape and slenderness of one's legs. Television programs, fitness videos, and magazine issues describe exercises and special diets that claim to target the legs exclusively. A beautiful *leg line,* as it is described in popular magazines and at the beauty salons, is not only thin (with no unsightly bulges from either fat or muscle), well-pedicured, hairless, and silky

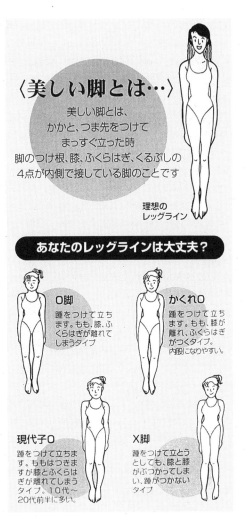

<美しい脚とは…>

美しい脚とは、
かかと、つま先をつけて
まっすぐ立った時
脚のつけ根、膝、ふくらはぎ、くるぶしの
4点が内側で接している脚のことです

理想の
レッグライン

あなたのレッグラインは大丈夫？

O脚
踵をつけて立ち
ます。もも、膝、ふ
くらはぎが離れて
しまうタイプ

かくれO
踵をつけて立ち
ます。もも、膝が
離れ、ふくらはぎ
がつくタイプ。
内股になりやすい。

現代子O
踵をつけて立ちま
す。ももはつきま
すが膝とふくらは
ぎが離れてしまう
タイプ。10代～
20代前半に多い。

X脚
踵をつけて立とう
としても、膝と膝
がぶつかってしま
い、踵がつかない
タイプ

20. In this pamphlet, distributed by a local aesthetic salon, aestheticians promise to remedy knock-kneed, bowed, or pigeon-toed legs to produce a beautiful "leg line."

smooth, but also perfectly aligned from ankle to hip. Magazines, fitness clubs, and beauty salons concur that correctly aligned legs should touch at four specific points: the ankle, the middle of the calf, the knee, and the upper thigh (Figure 20). Alas, it is the very rare woman whose legs fit these precise and nearly anatomically impossible specifications, but, never fear, magazines, aesthetic salons, and cosmetic stores offer miracle remedies, massages, and techniques to realign knock-kneed, bowed, flabby, or otherwise "misshapen" legs.

Given the desire for trim and proportionate legs, girdles and heavily elasticized reducers for stomachs, hips, and thighs are big sellers ("Slim

The Ideal Female Body   165

Down!" 1995; "Hip-Hugging Tights" 1997). In the United States, girdles are seldom worn by women in their teens, twenties, or thirties, but in Japan, nearly all women, young and old alike, wear some type of constrictive undergarment to reduce often imagined bulges and lumps. The astounding array of styles does not necessarily mean a choice in comfort. All girdles pinch, squeeze, and constrict, with the express purpose of contouring and molding. Some of the lighter-weight fabrics may be less constrictive, but the trade-off is that they are reputed to be less slimming. One 28-year-old member at Downtown Fitness explained the difference between heavy-weight ("hard") and light-weight ("soft") girdles: "There are soft girdles and hard girdles. I am wearing a hard girdle today. It looks better, but it's not good for you. I get lines on my stomach and legs after I wear it. Because I wear one every day, on the days I don't feel like wearing one, my pants don't fit!"

Popular bookstores carry manuals and magazines for selecting the right type of underwear to minimize, define, uplift, or pad. One such book is entitled *The Underwear Expert: Becoming More Beautiful* (1997); it offers step-by-step instructions for choosing the appropriate type of undergarment to wear with certain outfits or to complement certain body types. It characterizes underwear as "Not simply to wear under Western style clothing; we enjoy wearing underwear to show our bodies off beautifully" (39).[4] The book describes every type of undergarment conceivable and illustrates the proper way to choose and put on a girdle. In addition, it prescribes the specific types of figure-flattering undergarments, or *foundation* (in katakana) as it is called in Japanese, to best enhance a small-busted or large-hipped woman. The underlying premise is that all women can benefit from the right underwear, designed to mold the imperfect into the ideal. The opening quote for the chapter on "choosing underwear with a body type in mind" is particularly telling: "When enjoying various fashions, there are probably people who feel 'if only my stomach was a bit flatter . . .' or 'if only my breasts stood out a bit more . . .' In order to have the ideal style, struggling to diet is not the only option, you can also wear *foundation* to come closer to that ideal style. Here we will show you how to choose the right undergarments for your body type" (127). The chapter goes on to illustrate the range of figure flaws that can be "corrected" with the appropriate type of undergarment: breasts that are too large, too small, that sag or thrust too far forward; rib cages that stick out or stomachs that have too many rolls; hips and buttocks that are too wide or too narrow, too flat or too droopy. Although the ideal body is never described outright, it is perfectly clear what the ideal body is *not*. Nobody is perfect and no body is free of flaws, but the book assures readers that this litany of imperfections is no cause for undue alarm, endless exercising, or tiresome dieting, because the ideal body is just a girdle or a push-up bra away. The solution is both effortless and simple, albeit uncomfortable and expensive.[5]

The corset, push-up bra, and girdle have been used in other contexts as ways to control the sexuality of women. In the 1950s and 1960s, when girdle wearing in the United States was at its height, shaking legs and buttocks and bouncing breasts signaled unbridled sexuality, freedom, and a lack of restraint. "Good" girls wore girdles and bras; "bad" girls did not. The binding and ubiquitous girdle, prescribed for both old and young women in Japan, should be read as a way to constrain female sexuality. Cognizant of the implications of baring one's legs, at the fitness clubs in the suburban and more rural areas, many women in their early thirties and older wore flesh-colored tights under biking shorts for the sake of modesty. The moga, with their obi worn high, the body-con in their see-through, skimpy outfits, and the aerobicizers in their thong leotards present an alternative to bounded sexuality. Baring one's body, particularly one's buttocks, breasts, and legs, threatens patriarchal notions of morality.

Unlike in Japan, where donning foundation garments is an accepted and even requisite part of a woman's daily beauty ritual, women in the United States often resort to more permanent body modifications. The popularity of breast augmentation, liposuction, chemical peels, and even daily exercise regimes have taken the place of age-defying makeup and body-contouring underwear. Wendy Chapkis suggests that in the United States, where the now popular "natural look" has rendered girdles and thick makeup unfashionable and nearly obsolete, "older women must literally remake their bodies in the pursuit of beauty. Scientific skin care, cosmetic surgery and fitness programs promise to minimize the visible changes of living" (1986:9–10; see also Davis 1995). In Japan, however, where even high school girls admit to feeling undressed if they leave the house without tucking themselves into minimizing and uplifting undergarments and coating their face with a careful application of foundation, concealer, and lipstick, looking natural is not as important as looking "put together" (*kichinto*).

Of course, even in Japan, undergarments offering the illusion of a slim body may be enough for some, but other women do crave more permanent change. I want to emphasize that this craving or desire for thinness is not strictly psychological, but rather, culturally constructed. Bordo explains that desire must be considered in the context of advanced consumer capitalism, in which the ongoing struggle between repressing and indulging the desires of the body become metaphors for the repression and indulgence required of the consumer in an unstable market economy (1993:185–212). Liposuction, breast implants, and other cosmetic surgery are available in Japan, although they are less popular than in many areas of the United States. One upper-level fitness club manager told me that a well-known hospital was trying to establish a link with fitness clubs to avoid weight regain in liposuction patients.

In the back pages of most of the popular women's magazines, cosmetic surgeons do advertise breast implants, eyelid modification, and even liposuction. In the course of my fieldwork in Japan, however, I did not meet or speak with a single woman or man who had (or would admit to having) cosmetic surgery or even knew anyone who had. Most of the women I interviewed claimed that the typical (*futsu na*) woman did not seek cosmetic surgery; rather, it was only the popular tarentos, models, or television stars who desired and could afford surgery. Margaret Lock and Christina Honde (1990) have explored the cultural stigma against organ transplants and donors in Japan, which stems from a resistance to cutting into and invading the human body. The surprising lack of popularity of cosmetic surgery in general, and breast implants and liposuction in particular, despite a national trend in Japan toward effortless weight loss and body reshaping, may stem from this disinclination to slice into and introduce foreign material into the body.

Alignment is crucial, but a perfect leg line also requires trim ankles and slim thighs. Colorful descriptions of less-than-perfect legs tend to vary according to generation, but, regardless of age, most of the expressions are equally evocative and insulting in any context. The prewar generation refers to legs that are thick at the ankle and seem to run in a straight line from ankle to thigh as *daikon ashi* (turnip legs) for their striking resemblance to the Japanese turnip, which is large, thick, and elongated. As alluded to in the description of beauty ideals in the Taisho era, the daikon leg is thought to be an exclusively Japanese genetic trait; thus, this expression is used as a way to make racial distinctions and to once again elevate the American body type.[6]

In another, less racially charged example, a young woman revealed how she was given an embarrassing nickname at work. She laughingly labeled the incident as sexual harassment: "I know that I have fat legs. They are thick at the ankle and go straight up and down. In fact, in the office where I used to work, the men all used to call me 'elephant legs' or just 'elephant' because I have heavy, straight legs, just like an elephant. I thought this was mean, but it's okay, because I just said mean things right back!" Although sexual harassment cases are increasingly fought and won in the Japanese court system, blatant commentary on a woman's body or appearance in the office setting continues to be tolerated (White 1992:79; Sugawara 1996). Because success in the office is often tied to appearance and an easy-going manner (Vogel 1978), women may feel pressured not only to look their best but to hold their tongue.

Emi, a member at Downtown Fitness and a full-time employee at one of the largest esute in Japan, has also experienced on-the-job "encouragement" to lose weight: "When I first started working [at the esute], they told me at the interview that I was too fat and had to lose weight to work there. They ask for your height and weight and compare it to the chart, and if it's over, they tell you to lose weight. But of course, people like you and me have muscle, right? Which weighs more so our weight would be over, right? But that doesn't matter. They just tell you that . . . Even though I was working just at the business office [honsha] and not the shop, it is still very strict. But for the estheticians, it is even more strict. You know that they don't have any large size uniforms. I was so surprised, I couldn't believe it. What if you are tall, you would weigh more, right? Well, there would be no uniform to fit you."

Just as expressions vary according to generation, changes in body type are also said to be generational. Teenagers raised today are perceived to have longer and thinner legs than the generations that preceded them. One 35-year-old member described the Western standard: "I have a typical Japanese woman's body: short, big face, short legs, and wide hips. Young people's bodies are changing. They have small faces and are tall and thin. All the models have small faces. All American people have small faces too. If you noticed, old women and old men, they have big faces. It doesn't look good. A small face, big eyes, and a smallish but high nose . . . Black hair is a little heavy, it has a dark feeling, so people lighten their hair too." Some of the older women in the club commented that young Japanese girls "do not look Japanese."

Many suggest that the younger generation, born and raised at the peak of the prosperous bubble economy, benefited from a better, more "Westernized" diet and the change toward sitting in chairs rather than in the more traditional *seiza*.[7] Indeed, the protein-rich diet afforded by improvements in the economy did produce taller and more robust youth. On average, adolescents in 1989 were four inches taller than their grandparents, who were raised on a primarily carbohydrate-based diet prior to and during the war (Allinson 1997:139). Physical changes in the body are used as a template for measuring the changes and progress of Japan as a nation. Voluptuousness and height become symbolic of economic vitality and increased visibility in the global market economy.

Interestingly, similar reasons were cited for the improved physique of Japanese youth during the 1930s: "(a) sports; (b) an improved diet—that is, a Western diet, popularized by the military, consisting of more protein and fats; (c) the use of chairs in class rooms [as opposed to kneeling on the floor]; (d) and Western clothes" (Robertson 1997:12). Robertson examined how statistical studies, which compared the increased height and weight of Japanese children in the 1930s to results from studies conducted thirty years earlier, were used to "signif[y] a fully evolved race" which was based on the "definitive emergence of superior Japanese children" (12). In both the 1930s and today, physical changes in the body, particularly the female body, symbolize social, economic, and political changes in Japan. The physician's report for the winner of the 1931 Miss Japan contest "emphasized that she was taller than average and had 'the long legs of a 'new woman' . . . She's not an old style Japanese woman, but the embodiment of a healthy Japan" (15). In much the same way, younger Japanese today are thought to be moving away from the struggling Japanese way of life to a more affluent, Westernized lifestyle and therefore are perceived to be closer to the Western ideal of beauty: long-legged, tall, and thin.

As a foreigner, I served as an obvious target and a point of comparison to discuss and critique differences between the "Japanese" body and the "American" body. Reiko, a 25-year-old aerobics instructor, glancing down at my legs, exclaimed, "Your legs are so thin. They are like pencils. I'm so jealous, I wish I were thinner. Your legs are thin because you don't have any muscle. See, my legs are fat because they are so muscular." In this back-handed compliment, Reiko equated muscle and fat, believing both to be equally unattractive and undesirable. She grabbed my hand and led me into the staff room to measure my thighs and then her own with a tape measure. Another aerobics instructor at Downtown Fitness confirmed, "Without a doubt, most women want to lose weight in their legs and hips. Working in a sports club, I always hear members complain 'I want my legs to be thinner.' Trying to slim up one body part is really difficult, and most women don't understand this. We try to talk to them about fat percentages and health, but the only thing the women care about is measurements and the size of their legs [encircling her leg with an imaginary tape measure]."

Thinness at the club is defined by a healthy fat percentage, not by weight or pants size. The constant refrain in the clubs is that, although two people may be the same weight, the one with more muscle and less fat is healthier and will look thinner (Kaneko, Kubota, and Otaki 1995). The weight room staff has been known to criticize aerobics instructors for being thin but undeveloped, with upper bodies that are scrawny and undefined. The majority of Japanese women in the club, members and instructors alike, have a strong aversion to building muscles. They consider both muscles and fat to be big and bulky and thus equally undesirable.

Strength training for the legs, including squats, extensions, and curls, is generally viewed with distaste by most women, who are reluctant to build any muscle in their legs, even if their legs will look and feel thinner. Although the fitness staff encourage female members to use the weight machines to shape up calves and thighs, most of the members opt for their own version of spot slimming: riding the stationary bicycle set on zero resistance or using the weight machines with little or no weight. One female member explained, "In Japan, muscles are bad. Women don't want to use dumbbells because they don't want to get muscular arms. They say 'Eeww muscles, yuck.' Especially on their calves."

Tellingly, fitness clubs tend to advertise in sports and bodybuilding magazines and are noticeably absent from the pages of popular women's magazines. Advertisements for esute salons, on the other hand, monopolize a good portion of the available ad space in the fashion magazines directed at women. One of the staff members at Chiba Club tried to explain the discrepancy:

While it's true that fitness clubs don't advertise in young women's magazines, like *an-an*, they do advertise in magazines for sports-minded people, such as *Tarzan*, where the readers have an interest in fitness. If you look at women's magazines, you will see many ads for esute. This is because young Japanese women have a low fitness consciousness. When they want to shape up, they want to do so quickly and think of esute salons, not fitness clubs. Fitness clubs have an image of building muscle, and to young women this is very undesirable. Muscle equals fat. They want to be very skinny and not have any muscle. Sports clubs don't have women as their primary target, while esute target almost exclusively women. Fitness clubs target all age groups, and both men and women. If sports clubs had women as their primary target, then they would advertise in women's magazines.

This is not to say that the fitness advertisements do not conform to normative standards of beauty. In fact, as I have illustrated, the fitness club ad campaigns distinctly exploit the Japanese public's late-capitalist desire for catered service, quality leisure, improved health, and, most significant, beauty and body perfection.

Conclusions

Outlining parameters for body size, shape, and appearance, beauty ideals also prescribe acceptable feminine behavior and offer insight into cultural notions surrounding health, productivity, national identity, and gender roles. Beauty ideals are located at the intersection of patriarchy and capitalism. Patriarchy as an ideological paradigm with socioeconomic repercussions holds women responsible in part for their own subordination. As opposed to the practice of male domination, which clearly implicates men, patriarchy is an ideology that privileges maleness and masculinity over femaleness and femininity. Therefore, it is not that men and only men produce the demand for slender bodies and good legs, but that this cultural emphasis on unobtainable bodies for women reflects and produces a state of gender inequality, where men, in fact, do dominate.

This hegemonic emphasis on body part fixation, shapely legs, and youth highlights underlying contradictions between the emic notion of a mind and body synergy and the Western conception of mind and body dualism; the undying work ethic that has been used to characterize Japanese institutions since World War II and the desire for leisure and consumption that has defined the late-capitalist period; the uncriti-

cal consumption of Western cultural imports and the selective manipulation and construction of a national identity; and female empowerment and constraint. In the final chapter, I take up this last point of
the tension between control and constraint as experienced and enacted
through dieting and food refusal by young women in Japan.

Selfishly Skinny

or Selflessly Starving

When I asked members at both clubs the question, "Why do you work out?" the answers varied: to lose weight, to relax, to alleviate pain, to build body strength, to enjoy sports. But by far the most common answer by *young women* was "to lose weight." Although a certain number of men do exercise to lose weight and look better, it is the women and, in particular, the young women, whose fitness goals revolve around shedding pounds. The majority of young female club members narrowly define fitness as "diet" and frequent the clubs solely to mold a more perfect body. The fitness club, in one sense, is just another arena in which to strive for the body beautiful. Together with aesthetic salons and diet aids, the goal of molding a thin and balanced body is common.

This emphasis on thinness in contemporary Japan is unprecedented historically. As I explored in the previous chapter, robustness as a sign of productivity and fertility have been favored over thinness and its association with frailty throughout Japanese history, but particularly so in the Tokugawa, Meiji, and militaristic period of the late 1930s and early 1940s. Thinness made a brief appearance in the Taisho era as a way to resist restrictive notions of sexuality and the hegemonic association of femininity with the "good wife, wise mother" role, but was soon squelched under the strict militaristic regime. In the postwar period, moderation and control over one's appetite—delinked from hunger—accompanied the period of economic security and increased availability of food supplies for people all over Japan, from the center to the periphery.

The prosperous postwar period in Japan resulted in "the civilizing of appetite," as Mennell (1991) terms it. He argues that the overall shift toward delicacy and self-control as manifested in appetite was made possible by the reliability and availability of food and its more equal distribution among the social classes. Put simply, when there is not enough to eat, people do not have the luxury to refuse eating. Readily available food supplies enable appetite, or the desire to eat, to be separated from physiological hunger. Considered in light of the historical record, this recent emphasis on thinness is symptomatic of postwar changes in the political economy of Japan. Consumerism, where lifestyle, class, and worth are encoded in the products bought and displayed, creates a body that is "plastic" (Featherstone 1991:178).

With the discipline and effort of diet couched in the rhetoric of lifestyle and leisure, the body can be manipulated to achieve the idealized look. On the one hand, this desire for conformity seems to suggest a degree of false consciousness, in which consumers are the passive dupes of advertising and marketing. On the other hand, as Featherstone points out, "For individual family members to earn an independent income and be accorded the equality of independent consumers in the marketplace offered tangible freedoms, however limited and restricted they might turn out to be" (1991:175). Exercising control over appetite becomes a way to simultaneously reflect and critique notions of class, beauty, femininity, and power in contemporary Japan.

In this chapter, I begin by describing the striking attention given to female thinness, from the proliferation of diet aids to anecdotal evidence of fasting and eating disorders. As I illustrate, most of the aerobics instructors and club members reflected the national preoccupation with weight and thinness. To the Western eye, many Japanese women who struggle to lose weight appear quite thin or even skinny. In fact, when explaining my research to American friends and colleagues, I am often met with incredulous stares and comments that range from praise over the healthy Japanese diet and low caloric content of sushi to certainty that, excepting Sumo wrestlers, an obese or even overweight Japanese person is a rarity. It is crucial to remember, however, that thinness is culturally defined. What may appear thin to a Westerner can seem unbearably heavy to a Japanese woman, who compares her body unfavorably to friends and magazine photos. The definition of obesity, health, and beauty depends on local historical and cultural contexts, and it is this point that makes the cross-cultural examination of body image and ideals necessary.

88 Pounds: The Perfect Weight

The cultural obsession with thinness begins at an early age, as illustrated in the following anecdote of a young girl's embarrassment over and dislike of her own body. While in Japan, a friend taught me how to cook different Japanese dishes and would usually invite two of her neighbors, Naomi and Aya, to share in the festivities. Naomi, a 12-year-old student, particularly enjoyed the dinners as an escape from the drudgery of sixth-grade homework; Aya, a 24-year-old bank teller, always rushed in late, regaling us with tales of her mishaps at work. Despite the twelve-year age difference between Naomi and Aya, they were markedly similar in their poor body image and steady stream of complaints about being fat.

Naomi in particular seemed quite obsessed with the perceived imperfections of her body. Tall for her age, she had very smooth tanned skin and a sturdy muscular frame, which, although admired by family and friends, was a source of great misery to her. Even though she was very athletic and enjoyed sports of all kinds, she seemed to equate being tall with being fat. Because she was the tallest in her class and, in fact, even taller than Aya, Naomi complained about how fat she was and how she wished that she were shorter. Of course, looking different and standing out in elementary school is always difficult, perhaps particularly so in Japan, but the degree to which Naomi fixated on her weight when she was in no way overweight is significant.

In the span of two hours, the string of self-deprecating comments made by Naomi and Aya revealed an alarming lack of self-confidence and poor body image in girls so young. At the beginning of the meal, when Aya reached for a plate, she complained that her upper arm jiggled, to which Naomi immediately agreed, chiming in, "I hate waving good-bye because my arm shakes." When Aya made the off-hand comment that rice is fattening, Naomi wailed that she had a bigger bowl than everyone and looked extremely concerned. She fixated on the "fatness" of her wrists and demanded that we all hold up our wrists so that she could compare the sizes. Finally, after dinner, Naomi invariably clutched her stomach beneath her overalls and exclaimed, "I'm so fat."

Although Naomi admired Aya and modeled much of her behavior and comments on the older girl, she clearly had internalized this self-deprecation and, over the course of a two-hour dinner, had dissected herself from head to toe. For a 12-year-old to be that highly attuned to the size and shape of her body, comparing herself unfavorably to others and self-monitoring her food portions, illustrates the pervasiveness of the beauty and body ideal in Japan. Naomi has learned that big is bad and that an attractive woman is petite, thin, and small-boned. She has come to despise her height, muscle strength, and even the size of her bones, which mark her as physically powerful and therefore socially unacceptable.

For women larger than a size 6 by U.S. standards, shopping in Japan is often a depressing and futile experience. Although the selection and variety of shoes, accessories, cosmetics, and clothing can be mind-boggling, most department stores and boutiques in Japan carry a minimum range of sizes. Women's clothing generally can be found in three sizes only: small, medium, and large. Women who are tall, broad, or muscular simply cannot fit into a medium or even large size, and this prevents them from wearing the popular styles. Some of the more fashionable brands are made in "medium" only, but the "medium" is skimpy, cut short and tight in the sleeves, and binds in the waist. In the recent past, women's fashion trends have dictated tiny T-shirts with armholes that do not permit even the smallest biceps muscle development, tight bootleg pants, and high-heeled sandals and boots.

Unfortunately, the very few stores in Japan that stock unconventional sizes also tend to carry unconventional styles. Many of the larger women must resort to buying clothing from U.S. lines that are available in Japan or ordering from catalogues of other companies based abroad. Even maternity clothes tend to run in smaller than expected sizes. One of my Japanese friends, whom I first met in the United States and who is about 150 pounds at 5'5" and pregnant, complained, "Japanese women are all so small, I can't fit into any of the maternity bathing suits. I had to buy a LLL size at [one of the fitness clubs] made for old women. It was so embarrassing." This seems inconceivable to many North Americans, who can buy clothing in sizes ranging from 4 to 14 at most department stores and can purchase petite and plus-sizes at any number of specialty stores or separate departments.

The limited range of sizes clearly delineates the appropriate and accepted body size. If a woman is too large or too small to fit into the type of clothing advertised in the magazines or sold in the stores, she is made to feel that her body is the wrong size. Jeannie Lo, while living in the company dormitory and working as an office lady in Japan, noted this obsession with thinness and concluded that most women "aspired

21. The 1997 advertisement of the second-largest fitness club chain in Japan uses this exaggerated hourglass figure to market their "shape-up" campaign.

to rakelike thinness" (1990:69). In a 1997 advertising campaign run by the second-largest fitness club chain in Japan, the torso of a foreign woman with a black belt tightly cinched around her leotarded frame takes the hour-glass figure to its extreme (Figure 21). The result is a computer-enhanced image of a woman with a 10-inch waist, recalling the photograph of the "world's smallest waist" in the *Guinness Book of World Records.* As part of the campaign, this club also distributed belts printed with the phrase "Tone up, tone up" (*shime shime*) and an arrow pointing to the smallest belt hole size. The largest belt hole was marked with a tiny 68 cm (about 25 inches) and decreased incrementally to 58 cm (about 21 inches) as the goal. A friend of mine was given this belt when she was seven months pregnant and exclaimed that she couldn't even get the belt around one leg, let alone her huge stomach.

Forty kilograms (about 88 pounds) is the benchmark weight for many Japanese women, regardless of height, bone structure, or muscle definition. An almost magical number, not unlike the elusive and often imagined "five pounds too heavy" that plague women in the United States, 40 kilograms is held by many to represent a somewhat arbitrary but nonetheless powerful cultural standard for shaping women's body weight goals. At a women's physical education college in Japan, one student explained the allure of 40 kilograms: "At my school, the people who major in dance are really skinny. They all want to be 40 kilograms no matter what their height. At 160 centimeters [about 5 feet 2 inches], they all want to be 40 kilograms, so they don't eat anything and you can see them between classes, running around the track, trying to sweat. They are sickly skinny. It is more important for them to be skinnier than the average person because they want to fit into a leotard and look good."

But why 40 kilograms? As several members explained, many of the popular models and television stars publicly claim to be 40 kilograms, and that has come to set the standard. This round number has become part of the specific and narrow ideal by which beauty is measured. For many women, the ever-elusive 40 kilograms symbolizes success, accomplishment, happiness, and satisfaction. This unrealistic body weight can be physically dangerous for some and psychologically crippling for others. Women are burdened by feeling "If only I were 40 kilograms, then I would be" happy, beautiful, married—the list goes on and on. Practically, to fit into the styles she admires, and ideally, to conform to the images she internalizes, a woman may see altering her body as the only solution. Her goal becomes to lose inches or gain curves as quickly and easily as possible through exercise or, more commonly, through magical pills, creams, and fad diets.

Cake Sets and Fad Diets

Dieting in Japan is narrowly defined as radically cutting calories, similar to the diets in the United States ten years ago. In the United States, a high fat content has been deemed the ultimate dietary evil, usurping even nitrates, salt, and sugar, the evils of past years. Fat calories and cholesterol percentages are calculated and displayed on every product sold, from potato chips to canned vegetables, and even the most clueless shoppers are aware of the dangers of fat (which doesn't necessarily stop them from consuming the fat, of course). But the obsession with fat calories has not yet taken hold in Japan.[1] First of all, there are no FDA-like requirements that nutritional content labels be displayed on every foodstuff sold. Although some products in Japan carry these labels, the majority do not.[2] Second, the rows of Healthy Choice, Weight Watchers, and Lean Cuisine products, which boast reduced fat/sugar/salt and crowd the shelves of North American super-markets, are markedly absent in Japan. At best, the fat- and calorie-concerned shopper can purchase nonfat Yoplait yogurt and skim milk at most large supermarkets and department store basements, but convenience stores carry almost exclusively high-fat and high-calorie foods.

Most Japanese tend to conflate sugar with unhealthiness and high calories, while completely disregarding fat content. As one of the Chiba Club staff explained, "I was worried that the cheesecake I made last night wasn't sweet enough. I used a lot less sugar, because I wanted to make the cheesecake more *healthy* [in katakana]. When I tasted it, I didn't think it was sweet enough. I love cheesecake! Usually I can eat half by myself." It is significant that she chose to make her recipe more healthy by eliminating the sugar but not the cream cheese, despite the high fat, calories, and cholesterol found in the cheese and not in the sugar. I want to emphasize that many Americans, while militant about fat consumption, tend to overindulge in calories. I do not have the space nor the intent to conduct a cultural analysis of dieting and fitness in the United States, but I do want to caution the reader from concluding that North Americans are somehow less contradictory or more consistently health conscious. With equally high rates of obesity and fitness consciousness, the culture of the United States is just as plagued with inconsistencies as Japan's. But, of course, as in Japan, health, fitness, and diet map out according to class, gender, and occupation in the United States, where only certain privileged segments of the population have access to and resources for the healthiest foods and upscale exercise facilities.

Many Westerners (and many of the Japanese themselves) cling to the common notion of the "healthy" Japanese diet. Certainly the traditional, that is, the prewar diet of Japan, which was based on a balance of fresh vegetables, fish, and rice, is low in saturated fat, calories, and cholesterol and is undeniably healthy. But do the Japanese of prosperous, postwar Japan eat in the same Spartan way as their predecessors? Of course not. With the ready availability of almost any international product from tortilla chips to Häagen-Dazs and the increased technology and prosperity to produce their own fattening creations, the diet in contemporary Japan is far more varied but consequently far higher in calories, fat, and processed sugar.

Many Japanese officials recognize this shift and blame it on McDonald's, which has opened 399 restaurants in Japan since 1971, 100 of which are in the Tokyo area (Ohnuki-Tierney 1997). McDonald's is an easy scapegoat, as the most vivid example of the import of American fast food chains and products, but it is only part of the problem. The threat of Westernization is symbolized in the threat of the McDonald's takeover. A tension between nationalism and globalization is played out in the debate over the merits of a Japanese versus an American diet. Whether Western foods have "taken over" Japan is inconsequential; it is the perception that they have that is significant.

In fact, similar to the transformation of many foreign imports, food products have been selectively chosen and altered to suit the Japanese market. Ohnuki-Tierney (1997) has explored the way the McDonald's hamburger on a breaded roll is conceptualized and consumed as a snack, distinct from the rice-based meal in contemporary Japan. In fact, a second fast food restaurant, created in Japan and modeled on McDonald's, has taken the greasy hamburger one step further and sells merely a ball of deep-fried mayonnaise on a roll. Mayonnaise in Japan is ubiquitous, used on everything from eggs to dressing on salads. Unlike in the United States, where a group of diet-conscious young women may chat publicly over a virtuous coffee or a more decadent cappuccino, Japanese women usually order an afternoon "cake set," which includes, for a set price, a piece of whipped, sugary cake with a choice of coffee or tea. In fact, I conducted most one-on-one and group interviews in coffee shops over cakes and ice cream sundaes. The women I interviewed confided their desire to lose weight and their fixation on figure flaws as they dug into wedges of rich cake without a trace of irony or self-consciousness.

Indulgence, like dieting, is a way to claim identity and manipulate power. In Japan, enjoying sugary cakes and snacks is viewed as a decidedly feminine trait. Women, like children, are expected and encouraged to relish sweets, and those who do are constructed as cute and childishly attractive. Edwards explains: "Alcohol is considered one of the spicy foods which as a class are the province of adults, and which children are taught to avoid in favor of sweet ones. Cakes, as sweet foods, have a close association with children in Japan" (1987:66). The consumption of sweets, or what Kinsella terms "cute food," is particularly characteristic of the *burikko* (pretend child), the grown women who act naïve, coquettish, and innocent to appear attractive and to rebel against adult responsibilities (1995:231–232). The woman who prefers alcohol and salty snacks—the stereotypical indulgences of men—is viewed as

Selfishly Skinny, Selflessly Starving 181

masculine, aggressive, and "one of the boys," and the man who passes up a beer in favor of dessert may be characterized as sexually suspect, wimpy, or feminine.[3]

To satisfy contradictory cultural expectations that women should enjoy sweets but manage to maintain a skinny figure, many women resort to skipping meals or eating exclusively one type of food or drinking one type of beverage, such as eating only eggs or apples or drinking only kinoko (a type of seaweed) milkshakes. This narrow description of dieting leaves the door wide open for the pricey diet aids, teas, and restrictive meals that can be ineffective at best and dangerous at worst. According to a survey conducted by the Japanese National Milk Promotion Association in 1991, nearly 60 percent of young women in Japan are or have been on a diet ("Most Young Women Diet" 1991). The variety and number of diet products sold and the behavior of the female staff, members, and college students I observed in my fieldwork suggest that the percentages most likely have only increased.

Most women I spoke with in the clubs and at the universities had experimented with some type of dieting, either through metabolism-altering pills or, more commonly, by radically reducing caloric intake to produce speedy weight loss. Some members confided that they drank exclusively *oolong cha,* or Chinese tea, while dieting, as the tea is believed "to make the body cooler," thereby producing weight loss; others relied on chili peppers to raise the body temperature and increase metabolism. These beliefs are derived from the humoral theory of traditional Chinese medicine, which maintains that the body is affected by heat, cold, wetness, and dryness (Anderson 1997:82). Low-calorie foods such as lettuce and cabbage do not provide adequate nutrition during cold winter months and are therefore classified as "cooling," whereas "heating" foods, including ginger, pepper, and chilies, raise body temperature and are thought to burn calories. Although no longer actively practiced in China, traditional Chinese medicine has had lasting impact on folk beliefs of weight loss in Japan.

As one instructor at the fitness club explained, "Most of the women who diet are in high school or college, and they don't go to clubs and don't even know what the word diet means. They think that it means not eating and not exercising. They are just concerned with losing weight and don't care at all about fat percentage. They would eat nothing except sweets and snacks and think that that is a diet. These fad diets are weird. They are nonnutritious and not even proper dieting at all." Most fad diets can be sustained for only one to two weeks, as food choices are so limited in calories and necessary vitamins and minerals. Many dieters immediately regain the weight lost or *rebound*, as it is called in Japanese.

In 1995, NHK created a national sensation with the airing of the *Dumbbell Diet* ("Not So Dumb Belles" 1995). One middle-aged housewife at the suburban club tried to explain the appeal: "The Dumbbell Diet was shown on NHK about one to two years ago. Everyone from the young to the very old could do it, because it was so simple. It was extremely popular. My friends taped it off the TV and gave it to me. At first I did it with 1 kilogram weights, but because my arms jiggle when I wave good-bye, I increased to 5 kilogram weights. But this hurt my back, so I had to quit. I was so embarrassed that I had to stop because all my friends and everyone else could do it. I felt bad. Now, NHK has published books, magazines, and videotapes about it. It is really very popular. Diets in Japan become really popular because when one person hears that a new one works, the word spreads quickly, so everyone tries it." Nearly everyone I spoke to at the fitness clubs had heard of the Dumbbell Diet, and many had tried it. The books, magazines, and videos are still sold in stores, although sales have dropped off as the fad has leveled out. The *Dumbbell Diet* television program fits into the early morning niche for light exercise and stretching created by NHK just four years after television was introduced to Japan in 1953.

The *tamago* diet is probably one of the most well-known in Japan. Published by the National Hospital as a means to lose weight, it promises that "in just two weeks' time, this diet will cause the alteration of tissue within your body. The amount that you eat will not matter at all." I was given a copy of this controversial fad diet by one of the staff members at Chiba Club. She assured me that the diet worked and that I would lose weight if I stuck to the rules. The recommended time frame for the diet is two weeks and the predicted weight loss in this time is 10 kilograms or 22 pounds! The handout contains the printed warning: "If for some reason, you quit at any time, you must start over from the beginning of the diet." Containing seven menus for breakfast, lunch, and dinner, the entire diet is to be repeated two weeks in a row. The menu for day one is as follows:

Breakfast: one boiled egg, one grapefruit, one slice of toast,
     black coffee

| Lunch: | one boiled egg, a tomato, black coffee |
| Dinner: | one boiled egg; cucumber, carrot and celery salad (no dressing), *sukemono* [pickles] |

Not only is the diet high in fat and cholesterol because of the number of eggs, but the daily calories consumed total fewer than 350. The accepted recommended daily caloric intake by most doctors and nutritionists in both Japan and the United States is dependent on an individual's height, body size, and sex, but should never drop below 1,000 to 1,200 calories. Tantamount to starvation, this diet would cause anyone to lose weight, but would be virtually impossible to withstand for longer than the two weeks recommended. Furthermore, rebound is inevitable once the dieter goes back to his or her regular eating patterns.

Given the high incidence of weight regain and the dangers of depriving the body of the nutrients necessary for survival, dieting has become a bad word in fitness circles in the United States. Not surprisingly, the Japanese media have imported some of these concerns, seizing on certain inflammatory stories, such as Karen Carpenter's lifelong struggles with anorexia nervosa and her tragic death.

The Fasting Fitness Instructor:
Tension between Indulgence and Restraint

Given this overt attention to appearance and a national obsession with thinness, it is not surprising that a good number of female fitness instructors fast or exercise obsessively in an attempt to lose weight, and several pop metabolism-uppers every three to six hours. Other staff privately admitted that they had been to esute (aesthetic salons) to try to slim down, and still others confided to stints of employment by the salons prior to working at the fitness club. Despite (or more likely, because of) their experiences at the salons, very few of the staff believed that the esute produced results. In the staff room, one instructor remarked that she heard that the "before" and "after" photographs used in esute advertisements to illustrate weight loss following the program were actually taken in reverse order. That is, thin women are hired to take the "after" pictures first and then are paid to gain weight for the "before" pictures, photographed at a later date. Many noted that the women are positioned facing front for the "before" pictures, with stom-

22. Many fitness club staff and members pointed out the tricks of photography used in these advertisements for quick weight loss, noting that in the "after" pictures, the women are carefully made up, wearing high-heeled sandals and flattering bikinis.

achs pushed out and slouchy posture to exaggerate rounded stomachs and heavy hips, whereas the "after" photos are taken from a more flattering profile angle, with shoulders thrown back and stomachs pulled in (Figure 22).

On the job, club instructors preach against the ill effects of fad dieting, pills, and aesthetic salons, advocating exercise and a healthy diet instead. By no means hoodwinked, most of the staff frequent the aesthetic salons and department stores fully aware of the tricks of photography, the illusions of contour makeup and padded lingerie, and the short-lived results of fad dieting. It may be that the lure of losing weight effortlessly is so tempting that many of the instructors suspend disbelief, common sense, and professional experience on the off chance that a miracle will take place. It may also be that by frequenting the aesthetic salons, the primary competition of the fitness clubs, the instructors are financially and symbolically supporting the competitor as a way of thumbing their nose at the fitness club.

Some of the staff, despite their claims to be on a diet and their willingness to spend time and money on a variety of disreputable diet aids, snacked on junk food all day long. Many of the members brought *oben-*

Selfishly Skinny, Selflessly Starving 185

tou (boxed lunches), cookies, and snacks for a favorite instructor, and all the food wound up on this back room table to be consumed by the staff at a rapid-fire pace. Grabbing chips and cookies on their way out to pool duty or aerobics, most staff ate without guilt, never commenting about "ruining a diet" or "starting the diet tomorrow." The contradictions of fad dieting, binge eating, and exercise seem to support the claim that these acts should be interpreted in the context of power. Most of the instructors consistently and even simultaneously engaged in all forms of bodily indulgence, snacking on cookies while trading dieting tips and drinking a beer after exercising at a feverish rate to lose weight. The contradictions and seeming irrationality of these acts suggest that the body becomes a site of interplay between hegemony and resistance or indulgence and gratification.[4]

The pursuit of thinness is not simply a quest for beauty, but an active struggle over notions of selfhood, identity, and power. The contradiction between self-denial and self-indulgence reflects a larger struggle over women's roles in contemporary Japan. Bordo (1993) has examined U.S. women's struggles with their body as reflective of an underlying tension between the desire to give in to impulses and a need to repress cravings for instant gratification. She argues that a society that produces eating disorders that range from anorexia nervosa to obesity is symptomatic of the larger push-pull between resistance and indulgence that characterizes late-capitalist consumerism. Mennell agrees and notes, "Anorexia nervosa and obesity can be regarded as similar if opposite disturbances of the *normal* patterns of self-control over appetite now *normally* expected and necessary in prosperous Western societies" (1991:151; emphasis added). Although I agree with Mennell's general premise, my question is: "Normal" to whom and "normal" for whom? As Mennell illustrates, the emphasis on appetite control reflects a socioeconomic equalizing process, where food availability brings about more "even and 'all-round' self-controls over appetite" (151). He does an excellent job of accounting for the role of class in the determination of appetite control, but has less to say about why appetite control is also distinguished along gender lines.

This historically unprecedented attention to thinness *for women* in postwar Japan must be situated at the intersection of consumerism, capitalism, and patriarchal domination. As illustrated in the previous chapter, female beauty in Japan revolves around thinness, and the consumer market has accelerated to meet and define this desire. But to explain thinness only as a product of powerful market forces is to construct female consumers as mindless victims of advertising. While acknowledging the undeniable power of consumerism on determining and defining ideals, I choose to focus on the unconscious and conscious manipulation of power and gender roles through dieting and food refusal.

In late-capitalist societies such as the United States and Japan, consumerism produces and feeds a desire for the unobtainable body in order to sell products, and patriarchy contributes to the boundaries around normalcy and beauty in order to limit access to power. The impact of these forces on the construction of the ideal female body in the West has been thoroughly examined by scholars such as Bordo, Featherstone, and Turner. What can this localized study of Japan contribute to the field? By situating this discussion of thinness not only within larger, cross-cultural forces of patriarchy and consumerism but also within grounded constructions of the relationship between the mind and body, I assert that dieting and food refusal serve as powerful means to resist and comply with gender inequality and familial and societal expectations and roles for Japanese women.

Should we expect the fitness club staff to be exempt or somehow removed from the influences of the hegemonic culture that praises beauty and thinness at any cost? Should the staff, by virtue of their education, know better? Or are the staff more predisposed to caring about looks, health, and the body, and, thus, this more generalized preoccupation becomes even more exaggerated in the fitness club? I believe that the aerobics instructors are merely representative of the national fixation on looks that concerns so many young Japanese women, and increasingly men today. As Bordo asserts of the United States, "People *know* the routes to success in this culture—they are advertised widely enough—and they are not 'dopes' to pursue them. Often given the racism, sexism, and narcissism of the culture, their personal happiness and economic security may depend on it" (1993:30). The same can be said of Japan.

Anorexia Nervosa: An Exaggeration of the Norm

One cannot discuss this cultural predilection for thinness without linking it to a discussion of eating disorders, particularly anorexia nervosa. Primarily afflicting upper- to middle-class teenage girls and women, the disorder causes those afflicted to dramatically limit their food intake; they may also exercise obsessively and rely on purging and laxatives to lose weight. Although thinness is undeniably linked to the pursuit of beauty circulated by the media, it is also about tensions over power, inequality, and independence. I would characterize anorexia nervosa, bulimia, obesity, and other eating "disorders" as medicalized extremes of "normal" eating (or should I say noneating) habits among young women. Physiological, biological, and social factors determine where the line between disorder and diet is drawn. To focus on everyday thinness and daily dieting is to question and ultimately blur this line between normal and abnormal, healthy and ill, and order and disorder.

It is now generally accepted in psychoanalysis that many anorexic women use self-starvation as a means to exert control over their lives or to deny developing sexual maturation. The first case of anorexia nervosa in Japan was documented in 1960; it has since been diagnosed in increasing numbers ("Overcoming Eating Disorders" 1995:11). Appearing at the height of Japanese economic prosperity, the appearance of the disease accompanied widespread food availability. Bruch has observed that anorexia nervosa is not reported in countries with food shortages nor among impoverished subcultures in the United States (1997:13). In 1997, it was estimated that nearly 1 in 100 young Japanese women suffered from an eating disorder, an incidence rate comparable to that in the United States; that rate has only increased in the past four years (Efron 1997:A1).

In the past decade, anorexia nervosa has spread to the affluent populations of South Korea, Hong Kong, and Singapore, even appearing to a lesser degree in Taipei, Beijing, and Shanghai. In Singapore's trendy shopping district, a popular girl's T-shirt reads: "I've got to get into that dress. It's easy. Don't eat . . . I'm hungry. Can't eat breakfast. But I ought to . . . I like breakfast. I like that dress . . . Still too big for that dress. Hmm. Life can be cruel" (quoted in Efron 1997:A1). With the establishment of the Nippon Anorexia Bulimia Association (NABA) in 1987, the five hundred members struggling with eating disorders have had a place to seek help (Kuriki 1992:5). More recently, the Harajuku Counseling Center and Overeaters Anonymous have been established to offer individual and group therapy sessions, and in 2000, officials at the Health, Labor, and Welfare Ministry, recognizing the "drastic increase in the number of patients," made the commitment to establish medical centers across Japan to treat eating disorders ("Ministry to Set Up" 2000).

The high-profile death of Karen Carpenter in 1983, whose music has enjoyed remarkable longevity in Japan, ignited concerns over dieting and continues to be discussed on numerous daytime talk shows. Eating disorder specialists in Japan note that "young teenagers are being influenced significantly by fashion models, magazines, and entertainment industry figures from Westernized societies" ("Eating Disorders" 1989). One 24-year-old woman, a graduate student in the women's studies program at a Chiba university, explained: "Anorexia? You mean like Karen Carpenter? About one year ago, it became a hot topic and was discussed in the *dramas* [soap operas]. Everyone is very concerned that high school students have it. In magazines, television, and the *Wide Show*,[5] it is a common topic. It's very sensational, right? They show the skinny photographs [she sucks in her stomach to illustrate], so it has become a hot topic and now, because everyone is always dieting, dieting, now the mass media have informed us that there is this scary illness. Therefore, most people do know about it. So when someone doesn't eat, others say as a joke: 'Do you have anorexia?' [she laughs]."

Although these comments do indicate a certain attention to the sociocultural effects of Hollywood and the media on ideals of female beauty, it seems a bit facile to assume that the obsession with thinness is solely a function of Western or mass media hegemony. As I illustrate, thinness must be read for the sociological functions it serves in the particular context of Japan. As indicated in the previous chapter, the emphasis on proportions and thin legs is markedly distinct from the silicone-inflated, muscular bodies idealized in the West, which would also suggest that female skinniness might not mean the same thing in Japan as it does in the United States.

Psychologizing the Individual

Although anorexia is increasingly prevalent in Japan, most of the literature on eating disorders and body image has been produced by psychologists and aims at individual-focused prescriptions for treatment (e.g., Nakamura et al. 1990; Suematsu 1993; Takeda, Suzuki, and Matsushita 1993). Despite recent recognition of the widespread incidence of eating disorders in Japan by the Health, Labor, and Welfare Ministry, counseling is still not covered by insurance policies because anorexia "is not recognized as a medical problem" (Makino 1998). Frustrated with a psychological focus that ignores the sociocultural climate, one woman published an anecdotal article detailing her experience with anorexia nervosa in Japan. In her work, she describes the reaction of a doctor when she admitted that she was a recovered anorectic. His first question was: "Did you have a boyfriend at the time?" (Mukai 1989:631). Numerous scholars have examined eating disorders within the specific social, historical, and cultural contexts of the contemporary United States, Victorian England, and the Middle Ages (e.g., Bordo 1997; Brumberg 1997; Bynum 1987), but a sociological analysis of anorexia nervosa in postwar Japan has yet to be conducted.

Many psychiatrists in Japan point to stress as the primary cause of anorexia among young Japanese women (Imai 1993). Studying for college entrance exams, starting a new job, or marrying into a single-residence household can be cause for undue stress, which manifests itself in an eating disorder. Kaori is a 24-year-old woman who, at the time of my interview with her, had been a member at Chiba Club for five months. Smiling but somewhat shy, Kaori plays with a lock of hair as we talk. She is only slightly overweight but extremely self-conscious of her body and her self-described "chubby face." She joined Chiba Club in January, just days after quitting a strict fad diet in which she ate only green leafy vegetables for two months. Although Kaori lost 10 kilograms (22 pounds) on this vegetable diet, she since has gained back all of the weight and more.

In retrospect, Kaori acknowledges that fad dieting is extremely unhealthy. In fact, she finally decided to quit the diet, despite her "successful" weight loss, when she recognized the beginning signs of developing an eating disorder: "When I overeat, I feel really guilty [*tsumi*]. At that time, in December, it was the season for the 'end of the year' parties, so I was drinking a lot of alcohol and eating a lot of delicious foods. At these parties, I would eat so much and then return to my house, and even though it was late at night, even though it was midnight, I would open the refrigerator and think everything looks so delicious and eat even more. I would feel so guilty that I was trying so hard to be beautiful and even though I was trying so hard on my diet, I would ruin it at the party. So gradually I would feel so guilty that I would go throw up in the toilet. I would feel clean/pure [*sukkiri*] in my stomach. My body would feel good, but my heart would ache. I would think: 'This is awful. Why am I doing this?' And I would cry. I feel better now, but at that time, I was really sick."

Kaori was working in sales at the time and hated her job, primarily because she couldn't get along with her boss. Depressed and stressed at that time, Kaori explained that she tried to look more attractive to further her career: "Because my work was in sales and many customers came to the store, I wanted to have a more beautiful, thin body. Also, I wanted my face to look thinner and my stomach to be thinner." The stress described by Kaori reflects a larger tension over power and inequality in the workplace. Psychological stress over uncontrollable socioeconomic inequalities undeniably manifests itself in a concern with one's body. Rather than focusing on the stress suffered by the individual, as an anthropologist, I next concentrate on the social inequities that contribute to the near ubiquitous dieting in high schools, on college campuses, and in fitness clubs (see Nakagawa 1995; "The Latest News" 1995; "You Will Never Be Fat Again" 1996).

Cultural Explanations: Food and Power

The literature on thinness and eating disorders published in the West is more extensive than in Japan, reflecting a variety of perspectives that can be grouped into three categories: biomedical, psychological, and cultural models. Biomedical explanations cite hormonal, chemical, or other medical imbalances as responsible for a predilection for thinness, and psychological models find cause in familial relationships, socialization, and addictive tendencies. These models are useful for explaining why certain women develop anorexia nervosa and others do not, but for understanding the near universal concern over body weight in the United States and Japan, a sociocultural model is required. While most cultural and feminist explanations do not deny the effects of biology and familial socialization, they situate eating disorders within a larger, media-driven predilection for skinniness, a hegemonic emphasis on the equation of thinness and beauty for women, and larger socioeconomic expectations and roles for women.

To concentrate exclusively on thinness is to contribute to the static and objectified view of the female body: the thin body as a passive product subjected to the dominant standards of health and beauty. If we consider instead the acts of dieting and food refusal as either complicit or defiant reactions to the selfless and other-oriented construction of femininity in Japan, we come to recognize that these women maintain agency and power that, at times, is inadvertent and unconscious and, at other times, is intentional. The notion of dieting as empowering or at least agent-driven has been a theme common to feminist literature on anorexia nervosa in the West. Feminist anthropologists and historians have explained anorexia nervosa and systematic food refusal as a barometer of spirituality, sexuality, morality, self-restraint, and social status.

Situating the Self in a Social Network

Dieting in Japan represents, on the one hand, a form of resistance to traditional feminine roles, constructed as both productive and reproductive. Caring for one's own appearance rather than directing all one's energy to the care of others may be construed as defiant. The appetite, in the words of Brumberg (1997), becomes a voice for expressing displeasure with societal expectations and restrictions. To be well-fed in Japan is to be socially connected to one's community and one's family; for instance, a child's robustness is evidence of successful parental care. Many young women continue to live with their family until marriage, and their mother prepares the majority of their meals. While I was in the field, more than one mother expressed concern that her daughter was too skinny despite attempts to feed her nutritious and ample meals. A daughter who rejects these home-cooked meals is denying familial connections and dependency. Dieting becomes an expression not only of independence and self-sufficiency but also selfishness and antisocial tendencies. At the same time, because adult women in contemporary Japan and elsewhere are responsible for the care and feeding of others, young women who disassociate themselves from the consumption and preparation of food may be consciously or unconsciously postponing the responsibilities of adulthood.

On the other hand, food refusal by women can also be interpreted as complicit acceptance of ideological constructions of an other-oriented femininity. Food refusal must be distinguished from dieting, as the former is an act of social concern and the latter an act of self-concern. A woman who prepares and serves food but does not indulge is the epitome of selflessness. Indeed, as Bynum states, "Women prepare food and men eat it" (1987:191). Skinniness becomes symbolic of a clean, aesthetically pure nature, disconnected from the constant demands of physicality. A body without hunger is a body without needs. Similarly, Bynum points out, by not eating, a woman rids herself of the need to excrete, thereby preserving her feminine modesty (211). The young woman who is not hampered by the physical demands of the self is able to devote herself more fully to the care of others. Food refusal, conceived in this way, characterizes femininity.

Because of its inherent ties to familial dependency, care, and nurturing, food becomes an obvious tool for enacting resistance and acquiescence to familial, communal, and state relationships and responsibilities. The giving and receiving of food becomes a way of symbolically manipulating constructions of masculinity and femininity, independence and dependence, selfishness and selflessness, and child and parental roles. Thinness becomes synonymous with a certain type of femininity, defined as either self-centered and liberated or other-oriented and doting. These roles are neither bounded nor mutually exclusive, but are ambiguous and contradictory, as best seen in the all too common instance of Japanese women who divulge diet secrets while guiltlessly enjoying ice cream sundaes.

Evidence of the social body, in which boundaries between the self and others are fluid and overlapping, suggests that a Cartesian dualism is not at work here. But for those women who reject the care and feeding offered by their parents or the responsibilities of a future maternal role by attempting to reclaim their bodies for themselves, the notion of an individually bounded self de-linked from social networks may serve as the most effective path to independence. This rejection of normative roles is similar to the use of the hunger strike by Chinese student demonstrators as "an attempt to break away from the family and the state by constructing new boundaries around individual bodies, outlining a new and different conception of self in the process" (Brownell 1995:261). In both cases, the boundaries (or lack thereof) between mind and body are renegotiated as social relationships between children and parents, wives and husbands, and individuals and the nation are manipulated through food refusal and dieting.

Food not only plays a key role in the acquiescence and resistance to gender roles, it also defines and negotiates boundaries between families and communities. Counihan explains: "Manners and habits of eating are crucial to the very definition of community, the relationships between people" (1999:13). What roles do food, feeding, and dieting play in the construction of social relationships in Japan? Studies of the self in Japan stress the cultural and institutional significance attached to cultivating reciprocal relationships with others. At the risk of confirming cultural stereotypes about the "group-oriented Japanese," studies on early childhood education (Peak 1991), corporate management (Tobin 1992b), and marriage (Edwards 1989) do suggest strong socializing forces that reward the cultivation of social relationships. In Japanese preschools, the teacher's authority is de-emphasized so that children may learn to resolve conflict on their own in small groups, called *han*. These han are also instituted in large white-collar corporations, where authority is decentralized and management is farmed out to the smaller groups. These examples are not meant to suggest a structural-functionalist model of Japanese culture, where harmony serves to maintain social equilibrium. Certainly, as these scholars have illustrated, competition and hierarchy play as large a role as cooperation in the construction of self.

I turn now to an exploration of the tensions between cooperation and conflict and selflessness and selfishness, as they are played out through the control of the appetite and the distribution and consumption of food. Thinness as the tangible evidence of a woman's decision to refuse food represents both acquiescence and resistance to hegemonic constructions of femininity. As I illustrated in Chapter 4 and as Turner (1991b) argues in "The Discourse of Diet," control over diet contributes to the production of docile bodies in the service of capitalism; "A workforce which is not only sober but healthy is clearly desirable from the point of view of capitalist production" (164). But the manipulation of one's appearance through dieting and fashion also becomes a way to play with gender roles and power and, in the words of Kondo, serves as "a critically important political move if one's goal is to effect social transformation" (1997:7). Self-regulated and self-disciplined, a woman monitors her own eating habits as a way of expressing or performing femininity.

"Acting" Feminine

Judith Butler's (1993) notion of "performance" with regard to gender has been well accepted in the West. She subverts the idea that gender is a fixed and essentialized category, arguing that gender is a function of a social, political, and cultural context. Brownell has made the provocative observation that gender is not "performed" in the People's Republic of China, and asserts, "The idea that one might 'put on' and 'take off' one's gender is harder to comprehend in the Chinese cultural framework, in which gender is more closely tied to durable traits like social class and less tied to changeable traits like appearance" (1995:216). Are Brownell's arguments about gender as more fixed and less mutable applicable to Japan?

The performative nature of gender in Japan has been well-documented, from the age-old all-male Kabuki players who acted the parts of women to the more contemporary Takarazuka Revue, an all-female theater troupe who spend hours perfecting their exaggerated masculine and feminine roles (Robertson 1998). Dorrine Kondo (1997) explores the performance of race and gender in Asian American theater and the Japanese fashion industry. Although examples from theater point to the literal performance of gender, everyday examples of the burikko, a name given to Japanese women who act childlike as a way to appear more attractive and more feminine, indicate that gender construction in Japan is maleable as well as unconscious and hegemonic. Even in the PRC, Brownell indicates, with "the increasing availability of stylish clothes, cosmetics, hair salons, and fitness clubs" young people are playing with gender in new ways (1995:234).

In the following discussion of selfishly skinny and selfless starvation, I analyze what thinness tells us about women's roles, status, and power in contemporary Japan. I focus on both the acts of dieting and food refusal and the end result of thinness. Dieting can be interpreted as a conscious act of liberation from the other-oriented feminine standard, but, at the same time, food refusal can be a sign of complicity with normative standards of beauty and femininity, by which women are subordinated to the male gaze and evaluated solely on the basis of their appearance and selfless acts. By situating the performance of femininity within the particular context of patriarchal capitalism, the pursuit of thinness becomes more than just a psychological and biomedical disorder, more than merely the insidious domination of Hollywood, and more than just a mirror of the West. Thinness and dieting become emblematic of the tension and ambivalence over gender roles and notions of the self in Japan.

"The ideal body is a strong, healthy body"

Akiko is an attractive 48-year-old housewife who has been a long-time member at Chiba Club, a suburban fitness club located outside of Tokyo. She is friendly and personable, and struck up a poolside conversation with me while I was life-guarding at the club. When out of her bathing suit and swim cap, Akiko dresses impeccably but holds herself a bit stiffly, favoring her lower back. She strained her back more than fifteen years ago, but has finally decided to take action to strengthen her muscles and has been participating in a strength training class at Chiba Club twice a week. Our discussions over coffee often revolved around Akiko's worries and dreams for her two grown children, both of whom still live at home. Her daughter is 19 years old and is studying for the college entrance exam, and her son is 23 and suffers from autism.

Akiko is quite proud that her son can hold a steady job at a packing company but worries about what will happen to him when she and her husband grow too old to care for him. Like many of her female cohorts, she is exclusively responsible for caring for her dependent children and aging parents, and though she may desire relief from the responsibilities of providing round-the-clock care for her disabled son, alternatives simply are not available. In Japan, where day care centers, assisted living, and retirement homes continue to be stigmatized and underutilized, the responsibility of caring for dependent family members falls primarily to the female family members (see Bethel 1992). For many women in Japan, personal trips, hobbies, and work schedules revolve around their responsibilities as caregivers, whether of child or parent.

The weighty and life-long responsibilities of caring for a dependent son have made Akiko keenly aware of her own mortality and the importance of preserving good health, not only for herself but for her family. She believes that the way she feels is far more important than the way she looks: "The ideal body is a strong, healthy body. Young people care more about being beautiful, but to me a healthy body is more important. Both my daughter and I feel that being too skinny, like Rie Miyazawa,[6] who has anorexia nervosa—you can see her bones—is bad. It is very unhealthy. I make sure that my daughter eats well and that she eats a variety of foods and will know how to cook a variety of foods when she moves into her own apartment. But, as you may expect, she would like to be thinner! I don't have any confidence in my own body, because of my back pain. If the pain got better, I would be more confident."

To Akiko, an ideal body is active, strong, and eminently useful. The "skin-and-bones" body popular with many young people is unattractive to her because it looks unhealthy, weak, and useless. Akiko hopes that her daughter won't wait too long to have children, because she fears that she herself "will be all bent over and too old to help her [daughter] care for them." A dutiful wife and mother, Akiko has a middle-aged body inseparable from its uses, duties, and caregiving responsibilities. Lock (1993b) has examined the increasing medicalization of life-cycle changes, particularly the onset of menopause. She asserts that unlike in the United States, where the focus of medicalization for middle-aged women is "the projected cost of their illness and deaths," in Japan, the focus is on the potential cost of losing middle-aged women as caretakers: "Middle-aged women are expected above all to look after their bodies for the sake of the family, since physical labor is required of them as caretakers" (57). For older women, to diet in the pursuit of beauty is construed as selfish.

"You can't have a baby if you're too thin"

Just as the middle-aged female body is synonymous with caregiving, the young female body has a single function: that of childbearing. For young women, a healthy body is defined as a fertile body. This construction is also reminiscent of the rhetoric of prewar Japan, when "ordinary Japanese women were being encouraged to use their reproductive capabilities in the service of the state, and powerful corporations with the support of the state were looking for healthy, beautiful, unmarried, ordinary young women to serve as exemplars of the eugenically and racially ideal New Woman of the New Japan" (Robertson 1997:9).

The official policy at the clubs implies that pregnancy is a sacred but fragile condition that can be jeopardized by ignorant members and irresponsible instructors. Young or pregnant women are advised by concerned older members and the club staff to avoid severe dieting and excessive exercise. A 65-year-old female member criticized young women for dieting too much: "The ideal for women in Japan is very thin, and all the young women have become just too thin. They stop menstruating and can't have babies. It's so different than it was in the old days, when women had no trouble having babies. Now many women have a lot of trouble getting pregnant." As this member suggests, women who place themselves on restricted diets that are low in calories or necessary nutrients are regarded as selfish for placing a potential child's health at risk or for endangering their future prospects as mothers.

In a country where productivity is paramount, an unproductive body is deemed "unfit." Whether it is the mother who shirks her caregiving role, the individual confined to a wheelchair, or the person who has made the unorthodox decision not to marry and reproduce, there is little tolerance in Japan for those who do not contribute to the hegemonic demands of production and reproduction. The idealized female body, young or old, serves distinct political, social, and economic functions that benefit the state. A young body produces the able-bodied laborers and caregivers that support the economy; an older body shoulders the caregiving responsibilities that enable the state to avoid funding public facilities. The female body becomes public domain, where issues of health, fertility, and beauty become metaphors for the economic and social welfare of the state (Douglas 1966; Foucault 1979). Women who shirk their responsibilities, either as childbearers or caregivers, are constructed as selfish, unhealthy, and even unpatriotic.

"How will you cook for your husband and children?"

The control over diet becomes a way to exert control over the sexual division of labor and familial responsibilities. Labor, productive or reproductive, requires a certain physical strength that may be at odds with contemporary standards of beauty. If Akiko chose to diet, she would be privileging her looks or her desires over the needs of her children or parents. In the same way, overenthusiastic dieting by her daughter can be constructed not only as resistance to the construction of young women as future mothers but also as resistance to a mother's doting care. Akiko emphasizes her efforts to "make sure [her] daughter eats well and that she eats a variety of foods," for she clearly would feel to blame for her daughter's thin appearance: her daughter's health is a reflection on her success as a parent.

Although I was unable to interview her daughter, I can imagine that Akiko has not allowed her displeasure with her daughter's desire to be thinner to go unsaid, and therefore her daughter undoubtedly could use food refusal to her advantage. A young woman who rejects her mother's cooking is asserting her independence from both the family

unit and cultural expectations that she will assume a caregiving role.]
The manipulation of appetite by young Japanese women as a means
to assert control over their social circumstance bears a striking resemblance to the Chinese student demonstrators in Tiananmen Square, who
used mass hunger strikes as a way to reject the authority and "paternal"
care of both the Confucian family and the state: "Refusing food was an
act of rebellion against the family because in the Confucian scheme of
things, to damage the body inherited from one's parents was unfilial"
(Brownell 1995:260).

Similarly, Bynum illustrates how women in medieval Europe fasted
as a way not only to reject the authority of the late medieval church,
"an institution that made a tidy, moderate, decent, second-rate place
for women and for the laity" (1987:243), but also the authority of the
family. "Food-related behavior was central to women socially and religiously not only because food was a resource women controlled but because by means of food women controlled themselves and their world.
Bodily functions, sensations, fertility, sexuality; husbands, mothers,
fathers, and children; religious superiors and confessors; God in his
majesty and the boundaries of one's own 'self'—all could be manipulated by abstaining from and bestowing food" (194).

Brumberg observes a similar manipulation of appetite in Victorian
England, where insatiable hunger in young women was linked to lax
sexual mores: "It was incumbent upon the mother to train the appetite
of the daughter so that it represented only the highest moral and aesthetic sensibilities" (1997:166). Explicitly linked to the Cartesian mind-body dualism and its ties to Judeo-Christian tradition, constructions of
the body in the West are equated with sin, and, by extension, women
are linked with sinful sexuality. Therefore, as Bynum and Brumberg
illustrate, the rejection of corporality through fasting or appetite control becomes a way for a young woman to purify herself and elevate
her spirituality. As Judeo-Christian practices do not hold much sway
in contemporary Japanese ideology and because the divisions between
mind and body are not as consistently or historically dualistic, what are
we to make of the Japanese pursuit of thinness and how does dieting
and food refusal help us understand the relationship between the mind
and body in Japan?

Akiko's attempts to teach her daughter how to cook reflect the perpetuation of the ideological assumption that young women will inevitably assume the domestic responsibilities of the family. Many of the older women I met expressed concern over my inability to cook Japanese food and the fact that my mother was so far away and could not cook for me. "How will you cook for your husband and children?" they wondered aloud. Clearly distressed that I was 26 and yet unmarried, one woman offered to give me weekly cooking lessons in her home; it was during these three- to four-hour lessons that I was able to observe the importance of food and food preparation in Japanese women's lives.

My friend would spend hours preparing well-balanced meals for her family, only to have her husband show up late, her children demand that she pack their dinner "to go," and her rather inept American guest be unable to correctly reproduce the lessons the next week. Her frustration at the daily cooking and cleanup was evident as she sighed and said, "All this work and it goes unappreciated. Life as a housewife is harsh [*hidoi*]." It is no surprise that a young woman observing the frustrations of her mother might reject not only her mother's cooking but also any attempts to learn domestic skills, be it cooking, cleaning, or laundry, as a way to postpone this phase of her life for as long as possible. Many of my 20-something Japanese friends readily admitted to never having learned to cook, as their mother always prepared all of their meals. When I asked one club member what she would do when she finally moved to a home of her own, she responded wryly, "Well, I suppose I'll have to learn. Maybe my mother will bring meals over to me!"

Diets taken to the extreme result in the disappearance of all physical manifestations of maturity and adult sexuality. Cessation of menstruation and the gradual slimming down of womanly breasts and hips that are the inevitable consequences of radical dieting produce an approximation of the prepubescent form. Women afflicted with anorexia nervosa voice a fear of growing up, a disdain for their womanly bodies, and a desire to return to childhood. In the end, the "childlike" body of the dieter projects an image of immaturity, self-indulgence, and frailty. Like the anorexic who fasts as a way to reject all evidence of sexual maturity, skipping meals and spending one's own money on diet aids becomes a way to postpone adult responsibility.

Bynum (1987) has examined how women in medieval England used fasting as a way to refuse marriage proposals or cooking responsibilities. In Japan, this recent emphasis on thinness, indeed bone-thin skinniness, may indicate a larger rejection or postponement of patriarchal gender roles. Symptomatic of the national "never want to get married" trend among Japanese women, cooking and, by extension, eating home-cooked meals is tied to domestic drudgery. Like the moga of the Taisho era who used short hair and Western clothing as means to express independence and sexual freedom, contemporary women use dieting as a way to control their circumstances, to convey self-sufficiency, and to reject domestic and reproductive responsibilities. Food, prepared and controlled by women, becomes an apt medium by which to express displeasure with familial and societal standards of femininity.

It has been observed in multiple cross-cultural and historical contexts that the preparation of food by women is intrinsically linked to the feminine ideal, with an emphasis on other-orientation and selflessness. Bordo explores the cultural role of the mother in the United States, which revolves around the feeding and nourishing of others rather than the self (1993:118). Preparing food is viewed as an expression of love; self-indulgence is inappropriate and even shameful. DeVault has observed the difficulty of disentangling "care" and "work" in her research on distribution of household work in the United States: "Since feeding work is associated so strongly with women's love and caring for their families, it is quite difficult for women to resist doing all of the work" (1997:191). Similarly, Hughes asserts that the African American woman's, and particularly the African American mother's, "expressions of love, nurturance, creativity, sharing, patience, economic frustration, survival, and the very core of her African heritage are embodied in her meal preparation" (1997:272).

Most Japanese women go out of their way to serve others first, saving the most prized pieces for favored guests, friends, husband, and children. My cooking "instructor" always reserved the smallest and most aesthetically unappealing pieces for herself, sometimes neglecting even to serve herself a portion if she did not prepare enough or if one of her sons wanted more than his share. One woman struggling to lose weight at the club remarked wryly, "I had a leftover curry donut for breakfast. I don't really like them, but nobody ate it and I didn't want to waste it, so I ate it. The housewife has to eat all of the leftovers that nobody wants, so we get fat! We wind up having to pay money to lose the weight. It would be better to just waste money in the beginning and just throw the food away." I have seen young women remove food from their own plate, piling it onto the already loaded plate of a friend or boyfriend.

Admitting to dieting in public is embarrassing, as it seems vain and self-indulgent, but couching it in an expression of concern for others is a way to appear generous and selfless.

The symbol of the doting female is best illustrated in the memorable, albeit disturbing, scene in the Japanese movie *Tampopo*, where an emaciated and sickly woman, literally dying from exhaustion, rises from her death bed to prepare one last meal for her family before finally collapsing once the dinner has been served. Allison (1991) describes the time, attention, and creativity that Japanese mothers devote to the daily preparation of the obentou for their preschool children; these carefully prepared lunchboxes are then evaluated as symbols of a mother's dedication to the well-being of her children. In a tragic news story, a 15-year-old girl from northern Japan died of complications from anorexia "after wearing herself out while taking care of her disabled father and grandmother" ("Fifteen-Year-Old Dies" 1994) The head of the local children's counseling office expressed regret that things had progressed so far, concluding that "[her] disease was intricately linked to the family environment." It is significant to note that this "family environment," far from unique, mirrors that of countless other women in Japan. The act of giving away food, a resource readily available and associated with women, is illustrative of a complicity with normative standards of femininity as well as an undeniable form of social power. To deny one's appetite is a way to publicly announce one's roles as caregiver, mother, and doting wife or girlfriend.

Bodybuilding: A Selfish Indulgence

Although femininity is synonymous with selflessness in Japan, selflessness as a virtue is not gender-bound. Just as a woman who focuses exclusively on her own appearance through the strict monitoring of calories is perceived as indulgent, so is a man who spends an inordinate amount of time transforming his body through weight training. In fact, most Japanese men (and women) shy away from bodybuilding and bulk-building weight training exercise.[7] One club member explained, "Everything is better in moderation. It is one thing to lift weights, but quite another to bodybuild." Although the muscular frame has been idealized as the symbol of virility and masculinity in the United States, bodybuilding in both the United States and Japan has been characterized as an activity enjoyed by homosexuals, an unfortunate stigma that can serve as a strong deterrent for many.[8] Klein explains: "For all this heterosexual posturing, bodybuilding has long existed under a cloud of suspicion. Be it the inordinate vanity on the part of men (a quasi violation of blue-collar mores), the preoccupation with scantily clad, hairless-bodied men prancing about on stage, or an awareness that for all that size (form) there is little function behind bodybuilding, many outsiders see bodybuilders as sexually suspect. The view of vanity, male quasi nudity, and nontraditional activities, usually carried out with other men, may all be legitimate in bodybuilding subculture, but until recently, mainstream society tended to associate this with its clichéd sense of homosexuality" (1993:155).

In Japan, this stigma of homosexuality has another dimension beyond suspicions of sexuality: that of questionable productivity. As Edwards explains in his account of Japanese weddings, the heterosexual marriage is viewed as a requirement to enter adulthood, in which the man and woman in their "complementary incompetence" can become fully productive members of society (1989:120–127). Company promotions hinge on marriage as a demonstration that the employee is a responsible and fully functioning adult. A man who never marries is perceived as socially immature and unproductive. Homosexuality per se is not prohibited, provided that it is practiced discreetly and adulterously within the confines of a heterosexual marriage. Nevertheless, blatant demonstrations of homosexual practices and lifestyles are actively discouraged.

The Japanese bodybuilder, because of an exaggerated attention to appearance and physique, is generally considered odd. One Downtown Fitness instructor, who competed in amateur bodybuilding contests in Japan[9] and considered moving to the United States to compete professionally, confessed that the general public tends to view him as a misfit and even grotesque: "People always stare at me on the train and ask me if I'm American. If I worked at [Chiba Club] people would view me strangely, because very few Japanese men do bodybuilding. But here at [Downtown Fitness], because there are a lot of Americans here who understand bodybuilding, I don't stick out as much. They call me the 'Japanese Big-Boy.' You can tell a bodybuilder from people who just work out to look good. People who just want to look good don't bulk up their legs, because that wouldn't look good in the narrow pants that the models wear." Bodybuilders, like Sumo wrestlers, represent an exaggerated extreme far outside the desired and accepted body type. But unlike Sumo wrestlers, whose huge, fleshy frames distinguish them as some of the most popular and well-respected athletes in Japan, the bulky frame of bodybuilders is neither admired nor favored.[10]

The bulky muscles and finely honed physiques that represent the product of hard work, diligence, and motivation to the bodybuilders themselves brand the athletes as self-indulgent, narcissistic, and vain by society at large. Klein (1993) examines the qualities of narcissism, homophobia, and hypermasculinity that define and bind American bodybuilders as individuals and as a subculture. To be successful at bodybuilding, a minimum of two to three hours of serious weight training must be logged at the gym daily, not to mention seasonal attention to carbohydrate versus protein loading and year-round monitoring of fat intake. In a society where, as one bodybuilder explained, "unhealthy sarariiman fall asleep standing up on trains after getting drunk with coworkers," the bodybuilder is an anomaly. Devoting oneself to the timely and difficult task of perfecting and building muscle definition is seen not only as mindless, but as selfish, wasteful, and unproductive.

Just as aerobics teachers are denigrated by a society that privileges labor of the mind over labor of the body, bodybuilders are similarly ostracized—perhaps more so, because bodybuilders work alone. Unlike aerobics instructors who are employed by fitness clubs to lead classes, and unlike other athletes who may train alone but ultimately compete professionally, bodybuilding is an individual and amateur sport in Japan. Attracting few spectators and generating no national revenue or prestige, bodybuilding, when considered at all, is viewed as a sport for self-centered, less intelligent individuals who contribute nothing to society and receive little in return. But to the bodybuilders, it is the salariiman who should be pitied: "Humans are animals and they need to exercise. Modern people in Japan have no energy, they get money with their brains, but are not really happy. By using their body, they become more truly happy. Of course, they should study hard, but it is more important to be aware of health. Some people are skilled in studies and some in working the body. Salariiman are all sleepy because of all the desk work they do. It is sad, don't you think?"

Conclusions

The bodybuilder, the dieting adolescent, the domestically inclined housewife, and the "helpful" instructor who points out weight gain in her clients all illustrate the ideological emphasis on the fluid boundaries between self and other in Japan. The individual is part of a network of social obligations and familial responsibilities, which are projected onto the physical body. Body size is symbolic of social ties. To be painfully skinny or overly muscular is indicative of antisocial tendencies, a rejection not only of present familial and societal obligations but also of future roles and expectations. A young girl who diets is not simply conforming to fashion trends, but is asserting her independence from normative models of femininity, which are crafted as selfless and other-oriented. By eating out or not eating at all, the young woman has removed her body (and her self) from the care and influence of her family, thereby rejecting dependence on her father's earnings or her mother's cooking. Simultaneously, because extreme dieting affects menstruation, it becomes a very real way to postpone adult responsibilities. In these examples, it becomes increasingly difficult to perceive the relationship between mind and body in Japan as consistently fluid, harmonious, and interrelated.

Food refusal, on the other hand, can be interpreted as a confirmation of fluidity between self and other and mind and body in the Japanese context. A young woman who prepares food for her friends but does not partake or who heaps food onto the plates of others conforms to social expectations of the selfless female. She may derive pleasure and admiration from others and even power from her perceived generosity and conformity to the feminine ideal, because her self and her body are intrinsically linked to a social network. In this way, the mind and body are intertwined, as the self and the social network are intimately linked. The dualistic relationship that characterizes the West and that seems to play out in the dieting examples discussed above is inapplicable here. The varied cultural explanations for dieting and food refusal among young women in Japan represent the most recent manifestation of a long-standing negotiation over women's roles, femininity, and the construction of the mind and body in Japanese versus Western philosophy.

Conclusions

As the economic recession erodes the free time and resources of the ever dwindling pool of potential fitness club clientele, club managers struggle to attract and maintain members. Looking to the West, management continues to import and alter new trends in "American" fitness, but, given the mixed reception of American fitness in Japan, what does the future of the sport hold? Interestingly, the waves in fitness, at times, seem to be at odds with the larger economic cycles of business in Japan. Although the aerobics boom in the early and mid-1980s coincided with the unprecedented success of the Japanese economy, the securities and real estate collapse beginning in 1990 does not seem to have substantially affected the marketing and purchasing patterns of fitness club management. Even though recent years have ushered in dramatic corporate downsizing across Japan, fitness clubs continue to operate as if the prosperous 1980s had not faltered, continually upgrading equipment and introducing new programs. One of the newest fitness programs, introduced to Japan in 1996, is Spinning; it debuted in both of the clubs where I conducted research.

The introduction and ultimate failure of Spinning-style aerobics to the Japanese fitness scene presents an interesting case where globalization, invention, and reinvention intersect on the fitness club floor. Sleek and high-tech, Spinning bikes are unlike the sturdy, upright stationary bicycles that are ubiquitous in fitness clubs in Japan and the United States. Rather, they more closely resemble racing cycles, albeit stationary ones. The pedals and front wheel spin at extremely high speeds, hence the name. Complete with toe clips, adjustable handlebars, and tiny racing seats, Spinning bikes are designed to simulate outdoor speed cycling. Using specially selected mood music and visualization techniques, the American creators of Spinning aim to produce a full mind-body experience. Relying on the power of suggestion and the imagination, the instructor helps the class to visualize a grueling trek up Mount Fuji or a race along the beaches of Hawai'i by describing the smell of sea brine and the feel of the wind whipping back your hair. The challenge of jumping sand dunes and the ease of coasting down a mountainous terrain are simulated by standing or sitting on the bike or allowing the pedals to spin around with no added resistance.

As noted, the history of aerobics foreshadowed and set the precedent for the exaggeration and exploitation of the foreignness or, more precisely, the Americanness of Spinning. It should come as no surprise, then, that every advertisement for Spinning harkened back to its American origin, while instructor training workshops featured blond and blue-eyed instructors. One poster for Spinning at Chiba Club announced in Japanese: "The Hottest Program in the U.S.A," and written below in English, "New Trend in Fitness, Welcome to Spinning." Another read: "Arriving from L.A." (Figure 23). Chiba Club managers immediately assigned me to assist in the Spinning classes, crowing over the fact that they had an American assistant for an American class. Had I stayed longer in Japan, I am certain that I would have been appointed the primary instructor of Spinning at this suburban club. As it was, the management bemoaned the fact that I was not properly trained to teach the class on my own. Despite its budding popularity in the United States, I hadn't heard of Spinning prior to my stay in Japan. The manager was aghast at my ignorance: "Are you sure you are from America?" he asked half-jokingly, eyeing me incredulously.

The buildup preceding the introduction of Spinning was tremendous. Chiba Club sponsored numerous demonstrations and events to rev up interest in this new form of exercise. The first demonstration attracted a large crowd of onlookers. Before the demonstration, the instructor told us to act very enthusiastic and to count very loudly. Many of us had never tried Spinning before and grimaced with fatigue and discomfort as the instructor pushed us to show off for the audience. After the class, many of the instructors unthinkingly complained to the members about how grueling the exercise was and how uncomfortable the seats were. Although the members cooed sympathetically, they had also begun to develop negative impressions about Spinning.

Gradually the class size dwindled, and before we knew it, we had trouble reaching the three-person minimum required to hold the class.

23. The Americanness or California style of Spinning is used as a selling point to attract members, as seen in this poster announcing "Arriving from L.A."

The local and central club management were bewildered and angered by the low turnout and took aggressive measures to stir up interest. In the minutes before the class, the weight room staff was ordered to recruit (*kanshi suru*) participants. This recruitment boiled down to actively badgering members who were already involved in other activities such as basketball, weightlifting, or running on the treadmill. We were instructed to try to convince them to abandon their present activity to try a Spinning class. Most members simply refused, complaining that they had heard or had personal experience that Spinning was too difficult, too tiring, or too boring.

On the one hand, Spinning should have been a tremendous success, given the seeming ability to finesse the assured appeal of any American program with imagined Japanese ideological notions of mind and body fusion, using music, imagery, and even energy crystals (every instructor wears an energy crystal suspended by a leather strap around his or her neck) to create unity between body and spirit. But, as I have illustrated, although the Cartesian mind-body split characterizes conceptions of exercise in the West, mind-body fusion does not similarly influence Japanese understandings of fitness. In fact, the notion of an ideological marriage between mind and body serves as a red herring that detracts attention from other, more subtle constitutions of bodies and beauty in Japan.

At the same time, Spinning represented the importation of a Westernized stereotype of "Eastern" philosophy, reinterpreted in a Japanese context. And this reinterpretation failed miserably. Although the emphasis on mind-body unity has proven successful in the Japanese classes of yoga, Taichi, and visual relaxation, it is the relaxation offered by these classes rather than the mind-body fusion that is the source of their popularity. As one staff member explained, "The Japanese don't understand the mind-body link that is involved with Spinning. Perhaps in classes like VR [visual relaxation], it is the relaxation that is important, not the idea of being able to imagine but more the action of relaxation." Far from relaxing, the strenuous intensity of Spinning burns up to 600 calories per hour.

The simple choreography and hyperintense cardio workout that have made Spinning so popular in the United States are the same reasons Spinning has failed to catch on to the same degree in Japan. Even among the younger, more image-minded crowd at Downtown Fitness, the challenge of a workout lies in mastering fancy moves rather than in boosting stamina. The manager of Chiba Club explained this general aversion to intense aerobics at the local club: "I'm sure you have noticed that our aerobics schedule consists primarily of beginner classes. We try to encourage people to advance out of the beginning level, but they never do. We've tried taking a popular Friday night beginner class and replacing it with a more advanced Jog class or Body Shaping class, but everyone just quits and doesn't come. So now, we make a big point of saying that the Friday night class has been switched back to a beginner class. Even the pool, which is the most popular part of our club, is full of people who use it for walking rather than swimming, for rehabilitation."

This resistance to the hard work of working out in the fitness club is striking, but is it uniquely Japanese? That is, is this inconsistency any more unusual than the startling percentages of obesity coupled with a national fixation on diet and health that characterize the contemporary United States? One of the greatest contributions of anthropological analysis is the ability, as Ruth Benedict (1946) aptly puts it, to make the strange familiar and the familiar strange. Although I have not aimed to develop an extended cross-cultural comparison, it becomes inevitable that the inconsistencies that characterize the Japanese fitness club will be interpreted in light of the American case. It could be argued, for example, that Japanese women who confess diet secrets over a cake set are no different from Americans who virtuously order Diet Cokes with their hamburgers and hot fudge sundaes.

I do not mean to imply that American conceptions of health, beauty, and diet are free from contradictions; in fact, I began my research with the assumption that for both Japanese and North American readers, these inconsistencies are so apparent that pointing them out seemed redundant. The more interesting question became how bodies are constituted in the Japanese context despite or, more significant, because of these cross-cultural and local inconsistencies. What do grounded, everyday examples, such as the popularity of a sexy leotard, the disdain for muscles, or the failed introduction of Spinning, tell us about gender, beauty, the body, and the co-constitutive relationships between Japan and the West and the links between fitness and the larger socioeconomic context within Japan?

Purchasing twenty-five Spinning bikes at 30,000 yen ($250) apiece, for example, is not an effective way to cut costs in the fitness club. Requiring members to purchase yet another style of pricey spandex shorts, this time with a padded seat, may just serve as the proverbial straw that broke the camel's back. When the largest national banks and brokerage firms are closing their doors and declaring bankruptcy, the Japanese economy is on shaky ground. If the fitness clubs and aerobics programs continue to prioritize novelty, staying on the cutting edge of the fitness world, they will hasten their own failure, as more and more members simply will be unable to afford the sport and will be forced to drop out.

The clubs thus far have been able to maintain a steady membership by distinguishing themselves as simultaneously similar to other disciplinary institutions in Japan and decidedly unique spaces. On the one hand, the fitness boom has capitalized on the demands for entertainment, leisure, and conspicuous consumption that characterize the last part of the century. The layout of the fitness club structures and reflects widely held assumptions about luxury, hygiene, health, privilege, privacy, and gender. Employees and members are subjected to timetables, uniforms, and systematized choreography—the very same tactics of discipline that characterize other spaces of spiritual training in

Japan. This heavy-handed training of fitness club members and instructors and the constellation of meanings attached to aerobic exercise in Japan suggest that in the consumer-driven, patriarchal culture of late capitalism, the discipline of the body reflects and prescribes overlapping notions of beauty, gender, power, health, and sexuality.

Following a brief initial period when aerobics was originally imported to suit corporate desires for training an efficient and healthy workforce, sensationalism and sexiness, the hallmarks of objectified femininity, quickly began to characterize the aerobics boom in Japan. Female aerobics instructors, who cater daily to male managers and wealthy older clients, craft themselves in socially expected feminine roles as mothers, daughters, and sexual objects. Prescriptions of female beauty that revolve around thinness, youth, and good proportions are embodied in the trim, leotard-clad aerobics instructors and are implicitly or explicitly applied on the club floor. For some young women, refusing to eat becomes a way to realize this unrealistic beauty ideal and to comply with societal expectations that women should be selfless and other-oriented. The fitness club, from this perspective, seems no different from countless other institutions in Japan that categorize and control people according to strict hierarchies based on gender, age, and educational level.

On the other hand, the fitness club presents a strikingly unique space where cultural expectations are inverted. Unlike the Zen monastery, the corporate hardship courses, or the cram school, where discipline of the mind produces discipline of the spirit, fitness club instructors and managers insist on thinness, synchronicity, and self-reflection for the sake of the workout and fail to connect success at the club with success in the office or in the home. In the club, the links between exercise and spiritual fortitude, exercise and productivity, and exercise and mental relaxation are weakly defined, inconsistent, and underemphasized. Because the clubs strive to be "Western" and neglect to incorporate certain elements of Japanese philosophy that at least ideologically forge ties between mind and body, the demands in the club for effort and exertion do not resonate. The club advocates neither a Cartesian-derived separation of mind and body that characterizes the West nor Japanese conceptions of a mind-body synthesis.

Although disciplinary tactics superficially echo those found in other institutions both in Japan and the United States, members are encouraged to "work at their own pace" and to enjoy themselves. Official rhetoric at the fitness club emphasizes muscular and healthy bodies, a perspective that stands in direct opposition to societal and media calls for bone-thin skinniness at any cost. The female service employees, while compliant on-stage, co-opt traditionally masculine behavior after-hours as a way to challenge gender and age-based biases in the workplace. Even the sexy leotard, while on the one hand trivializes women's exercise, simultaneously liberates the body and sexuality of its wearer. It follows then that many young female club members and instructors employ dieting as a way to reclaim their body and to define themselves as individuals, distinct from social networks and responsibilities. In these ways, the fitness club should be viewed as an unusual institutional space where cultural norms are challenged.

In this ethnographically grounded analysis of American-inspired fitness clubs in a Japanese context, I have illustrated the ways ideological debates over national identity, hygiene and health, discipline, power within the corporate hierarchy, definitions of leisure, work, and home, and idealized gender roles are enacted and experienced through the female body.

Notes

Introduction

All translations are my own unless otherwise noted.

1 Aesthetic salons provide a variety of oil and cream treatments, low-grade electric shock massages, and chiropractic manipulations in the pursuit of beauty. Located in department stores, by train and subway stations, and even in fitness clubs, the salons cater to an almost exclusively female clientele.

2 There have been several statistical studies conducted on leisure and sports in contemporary Japan. The two most well-known are the *Leisure White Papers* and the *Marketing Data of Leisure Industry and Daily Life*. *Leisure White Pages* is published annually by the Leisure Development Center; I draw on statistics from the 1996 and 1997 volumes, the period in which I was conducting fieldwork. The *Marketing Data of Leisure Industry and Daily Life* is compiled by the Ministry of Economy, Trade and Industry and is published only every three years. To correspond to the period in which I conducted research in Japan, I have relied on the volume published in 1994. The statistics from this volume are very comprehensive and detailed, but one must bear in mind that the data are several years old. I use these statistics only for background on the larger demographics of leisure and fitness in Japan and hope that the ethnographic portion of this book will more than supplement the older statistics.

3 For the more current data on Japan, I have contacted Ms. Tomoko Iwai at Club Management Network (CMN) in Japan, which publishes the only magazine specializing in health management in Japan and supplies statistics to the *Leisure White Papers*. The Fitness Industry Association of Japan (FIA Japan), which is made up of about nine hundred different clubs, focuses its research on a different subject each year. The International Health, Racquet and Sportsclub Association (IHRSA) compiles annual statistics on the state of the fitness industry in Japan. A portion of these statistics is

available to the public on their Web-page, but for more detailed data "Profiles for Success" is published annually for purchase.

4   During the year 1996–1997, the exchange rate was approximately 120 yen to the U.S. dollar. I use this conversion rate to calculate approximate dollar amounts throughout the book.

5   According to the Leisure Development Center, a group affiliated with the Ministry of International Trade and Industry, the number of Japanese participating in aerobics, jazz dance, and other fitness activities tumbled from a peak of 5.3 million in 1989 to 4 million in 1995 ("Only the Fittest" 1996:17). Numbers currently stand at around 3 million participants.

6   The names of clubs, members, and staff have been changed to protect the privacy of those involved.

7   Written in *katakana, office lady* or OL is the Japanese term for secretary or lower-level office assistant; *sarariiman* refers to the typical white-collar businessman employed by a large company.

8   Ninety-five percent of the members at Downtown Fitness are in their twenties and 60 percent are women.

9   The word *silver* in Japanese refers to the elderly population.

10 During an earlier stay in Iwate Prefecture in 1992–1993, I taught a weekly aerobics class in a community center. In general, community centers, which are popular in the more rural locations across Japan, do not have aerobics studios, and thus many of the classes must be held in sprawling gymnasiums with terrible acoustics. People in the back row have trouble hearing the verbal cues of the instructor, let alone the tinny music coming from the portable cassette player. The participants were generally housewives in their late twenties and thirties, most of whom brought along their toddlers, who played on the fringes of the class. The mothers were constantly stopping in the middle of the routine to tend to a crying or bored child underfoot. One woman explained, "I used to go to [one of the big fitness club chains] before I was married, but since having my child it is hard to go as often. [The fitness club] branch near me doesn't have a baby-sitting service, so I could only go when my husband was here to watch my son. That's not very often [laughs]! So that's why this class [at the community center] is so good." Even though baby-sitting is quite uncommon in Japan, most Japanese fitness clubs do not provide nurseries. But here at the community center's informal class, all of the women participated in child care, tending to the children closest to them. The atmosphere was relaxed, friendly, and communal, quite unlike the sterile, rushed feel of the downtown clubs.

11 Clark (1992) observes a similar correlation between time of day and type of clientele in the public bathhouses of Japan.

12 Aerobics and Fitness Association of America (AFAA) is the most well-regarded aerobics instruction certification and training program in the United States. It opened a branch in Japan, called AFAA Japan, in 1988.

13 Of course, as Klein notes, full explanations may be elusive in any field setting: "To assume that people are telling the truth is naïve, since it assumes that toying with the fieldworker out of playfulness or boredom, or misleading him to keep him away from potentially damaging information, is not in the 'native's' mind" (1993:29).

14 Brannen explores the treatment and role of the *gaijin*, or foreign employee, at Tokyo Disneyland (1992:230).

15 Monastic aestheticism characterizes not only Japan, as the movement advocated by mid-nineteenth-century British proponents for "muscular Christianity" indicates. Muscular Christianity refers to the efforts made by Charles Kingsley and other Englishmen to disrupt associations between spiritual purity and bodily spareness that had characterized the Christian legacy of Cartesian dualism. By advocating a muscular, healthy, and robust body as evidence of spiritual devoutness, muscular Christianity recast prior sanctions on physical activity in a religious light.

16 Certain corporations have formed alliances with larger fitness club chains and have purchased corporate memberships for their employees. But for the most part, these alliances are seldom forged and little used.

17 To satisfy the Japanese desire for relaxation, the "health center," a cross between a fitness club and a *sentou,* the traditional public bath, has emerged as a popular new trend in the past few years. Offering a variety of hot, cold, and medicated baths, plus exercise equipment, massage chairs, and workout rooms, these facilities have been so successful that, according to Clark (1992), they have revived the declining public bath industry. Clark asserts that when the number of health centers is "combined with remaining *sentou* the number of public bathing facilities is greater than ever before" (96). Fitness club managers do not seem too concerned about this emerging industry and maintain that the distinguishing feature of the club is its emphasis on fitness.

18 It is important to note that this notion of "going for the burn" has been somewhat phased out in the United States as well. Characteristic of the joint-jarring, high-impact aerobics of the Jane Fonda era in the 1980s, when pain and exertion were encouraged and expected, the notion of "no pain, no gain" has become anachronistic. New trends of fitness in the United States, which include yoga, Tae-bo, and Pilates, stress low-impact and fluid movements.

1. The History of Aerobics in Japan: The Sexy American Import

1 The Japanese term *maniac* (written in katakana) refers to an exercise enthusiast.

2 Of course, fitness clubs in the United States also sell a variety of exercise

wear and nutritional supplements to increase revenue. Klein describes the array of products in his ethnographic study of professional bodybuilders in southern California: "The economic program of most elite gyms is deepened by the sale of a fairly diverse array of gym sporting goods, which are the mainstay of elite gyms. They typically include a range of T-shirts . . . sweat clothes, belts, and wraps of various sorts, and specialty items such as satin jackets, hats, bags, coffee mugs, and fashion items. . . . These items are adorned with the particular gym's logo" (1993:88). The Japanese fitness club, however, offers a much greater variety of products displayed in a larger area of space relative to the club, suggesting a greater attention to consumption.

3 In one of the more well-known examples, Demings received expert status in the 1970s for his introduction and implementation of the U.S. system of quality control. Designed to standardize and improve production, managing control and problem-solving responsibilities are distributed among self-regulating labor circles made up of the workers themselves. Although the concept of quality circles originated in the United States, the unequal distribution of power between laborers and management in the West precluded acceptance of an equal distribution of authority.

4 Similarly, both of these movies, in addition to *Perfect*, which stars John Travolta and Jamie Lee Curtis in a sensational and sexy fitness club scene in Los Angeles during the 1980s, and the music video *Let's Get Physical* by Olivia Newton John, were responsible in part for igniting a fitness boom in the United States around the same time.

2. The Discipline of Space

1 Foucault's discussion of the discipline of time is also relevant to the fitness club, but is discussed in the next chapter, on the discipline of the body.

2 The panopticon is a "tower pierced with wide windows that open onto the inner side of the ring; the peripheric building is divided into cells, each of which extends the whole width of the building; they have two windows, one on the inside, corresponding to the windows of the tower; the other, on the outside, allows the light to cross the cell from one end to the other. . . . By the effect of backlighting, one can observe from the tower, standing out precisely against the light, the small captive shadow in the cells of the periphery" (Foucault 1979:200).

3 Eskes, Duncan, and Miller (1998) have likened the self-monitoring characteristic of the panopticon to women's fitness efforts in the contemporary United States. They argue that many women partake in beauty practices because they feel examined and judged by their appearance.

4   Trains and train stations are prime advertising spots in Japan, frequented by tens of thousands of commuters who stream through the stations daily (see Ivy 1988). Many clubs place flyers in popular newspapers or offer free tissues on street corners with the chosen image emblazoned on the packaging. The particularly successful chains can afford to run promotional videos on the large-screen monitors that sit atop the high-rise buildings in front of the bustling Shibuya subway station. Fitness club advertisements, however, are noticeably absent from fashion magazines and popular women's magazines.

5   SMAP is the name of an all-male music group, popular in the mid- to late 1990s. The band members are young and good-looking and have quite a following among teenage girls.

6   Sato (1991) draws on the metaphor of the theater to explain the performance aspect of motorcycle gangs in Japan.

7   Downtown Fitness in Roppongi was the most flirtatious of all of the clubs I visited, and I attribute this phenomenon to the high percentage of foreign members at this branch.

8   The reluctance to bulk up is true to some degree for men as well. Men who concentrate on their body too much, such as bodybuilders or even heavily muscular noncompetitors, are regarded as vain and self-indulgent. The general population tends to consider a very bulky frame to be grotesque.

9   *Nomunikeshon* is a combination of the Japanese word *nomu,* which means to drink, and the English word "communication" and refers to the after-hours networking required to be successful in a corporate job.

10 Given the symbolic impurity of the lower body, many Japanese even launder clothing that is worn above the waist separately from that worn below the waist (Ohnuki-Tierney 1984:30).

11 Some of the clubs, such as Roppongi Downtown Fitness, do hire a two- to three-person cleaning staff, whose job is to keep the locker rooms, bathrooms, pool area, and aerobics studios tidy. Even at these clubs, however, the *arubaito* polish weight room equipment daily and clean the pool area on a monthly basis. But they are free from doing the most despised jobs of shower-stall scrubbing and toilet-bowl cleaning. The staff at Chiba Club envied the Downtown Fitness staff, who were hired for counseling and little else. The staff responsibilities at each club vary according to branch location and contribute to the reputation and hierarchical standing of the club. Downtown Fitness consistently comes out on top.

12 The Takarazuka Revue is an all-female theater troupe that performs large-scale musical revues, to the delight of their tremendous fan base. See Robertson (1998) for a detailed examination of the troupe.

13 Public talk about bodily functions and secretions is quite open and acceptable in Japan. New member questionnaires at the fitness clubs and *esute*

(aesthetic salon) inquired about daily bowel movements, and staff openly discussed constipation and diarrhea with members and with each other in the back room. Japanese comic books and cartoons even feature the heroes passing gas or defecating on an enemy as a form of offensive attack. Brannen describes an incident at Disneyland that supports this phenomenon: "When the trunk of a huge (strategically positioned) African elephant fails to spray the cruise boat's passengers with water, the Tokyo Disneyland ride operator explains that luckily for them the elephant's trunk is stopped up with *hanakuso* (snot). Humorous references to *kuso* (a vulgar generic suffix attached to the names of various bodily orifices from which mucus or excrement is expelled) are commonplace among children and adults in Japan, where people are much less inhibited about bodily functions than in the United States" (1992:226).

14 The English expression "blood, sweat, and tears" and the Chinese idiom "putting out blood and sweat" have no equivalent in Japanese. The closest expression that I could find to illustrate the symbolism of sweat and its relationship to hard work is the phrase *ase no kesshou* (the crystal of sweat), meaning the fruits of one's labor.

3. The Discipline of Bodies

1 See Whiting (1990) for a Nihonjinron depiction of Japanese baseball. Kelly (1998) resists national characterization through sport in his current work on baseball.

2 The training courses in Japan are markedly distinct from the U.S. certification programs. Comprehensive training programs that provide students with the practical training and anatomical theory to pass the national aerobic certification exams are the exception in the United States. Because graduation from an expensive and time-consuming training program does not guarantee national certification by AFAA or IDEA, which is required to be an instructor at almost all U.S. clubs, the majority of instructors-to-be in the United States choose to forgo the $500 training programs and apply directly to AFAA or IDEA for testing and certification. Because the national certification workshops consist of instruction over the course of an intensive two-day weekend, the bulk of the preparation for the exams must be completed by the individual in his or her home prior to attending the workshop. In both Japan and the United States, successful instruction requires self-motivation. Although the most diligent and successful instructors in both countries do attend training programs, workshops, and conferences to keep their knowledge up-to-date and their choreography innovative, others can squeak by with a minimum of credentials, training, and preparation.

3 AFAA opened its Japan branch in 1988 in a licensing agreement with Seibu/Saison to become the largest competitor of JAFA.

4 The process of making the kintaro candy is similar to that of slicing a sushi roll. That is, this small round candy is cut from one long cylinder, so that each round sweet has the same picture on the front and the back as others cut from the same roll.

5 Similarly, it is no coincidence that technicians in Japanese beauty salons wear white lab coats when administering massages or facials. These jackets, similar to the coats worn by doctors, are intended to attach prestige and credibility to what may otherwise be considered a suspect procedure. Goffman describes perfume clerks in the United States who wear white lab coats "to provide the client with an understanding that the delicate tasks performed by these persons will be performed in what has become a standardized, clinical, confidential manner" (1959:26).

6 It is important to note, however, that despite a desire for allegiance with the medical world, there are obvious gaps between the ambitions of the fitness clubs and their day-to-day programs and instruction. Staff explanations seem somewhat superficial, their analyses incomplete, and their technique inconsistent and sometimes dangerous. In some cases, the staff is simply untrained for the responsibilities they are required to undertake. For example, in the diet class at Chiba Club, despite its billing as a course designed for people interested in losing weight and learning how to eat and exercise properly, there was absolutely no diet instruction and the main instructor was an office worker rather than a qualified aerobics instructor.

7 The signs above the tanning beds in the Japanese fitness clubs make the claim: "Safer than the Sun . . . Our tanning machines cut out the dangerous UV-C rays and emit only UV-A and appropriate amount of UV-B." Scientific research has proven, however, that UV-B rays do burn the skin. This type of ray actually causes the most skin damage and is responsible for skin cancer. UV-A rays, although safer than the burning rays, cause significant damage if the skin is exposed for longer than ninety minutes.

8 During this classical period, the face, meticulously dissected from eyebrows to lips, was subjected to public scrutiny and judged accordingly, but a specific body size and shape, cloaked under voluminous robes, was not prescribed in the strict class-based beauty ideal. Nobles in particular expressed an aesthetic aversion to the unadorned nude body and wore multiple layers of clothing to conceal their nakedness. Members of the Heian court wore at least twelve layers of unlined solid-colored silk robes, and skill at matching colors identified noble breeding. Like pale skin, the voluminous silk kimonos and floor-length hair, both of which inhibited movement, distinguished the luxury-driven and largely sedentary lifestyle of the aristocracy. Both men and women celebrated the extravagance of style and projected their artistic aesthetics and social snobbery onto the makeup and

clothing they wore. Morris summarizes the nobles' devotion to beauty: "Despite the influence of Buddhism, Heian society was on the whole governed by style rather than by any moral principles, and good looks tended to take the place of virtue" (1964:207). The emphasis on white skin, luxurious hair, and opulent gowns favored by the Heian aristocracy had a profound influence on definitions of female beauty for that period and in the centuries that followed.

9   This instructor's entry is not typical in its length and great attention to detail. She allowed me to read over her shoulder as she wrote and thus, with an audience in mind, probably wrote with far more care than usual.

10 Nichter and Vuckovic coin the phrase "fat talk" to discuss the common lament among white, middle-class adolescent females of "I'm so fat." Fat talk discourse is used by these girls as a means to fit in with their peers, diffuse guilt about overeating, or fish for compliments (1994:109–131). I am using the phrase fat talk in a slightly broader way to refer not only to self-deprecating comments but also to criticism of others.

11 An exception to general social decorum in the United States that prohibits commenting on another's body size and appearance occurs in the world of professional bodybuilding. Klein describes how competitors comment on one another's physique, pinching stomachs for evidence of fat and admiring or criticizing one another's musculature in the mirror. The bodybuilders use criticism and compliments to psych out an opponent and to offer support to a friend (1993:77). Open discussion of the body is seldom tolerated in the United States outside this unique subculture.

12 On a prime-time television special aired in October 1996, entitled *Aitai* [I want to be reunited], men and women were reunited on air with past loves, for better or worse. After the reunion, a panel of popular celebrities commented on the success or failure of the renewed relationship, offering advice, counsel, or congratulations to the couples. In one instance, a 30-year-old woman wanted to remeet her high school sweetheart, who unfortunately had no desire to date again, let alone marry her as she had hoped. When the woman came back on the show after her rejection to speak with the panel of celebrities, she was subjected to pity and condescension, which centered on what they described as her "fat and unattractive" appearance. One female celebrity cautioned, "At age 30, it is natural to be worried about getting married. You should be worried, but I want to help you. The first thing I would do would be to put you on a diet program." The audience and other members of the panel laughed merrily, and the humiliated woman bowed and said thank you. The public critique of the woman's body on national television is not only accepted, but is a source of amusement for others. Criticism in the guise of well-meaning advice is all the more insidious and debilitating when the woman has no choice but to thank her advisor gracefully. Indeed, the woman's ability to distance her

emotions and accept criticism about the size and shape of her body suggests a certain mind-body detachment, which the ideological formulation of a Japanese mind-body union does not take into account.

4. Cigarettes and Aerobics: Frustrations with Gender Inequities in the Club

1   One prominent club chain recently promoted a woman to the position of branch manager at their smallest club. The management decided to try the unorthodox practice of employing a female in their least demanding facility. This branch is the only club that is not located in a downtown area and is consequently populated by older women, who, as one female staff member explained, "are very meek [otonashii] and complain very little." The promotion was quite surprising to many of the staff, including the newly promoted woman herself. According to some of the employees at the branch, the female manager is performing quite well but has encountered a bit of trouble from the male assistant manager. According to some instructors, he is unaccustomed to and uncomfortable working under a woman's direction.

2   The stereotype of the loyal and long-term employee who is rewarded with "lifetime employment" and tenure-based promotions characterizes the jobs of the remarkable few who are employed by large white-collar companies. In fact, the majority of workers in Japan are employed either at small to medium-size companies, at independent or family-run businesses, or as peripheral part-time (arubaito) staff. None of these workers enjoys the job security, benefits, and steady salary raises offered in the large firms.

3   With a curriculum most similar to departments of physical education in U.S. universities, Taiiku Daigaku offer courses in performing and teaching gymnastics, volleyball, tennis, judo, and even aerobics. The curriculum also includes courses on exercise physiology, nutrition, and sports medicine. Students choose among majors in gymnastics, health, sport, and the arts (jazz, tap, ballet, or traditional Japanese dance). Although some graduates are qualified to teach physical education or work as nutritionists or physical therapists, unlike vocational schools or even academic universities, the PE college education does not prepare students for a particular career. Consequently, these colleges are not well-regarded, and graduates tend to have difficulty getting jobs above entry level or outside of the industries of sports and dance.

4   This is true for the United States and other industrialized countries, as well. See Dudley (1994) and Douglas (1986).

5   Unlike Chiba Club, Downtown Fitness had no training course per se. Incoming staff simply spoke informally with other staff about club rules and

responsibilities and accompanied the more experienced staff as they counseled the members, until they got the hang of it. Gradually, the new employees assumed more and more responsibilities and duties until they were full-fledged staff members.

6 As a foreigner (and an unpaid one at that), I was given some slack and permitted to write the names phonetically.

7 Many of the foreign members in the Japanese clubs, although initially polite, became quite curt when a staff member interrupted them for the third time during a workout.

8 Ohnuki-Tierney notes, however, that unlike in the United States, "Paradoxical though it may sound, doctors in Japan assume total responsibility for their patients yet remain nonauthoritative by accommodating 'human factors'" (1984:208). Doctors rely on the extended network of the family and friends of the patient to help prepare meals, note changes in the patient's condition, and contribute to round-the-clock care and support of the patient (194–208).

5. Young, Proportionate, Leggy, and Thin: The Ideal Female Body

1 A decree by military leader Hideoyoshi in the middle of the sixteenth century confined prostitution and "red-light" entertainment to specific areas that came to be known as the mizu shobai, or floating world.

2 The Roppongi fitness club has neither the facilities nor the staff to contend with this high percentage of non–Japanese speakers. The local management is currently struggling to find a solution. Branch managers do not believe that this so-called problem will disappear, nor do they want it to, as a large percentage of their revenue comes from the foreign community. But upper management in the main office do not want to recognize the foreign members, opting instead to ignore the issue rather than to capitalize on it.

3 For bodybuilders in the United States, dissection and evaluation of body parts is quite excessive. Klein explains how professional bodybuilders in California isolate muscle groups or specific parts to be worked and pumped: "For bodybuilders the view of the body as distinct from the self, and the view of the body as partible (separated into distinct parts) works to enable the bodybuilder to establish a sense of self-mastery. Body parts are specialized, named, and acted upon, all in the name of fashioning a championship physique. Hence, arms, back, legs, and so forth are separated out and worked on individually. Days of the week are devoted to exercising one or another body part, even named after that part—e.g., 'Tuesday is leg day'" (1993:244).

4 The book also offers an abbreviated history of underwear in Japan and

contrasts the type of undergarments worn with a kimono to the brassieres, girdles, and slips worn under "Western" clothes. See also Ueno (1990) for a feminist critique of the marketing and consumption of underwear in Japan.

5 The Wonder Bra costs about 40 U.S. dollars in Japan, and many of the girdles are even more expensive.

6 Kaw (1994) explores the politics of cosmetic eye surgery among Asian American women who desire a more "Western" look.

7 *Seiza* is the traditional way of sitting in Japan, kneeling with the buttocks resting lightly on the ankles.

6. Selfishly Skinny or Selflessly Starving

1 Given the widespread predisposition toward lactose intolerance and a national concern over osteoporosis, many Japanese products emphasize the addition of calcium rather than the omission of fat. Bread, juice, and even cookie brands advertise calcium supplements in their products.

2 This is rumored to change in coming years, as the Health, Labor, and Welfare Ministry has considered passing a bill to require nutritional labels.

3 However, S. Smith indicates that in a recent survey of the youth market, both young men and women "are seeking lighter-tasting drinks, which are thought to be *healthier*" (1992:153; emphasis added).

4 Klein's (1994) ethnographic study of professional bodybuilders reveals a similar striking discrepancy between image and practice. The image of the bodybuilder is virile, healthy, self-reliant, and aggressively heterosexual but, Klein explains, "Although each of these ideal projections has more than a kernel of truth to it, each also contains a measure of its opposite found in patterned behavior. Hence, self-reliance bespeaks subjected dependency; healthy lifestyles conceal physiologically dangerous practices; and heterosexual appeal belies the existence of homosexual practices" (140). The contradictions between the strong, tanned, and healthy image and the reality of the steroid-dependent and insecurity-ridden athlete can be compared to inconsistencies that characterize aerobics instructors in Japan.

5 *Wide Show* is a morning news and talk show that is perhaps most similar to *Good Morning America* in the United States.

6 Rie Miyazawa is a popular television star who is well-known for losing a great deal of weight. Her engagement and subsequent breakup with the famous Sumo champion Takenahada has made her an extremely high-profile celebrity. Rumored to have anorexia nervosa, Miyazawa is central to any discussion on excessive dieting in Japan.

7 See Yato (1967) for an account of bodybuilding in Japan.

8 Some Japanese club members indicated in hushed voices that bodybuilders

are rumored to have small penises. One young woman whispered with a giggle, "Big bodies, but not much down there."

9 Bodybuilding is not a professional sport, as it is in the United States; as a result, even the national competitions are nearly empty of spectators, save relatives and close friends. I attended the Japan Open bodybuilding competition held in September 1997. Men and women competed in several categories: novice, mixed pairs, local, master's (over age 40), and the national finals. Out of the fifteen women competing, two were instructors at Downtown Fitness. Interestingly, the winner of the female competition had the largest and most bulky frame, which is not to say the most muscle definition. In fact, my bodybuilding friend pronounced her quite "soft" (*amai*). Clearly, the large body type, which is the ideal in the bodybuilding contest, is quite distinct from the body ideal for the average woman. See M. Lowe (1998), S. Butler (1997), and Klein (1994) for a discussion of women's bodybuilding in the United States, where slimmer, more well-defined silhouettes usually win over bulk and mass.

10 Interestingly, women's pro wrestling has attracted an enormous following in recent years. Athletes such as Cuty Shuta are extremely popular and have become television tarentos, adored by fans nationwide. The fleshy, large frames necessary for wrestling are not consistent with the body ideal aimed at the average woman; nevertheless, these pro wrestlers clearly have a certain appeal. Even the nickname Cuty, while perhaps an ironic allusion to a diminutive and adorable demeanor and appearance, does suggest an acknowledgment of her attractiveness. Klein, in his treatment of female bodybuilders, suggests that feminist readings of the muscular female bodybuilder as actively resisting hegemonic stereotypes of femininity might be incomplete and somewhat superficial: "Although the bodybuilders distance themselves from societal norms for women's bodies, they do not seek to repudiate the traditional notion that it is desirable for women to be objectified" (1993:190). Are the female bodybuilders and wrestlers popular in spite of their size or because of it? How these female wrestlers fit in with more general body ideals is a subject that must be explored at greater length.

Bibliography

Aim, Richard. 1989. "Ease Up: Workaholics Told to Relax." *Orange County (CA) Register*. 13 Aug. LO1.

Allinson, Gary D. 1997. *Japan's Postwar History*. Ithaca, NY: Cornell University Press.

Allison, Anne. 1991. "Japanese Mothers and *obentō*: The Lunch-box as Ideological State Apparatus." *Anthropological Quarterly* 64 (October):194–208.

———. 1993. "A Male Gaze in Japanese Children's Cartoons, or Are Naked Female Bodies Always Sexual?" *Working Papers in Asian/Pacific Studies*. Durham, NC: Asian Pacific Institute, Duke University.

———. 1994. *Nightwork: Sexuality, Pleasure, and Corporate Masculinity in a Tokyo Hostess Club*. Chicago: University of Chicago Press.

Alter, Joseph. 1992. *The Wrestler's Body: Identity and Ideology in North India*. Berkeley: University of California Press.

———. 1993. "The Body of One Color: Indian Wrestling, the Indian State, and Utopian Somatics." *Cultural Anthropology* 8(1):49–72.

Anderson, E. N. 1997. "Traditional Medical Values of Food." In *Food and Culture: A Reader*. Carole Counihan and Penny Van Esterik, eds. New York: Routledge. 80–91.

Arai, Paula Kane Robinson. 1999. *Women Living Zen: Japanese Soutou Buddhist Nuns*. New York: Oxford University Press.

Atsumi, Reiko. 1988. "Dilemmas and Accommodations of Married Japanese Women in White-Collar Employment." *Bulletin of Concerned Asian Scholars* 20(3):54–62.

Bachnik, Jane. 1992. "Kejime: Defining a Shifting Self in Multiple Organizational Modes." In *Japanese Sense of Self*. Nancy Rosenberger, ed. Cambridge, England: Cambridge University Press. 153–172.

Back in Shape: Akino Yoko's Special Diet. 1994. Videotape. Yoko Akino, narr. Pony Canyon, Inc.

Banet-Weiser, Sarah. 1999. *The Most Beautiful Girl in the World: Beauty Pageants and National Identity*. Berkeley: University of California Press.

Bartky, Sandra Lee. 1990. *Femininity and Domination: Studies in the Phenomenology of Oppression*. New York: Routledge.

Becker, Anne E. 1995. *Body, Self, and Society: The View from Fiji*. Philadelphia: University of Pennsylvania Press.

Ben-Ari, Eyal. 1994. *Body Projects in Japanese Childcare: Culture, Organization, and Emotions in Preschool*. Richmond, VA: Curzon.

———. 1998. "Golf, Organization, and 'Body Projects': Japanese Business Executives in Singapore." In *The Culture of Japan as Seen through Its Leisure*. Sepp Linhart and Sabine Fruhstuck, eds. Albany: State University of New York Press. 139–161.

Benedict, Ruth. 1946. *Chrysanthemum and the Sword: Patterns of Japanese Culture*. Boston, MA: Houghton Mifflin.

Benjamin, Walter. 1969. "The Work of Art in the Age of Mechanical Reproduction." In *Illuminations*. Hannah Arendt, ed. New York: Schocken Books. 217–251.

Bethel, Diana. 1992. "Alienation and Reconnection in a Home for the Elderly." In *Re-made in Japan: Everyday Life and Consumer Taste in a Changing Society*. Joseph Tobin, ed. New Haven: Yale University Press. 126–142.

Bordo, Susan. 1993. *Unbearable Weight: Feminism, Western Culture, and the Body*. Berkeley: University of California Press.

———. 1997. "Anorexia Nervosa: Psychopathology as the Crystallization of Culture." In *Food and Culture: A Reader*. Carole Counihan and Penny Van Esterik, eds. New York: Routledge. 226–250.

Bourdieu, Pierre. 1977. *Outline of a Theory of Practice*. Cambridge, England: Cambridge University Press.

Brackenridge, Celia, ed. 1983. *Body Matters: Leisure Images and Lifestyles*. Leisure Studies Association. Eastbourne: University of Brighton.

Brain, Robert. 1979. *The Decorated Body*. New York: Harper and Row.

Brannen, Mary Yoko. 1992. " 'Bwana Mickey': Constructing Cultural Consumption at Tokyo Disneyland." In *Re-made in Japan: Everyday Life and Consumer Taste in a Changing Society*. Joseph Tobin, ed. New Haven: Yale University Press. 216–234.

Brinton, Mary C. 1992. "Christmas Cakes and Wedding Cakes: The Social Organization of Japanese Women's Life Course." In *Japanese Social Organization*. Takie Sugiyama Lebra, ed. Honolulu: University of Hawai'i Press. 79–107.

———. 1993. *Women and the Economic Miracle: Gender and Work in Postwar Japan*. Berkeley: University of California Press.

Brownell, Susan. 1995. *Training the Body for China: Sports in the Moral Order of the People's Republic.* Chicago: University of Chicago Press.

Bruch, Hilde. 1997. "Body Image and Self Awareness." In *Food and Culture: A Reader.* Carole Counihan and Penny Van Esterik, eds. New York: Routledge. 211–225.

Brumberg, Joan Jacobs. 1988. *Fasting Girls: The History of Anorexia Nervosa.* New York: Plume.

———. 1997. "The Appetite as Voice." In *Food and Culture: A Reader.* Carole Counihan and Penny Van Esterik, eds. New York: Routledge. 159–179.

Buckley, Sandra. 1991. "Penguin in Bondage: A Graphic Tale of Japanese Comic Books." In *Technoculture.* Constance Penley and Andrew Ross, eds. Minneapolis: University of Minnesota Press. 163–193.

———. 1993. "Altered States: The Body Politics of 'Being-Woman.' In *Postwar Japan as History.* Andrew Gordon, ed. Berkeley: University of California Press. 347–372.

Butler, Judith. 1993. *Bodies That Matter: On the Discursive Limits of "Sex."* New York: Routledge.

Butler, Susan. 1997. "Revising Femininity? Review of Lady, Photographs of Lisa Lyon by Robert Mapplethorpe." In *Looking On: Images of Femininity in the Visual Arts and Media.* Rosemary Betterton, ed. London: Pandora. 120–126.

Bynum, Caroline Walker. 1987. *Holy Feast and Holy Fast: The Religious Significance of Food to Medieval Women.* Berkeley: University of California Press.

———. 1997. "Fast, Feast, and Flesh: The Religious Significance of Food to Medieval Women." In *Food and Culture: A Reader.* Carole Counihan and Penny Van Esterik, eds. New York: Routledge. 138–158.

Chaney, David. 1996. *Lifestyles.* New York: Routledge.

Chapkis, Wendy. 1986. *Beauty Secrets: Women and the Politics of Appearance.* Boston: South End Press.

Chernin, Kim. 1981. *The Obsession: Reflections on the Tyranny of Slenderness.* New York: Harper.

Cherry, Kittredge. 1987. *Womansword: What Japanese Words Say about Women.* Tokyo: Kodansha International.

Chow, Rey. 1993. *Writing Diaspora: Tactics of Intervention in Contemporary Cultural Studies.* Bloomington: Indiana University Press.

Clammer, John. 1995. "Consuming Bodies: Constructing and Representing the Female Body in Contemporary Japanese Print Media." In *Women, Media, and Consumption.* Lisa Skov and Brian Moeran, eds. Honolulu: University of Hawai'i Press. 197–219.

Clark, Scott. 1992. "The Japanese Bath: Extraordinarily Ordinary." In *Remade in Japan: Everyday Life and Consumer Taste in a Changing Society.* Joseph Tobin, ed. New Haven: Yale University Press. 89–105.

Clifford, James. 1988. *The Predicament of Culture: Twentieth-Century Ethnography, Literature, and Art.* Cambridge, MA: Harvard University Press.

"Clubs Shift from Weight-lifting to Weight-watching: Fitness Clubs Offer More Health, Beauty Services." 1995. *Nikkei Weekly.* 30 Oct. 20.

Club Management Network [CMN]. 2001. Fitness Club Web page.

Cole, Cheryl. 1994. "Resisting the Canon: Feminist Cultural Studies, Sport, and Technologies of the Body." In *Women, Sport, and Culture.* S. Birrell and C. Cole, eds. Champaign, IL: Human Kinetics. 5–30.

Cooper, Kenneth. 1968. *Aerobics.* New York: M. Evans.

Counihan, Carole M. 1999. *The Anthropology of Food and Body: Gender, Meaning, and Power.* New York: Routledge.

Creighton, Millie R. 1992. "The *Depaato:* Merchandising the West While Selling Japaneseness." In *Re-made in Japan: Everyday Life and Consumer Taste in a Changing Society.* Joseph Tobin, ed. New Haven: Yale University Press. 42–57.

———. 1995. "Imaging the Other in Japanese Advertising Campaigns." In *Occidentalism: Images of the West.* James Carrier, ed. Oxford: Clarendon Press. 135–160.

Dalby, Liza. 1983. *Geisha.* Berkeley: University of California Press.

Davis, Kathy. 1995. *Reshaping the Female Body: The Dilemma of Cosmetic Surgery.* New York: Routledge.

Deem, Rosemary. 1986. *All Work and No Play? The Sociology of Women and Leisure.* Philadelphia, PA: Open University Press.

DeVault, Majorie. 1997. "Conflict and Deference." In *Food and Culture: A Reader.* Carole Counihan and Penny Van Esterik, eds. New York: Routledge. 180–199.

Doi, Takeo. 1973. *The Anatomy of Dependence.* Tokyo: Kodansha.

Donohue, John J. 1991. *The Forge of the Spirit: Structure, Motion, and Meaning in the Japanese Martial Tradition.* New York: Garland.

Douglas, Mary. 1966. *Purity and Danger: An Analysis of the Concepts of Pollution and Taboo.* London: Routledge.

———. 1970. *Natural Symbols: Explorations in Cosmology.* London: Routledge.

———. 1986. *How Institutions Think.* Syracuse, NY: Syracuse University Press.

"Dressing Well for Exercise: Aerobic Dance" [Taiku no Kikonashi: Earobikusu Dansu]." 1997. In *Tarzan.* 26 Mar. 78–79.

Dudley, Kathryn Marie. 1994. *The End of the Line: Lost Jobs, New Lives in Postindustrial America.* Chicago: University of Chicago Press.

"Eating Disorders in Japan and Russia." 1989. PR Newswire. 17 Jan.

Edwards, Walter. 1987. "The Commercialized Wedding as Ritual." *Journal of Japanese Studies* 13(1):51–78.

————. 1989. *Modern Japan through Its Weddings: Gender, Person, and Society in Ritual Portrayal*. Stanford: Stanford University Press.

Efron, Sonni. 1997. "Eating Disorders Go Global." *Los Angeles Times*. 18 Oct. A1.

Eichberg, Henning. 1998. *Body Cultures: Essays on Sport, Space and Identity*. John Bale and Chris Philo, eds. London: Routledge.

Eskes, Tina B., Margaret Carlisle Duncan, and Eleanor M. Miller. 1998. "The Discourse of Empowerment: Foucault, Marcuse, and Women's Fitness Texts." *Journal of Sport and Social Issues* 22:3 (August): 317–344.

Faludi, Susan. 1991. *Backlash: The Undeclared War against American Women*. New York: Doubleday.

Featherstone, Mike. 1991. "The Body in Consumer Culture." In *The Body: Social Process and Cultural Theory*. Mike Featherstone, Mike Hepworth, and Bryan S. Turner, eds. London: Sage. 170–196.

Fields, George. 1983. *From Bonsai to Levi's—When West Meets East: An Insider's Surprising Account of How the Japanese Live*. Chicago: Mentor.

————. 1989. *The Japanese Market Culture*. Tokyo: Japan Times.

"Fifteen-year-old Dies after Being Family Caretaker." 1994. Japan Economic Newswire. 26 Dec.

"Fitness Clubs Broaden Services to Ensure their Fiscal Health." 1992. *Nikkei Weekly*. 18 Jan. 18.

"Fitness Now and Then: A Look Back at the Ten-Year History of Aerobics in Japan [Fitness Now and Then: Nihon no Earobikusu Juunen no Rekishi o Furikaeru]." 1991. *Fitness Journal*. Nov. 7–23.

Foster, Patricia, ed. 1994. *Minding the Body*. New York: Doubleday.

Foucault, Michel. 1979. *Power, Truth, Strategy*. Sydney: Feral.

————. 1980. *Power/Knowledge: Selected Interviews and Other Writings, 1972–1977*. Colin Gordon, trans. New York: Pantheon.

————. 1995. *Discipline and Punish: The Birth of the Prison*. Alan Sheridan, trans. New York: Vintage.

Frykman, Jonas. 1993. "Becoming the Perfect Swede: Modernity, Body Politics, and National Processes in Twentieth-Century Sweden." *Ethnos* 58(3–4):259–274.

Fukuzawa, Rebecca Irwin. 1996. "The Path to Adulthood According to Japanese Middle Schools." In *Teaching and Learning in Japan*. Thomas P. Rohlen and Gerald K. Le Tendre, eds. Cambridge, England: Cambridge University Press. 295–322.

Funabashi, Kuniko. 1995. "Pornographic Culture and Sexual Violence." In *Japanese Women: New Feminist Perspectives on the Past, Present, and Future*. Kumiko Fujimura-Fanselow and Atsuko Kameda, eds. New York: Feminist Press. 255–264.

Furman, Frida Kerner. 1997. *Facing the Mirror: Older Women and Beauty Shop Culture*. New York: Routledge.

Gal, Susan. 1995. "Language and the 'Arts of Resistance.' " *Cultural Anthropology* 10(3):407–424.

Geertz, Clifford. 1988. *Works and Lives: The Anthropologist as Author*. Stanford: Stanford University Press.

Ginsberg [Spielvogel], Laura. 2000. "The Hard Work of Working Out: Defining Beauty and Leisure in a Japanese Fitness Club." *Journal of Sport and Social Issues* 24:3 (August). 260–281.

Goffman, Erving. 1959. *The Presentation of Self in Everyday Life*. New York: Doubleday.

———. 1961. *Asylums*. Garden City, NY: Anchor.

Greenbie, Barrie. 1988. *Space and Spirit in Modern Japan*. New Haven: Yale University Press.

Greenlees, John. 1994. "Women: The Leisure Principle: Meet the Japanese Yenjoy Girls Who Just Wanna Have Fun." *The Guardian*. 17 May. T16.

Guttmann, Allen, and Lee Thompson. 2001. *Japanese Sports: A History*. Honolulu: University of Hawai'i Press.

Hamabata, Mathews Masayuki. 1990. *Crested Kimono: Power and Love in the Japanese Business Family*. Ithaca, NY: Cornell University Press.

Harada, Munehiko. 1994. "Towards a Renaissance of Leisure in Japan." *Leisure Studies* 13(4):277–287.

Hardacre, Helen. 1986. *Kurozumikyo and the New Religions of Japan*. Princeton, NJ: Princeton University Press.

Hargreaves, Jennifer. 1994. *Sporting Females: Critical Issues in the History and Sociology of Women's Sports*. London: Routledge.

Hasegawa, Mina. 1992. "Elderly Due Tax Breaks for Health-Club Visits: Ministry Authorizes Select Fitness Centers." *Nikkei Weekly*. 30 Nov. 10.

Hata, Osamu, and Norio Umezawa. 1995. "Use of Fitness Facilities, Equipment, and Programs: A Case Study of a Japanese Fitness Club." *Journal of Sport Management* (9):78–84.

Havens, Thomas R. H. 1994. *Architects of Affluence: The Tsutsumi Family and the Seibu-Saison Enterprises in Twentieth-Century Japan*. Cambridge, MA: Harvard University Press.

Hendry, Joy. 1993. *Wrapping Culture: Politeness, Presentation, and Power in Japan and Other Societies*. Oxford: Clarendon Press.

"Hip-Hugging Tights Post Firm Sales: Designer Updates Girdle by Using Modern Fibers." 1997. *Nikkei Weekly*. 3 Feb. 11.

Horioka, Charles Yuji. 1993. "Consuming and Saving." In *Postwar Japan as History*. Andrew Gordon, ed. Berkeley: University of California Press. 259–292.

Hughes, Marvalene H. 1997. "Soul, Black Women, and Food." In *Food and Culture: A Reader*. Carole Counihan and Penny Van Esterik, eds. New York: Routledge. 272-280.

Igarashi, Yoshikuni. 2000. *Bodies of Memory: Narratives of War in Postwar Japanese Culture, 1945-1970*. Princeton, NJ: Princeton University Press.

"I Love Aerobics." 1986. *Fitness Journal* (Nov.): 2-3.

Imai, Kanichi. 1993. "Help for the Mother Who Has an Anorexic Daughter. [Kyoshokubyou no Musume o Motsu Hahaoya no Enjo]." *Journal of Japanese Clinical Psychology* 11(1):25-35.

International Health, Racquet, and Sportsclub Association. 2001. Web page.

Ivy, Marilyn. 1988. "Tradition and Difference in the Japanese Mass Media." *Public Culture* 1(1):21-29.

———. 1993. "Formations of Mass Culture." In *Postwar Japan as History*. Andrew Gordon, ed. Berkeley: University of California Press. 239-258.

Jacobson, Bobbie. 1981. *The Ladykillers: Why Smoking Is a Feminist Issue*. London: Pluto Press.

———. 1986. *Beating the Ladykillers: Women and Smoking*. London: Pluto Press.

"Japan Eyes Health Insurance Coverage for Fitness Clubs." 2001. Japan Economic Newswire. 3 Apr.

Jordan, Mary. 1997. "In Search of an Anesthetic Experience." *Washington Post*. 24 Nov. B1, B5.

"Jumping into New Career as Aerobics Teacher No Easy Feat: More Applicants Than Available Jobs at Most Health Clubs." 1996. *Nikkei Weekly*. 2 Dec. 18.

Kaneko, Motoko, Hisako Kubota, and Chikako Otaki. 1995. "Learning What to Eat to Lose Fat and Build Muscle [Shibou o Otoshi Kiniku o Tsukeru Shokujigaku]." *Fitness Journal*. (8 Aug.): 7-21.

Kaplan E. Ann. 1987. "Feminist Criticism and Television." In *Channels of Discourse: Television and Contemporary Criticism*. Robert Allen, ed. Chapel Hill: University of North Carolina Press. 211-253.

Kasulis, Thomas P. 1993a. Introduction to *Self as Body in Asian Theory and Practice*. Thomas P. Kasulis, Roger T. Ames, and Wimal Dissanayake, eds. New York: State University of New York Press. i-xxii.

———. 1993b. "The Body—Japanese Style." In *Self as Body in Asian Theory and Practice*. Thomas P. Kasulis, Roger T. Ames, and Wimal Dissanayake, eds. New York: State University of New York Press. 299-319.

Kaw, Eugenia. 1994. " 'Opening Faces': The Politics of Cosmetic Surgery and Asian American Women." In *Many Mirrors: Body Image and Social Relations*. Nicole Sault, ed. New Brunswick, NJ: Rutgers University Press. 241-265.

Kawahara, Kazue. 1995. "Notes on the Introduction and Dissemination of 'Fitness' in Japan ['Fuittonesu' Genshou e no Shiten]." *Japan Journal of Sport Sociology* (3):38–45.

Kelly, William. 1992. "Tractors, Television, and Telephones: Reach Out and Touch Someone in Rural Japan." In *Re-made in Japan: Everyday Life and Consumer Taste in a Changing Society.* Joseph Tobin, ed. New Haven: Yale University Press. 77–88.

———. 1993. "Finding a Place in Metropolitan Japan: Ideologies, Institutions, and Everyday Life." In *Postwar Japan as History.* Andrew Gordon, ed. Berkeley: University of California Press. 189–216.

———. 1998. "Blood and Guts in Japanese Professional Baseball." In *The Culture of Japan as Seen through Its Leisure.* Sepp Linhart and Sabine Fuhstuck, eds. Albany: State University of New York Press. 95–111.

Kidwell, Claudia Brush, and Valerie Steele. 1989. *Men and Women: Dressing the Part.* Washington, DC: Smithsonian Institution Press.

Kinsella, Sharon. 1995. "Cuties in Japan." In *Women, Media, and Consumption.* Lisa Skov and Brian Moeran, eds. Honolulu: University of Hawai'i Press. 220–254.

Klein, Alan M. 1993. *Little Big Men: Bodybuilding Subculture and Gender Construction.* New York: State University of New York Press.

———. 1994. "The Cultural Anatomy of Competitive Women's Bodybuilding." In *Many Mirrors: Body Image and Social Relations.* Nicole Sault, ed. New Brunswick, NJ: Rutgers University Press. 76–104.

Kondo, Dorrine. 1990. *Crafting Selves: Power, Gender, and Discourses of Identity in a Japanese Workplace.* Chicago: University of Chicago Press.

———. 1992. "The Aesthetics and Politics of Japanese Identity in the Fashion Industry." In *Re-Made in Japan: Everyday Life and Consumer Taste in a Changing Society.* Joseph Tobin, ed. New Haven, CT: Yale University Press. 176–203.

———. 1997. *About Face: Performing Race in Fashion and Theatre.* New York: Routledge.

Kotani, Hiroshi. 1998. "Health Clubs Doing Back Flips to Attract Customers in Lean Times." *Nikkei Weekly.* 6 Apr. 10.

Kuriki, Chieko. 1992. "Japanese Phenomenon: Eating Disorders Make Their Painful Arrival." *Chicago Tribune.* 13 Sept. N5.

Kyuzo, Takenoshita. 1967. "The Social Structure of the Sport Population in Japan." *International Review of Sport Sociology* 2:5–18.

"The Latest News on Summer Diets [Natsu no Daietto Saishin Niyuusu]." 1995. *Fytte* (Tokyo). Aug. 6–33.

Lebra, Takie. 1984. *Japanese Women: Constraint and Fulfillment.* Honolulu: University of Hawai'i Press.

———. 1992. "Self in Japanese Culture." In *Japanese Sense of Self.* Nancy

Rosenberger, ed. Cambridge, England: Cambridge University Press. 105–120.

Leisure White Papers. 1996. [*Rejyaa Hakusho '96*]. Tokyo: Youkakaihatsu Sentaa.

Lenskjy, Helen. 1986. *Out of Bounds: Women, Sport and Sexuality.* Toronto: Women's Press.

"Let's Become a Body That Doesn't Get Fat Again! [Nido to Futoranai Karada ni Naroo!]" 1996. In *an-an.* (Tokyo). 15 Nov. 6–31.

Linhart, Sepp, and Sabine Frühstück, eds. 1998. *The Culture of Japan as Seen through Its Leisure.* Albany: State University of New York Press.

Lo, Jeannie. 1990. *Office Ladies, Factory Women: Life and Work at a Japanese Company.* New York: M.E. Sharpe.

Lock, Margaret. 1993a. *Encounters with Aging: Mythologies of Menopause in Japan and North America.* Berkeley: University of California Press.

———. 1993b. "Ideology, Female Midlife, and the Greying of Japan." *Journal of Japanese Studies* 19(1):43–78.

Lock, Margaret, and Christina Honde. 1990. "Reaching Consensus about Death: Heart Transplant and Cultural Identity in Japan." In *Social Science Perspectives on Medical Ethics.* G. Weisz, ed. The Hague: Kluwer Academic. 99–119.

Longstreet, Stephen, and Ethel Longstreet. 1970. *Yoshiwara: The Pleasure Quarters of Old Tokyo.* Tokyo: Yenbooks.

Lowe, Donald M. 1995. *The Body in Late-Capitalist USA.* Durham, NC: Duke University Press.

Lowe, Maria R. 1998. *Women of Steel.* New York: New York University Press.

"Making a Beautiful Body in '95: Leg Slimmers [Utsukushii Boteii Tsukuri '95: Ashi Yaseesute]." 1995. *Can-Cam* (Tokyo). 10 June. 44–75.

Makino, Catherine. 1998. "Realizing When Thin Is No Longer In." *Japan Times.* 10 Dec.

Mankekar, Purnima. 1993. "National Texts and Gendered Lives: An Ethnography of Television Viewers in a North Indian City." *American Ethnologist* 20(3):543–563.

Marcus, George, and Michael Fischer. 1986. *Anthropology as Cultural Critique.* Chicago: University of Chicago Press.

Marketing Data of Leisure Industry and Daily Life. 1995. [*Rejaa to Raifu: Maaketeingu Deeta*]. Tokyo: Sougou Yunikomu Kabushikigaisha.

Marsh, Alan, and Stephen McKay. 1994. *Poor Smokers.* London: Policy Studies Institute.

Martin, Emily. 1987. *The Woman in the Body: A Cultural Analysis of Reproduction.* Boston: Beacon Press.

Matsuzaki, Tsuyoshi. 1997. "Exercise Show Mirrors Changing Times." *Daily Yomiuri* (Tokyo). 16 Oct. 18.

McVeigh, Brian. 1995. "The Feminization of Body, Behavior, and Belief: Learning to Be an 'Office Lady' at a Japanese Women's College." *American Asian Review* 13(2):29–67.

———. 1996. "Commodifying Affection, Authority and Gender in the Everyday Objects of Japan." *Journal of Material Culture* 1(3):291–312.

———. 1997. "Wearing Ideology: How Uniforms Discipline Minds and Bodies in Japan." *Fashion Theory* 1(2):189–214.

Mennell, Stephen. 1991. "On the Civilizing of Appetite." In *The Body: Social Process and Cultural Theory.* Mike Featherstone, Mike Hepworth, and Bryan S. Turner, eds. London: Sage. 126–156.

Miller, Laura. Forthcoming. "Busting Out: Mammary Mania in Japan and the U.S." In *Tsunami Pop: American Culture and the Pacific Rim.* George Lewis, ed. Bowling Green, OH: Popular Press.

Millum, Trevor. 1975. *Images of Women: Advertising in Women's Magazines.* Totowa, NY: Rowan and Littlefield.

"Ministry to Set Up Medical Centers for Eating Disorders." 2000. Japan Economic Newswire. Lexis-Nexis. 18 Dec.

"Modern Women's Number One Desire: The Reality of 'Wanting a Small Face' [Genzai Josei no Ichiban no Nozomi: 'Chisai Kao ni Naritai' o Genjitsu ni]." 1997. *an-an* (Tokyo). 24 Jan. 5–31.

Morris, Ivan. 1964. *The World of the Shining Prince.* New York: Penguin.

"The Most Common Worry of Women about Their Bodies Are Their Legs, But Without a Doubt We Will Make Them Beautiful [Onna no Karada no Nayami wa Ashi ni Shuuchuu, Demo Kanarazu Kirei ni Naru]." 1997. *an-an* (Tokyo) 25 Apr. 5–31.

"Most Young Women Diet." 1991. *Daily Yomiuri* (Tokyo). 10 May. 2.

Mukai, Takayo. 1989. "A Call for Our Language: Anorexia from Within." *Women's Studies International Forum* (12):613–638.

Murakami, Maki. 1991. "Made to Order." *Look Japan.* May. 46.

Nakagawa, Hisako. 1995. *Hisako Nakagawa's Lose Ten Kilograms in Four Months! [Nakagawa Hisako No Yon ka Getsu de Juu Kiro Yaseru!]* an-an Daieto. Tokyo: Magashin Hausu Kabushikigaisha.

Nakamura, Konoyu, Kazuko Takeuchi, Syuji Kurita, and Megumi Yama. 1990. "The Mother's Counseling of Anorectic Patients [Shinkeiseishokuo mofushinbyousha no Hahaoya Kaunseringu]." *Journal of Japanese Clinical Psychology* 8(1):38–47.

Nakamura, Yumi. 1996. "Sports Policy in Japan." *National Sports Policies: An International Handbook.* Lawrence Chalip, Arthur Johnson, and Lisa Stachura, eds. Westport, CT: Greenwood Press. 286–316.

Nichter, Mimi, and Nancy Vuckovic. 1994. "Fat Talk: Body Image among Adolescent Girls." In *Many Mirrors: Body Image and Social Relations.* Nicole Sault, ed. New Brunswick, NJ: Rutgers University Press. 109–131.

Nolte, Sharon H., and Sally Ann Hastings. 1991. "The Meiji State's Policy toward Women, 1890–1910." In *Recreating Japanese Women, 1600–1945*. Gail Lee Bernstein, ed. Berkeley: University of California Press. 199–216.

"Not So Dumb Belles and Beaus." 1995. *Japan Times Weekly International Edition*. 4–10 Dec. 17.

Oga, Jun. 1998. "Business Fluctuation and the Sport Industry in Japan: An Analysis of the Sport Industry from 1986 to 1993." *Journal of Sport Management* (12): 63–75.

Oga, Jun, and Kazuhiko Kimura. 1993. "Recent Trends in the Sports Industry in Japan." *Journal of Sport Management* (7): 249–255.

Ogasawara, Yuko. 1998. *Office Ladies and Salaried Men: Power, Gender, and Work in Japanese Companies*. Berkeley: University of California Press.

O'Hanlon, Michael. 1989. *Reading the Skin: Adornment, Display, and Society among the Wahgi*. London: British Museum Publications.

Ohnuki-Tierney, Emiko. 1984. *Illness and Culture in Contemporary Japan*. Cambridge, England: Cambridge University Press.

———. 1997. "McDonald's in Japan: Changing Manners and Etiquette." In *Golden Arches East: McDonald's in East Asia*. James Watson, ed. Stanford: Stanford University Press. 161–182.

"Only the Fittest Sports Centers Survive." 1996. *Nikkei Weekly*. 10 June. 17.

Ortner, Sherry. 1995. "Resistance and the Problem of Ethnographic Refusal." *Society for Comparative Study of Society and History* 37(1):173–193.

"Overcoming Eating Disorders." 1995. *Daily Yomiuri* (Tokyo). 28 Oct. 11.

Park, Roberta J. 1994. "A Decade of the Body: Researching and Writing about the History of Health, Fitness, Exercise, and Sport, 1983–1993." *Journal of Sport History* 21(1):59–82.

Peak, Lois. 1991. *Learning to Go to School in Japan: The Transition from Home to Preschool Life*. Berkeley: University of California Press.

Perfect Body: Yoko Akino's Special Diet. 1995. Videotape. Yoko Akino, narr. Pony Canyon, Inc.

Radner, Hilary. 1995. *Shopping Around: Feminine Culture and the Pursuit of Pleasure*. New York: Routledge.

"Report on Fitness Trends." 1997. *International Market Insight Reports*. 18 Dec. Business Section.

Reynolds, David K. 1980. *The Quiet Therapies: Japanese Pathways to Personal Growth*. Honolulu: University of Hawai'i Press.

Robertson, Jennifer. 1991. "Theatrical Resistance, Theatres of Restraint: The Takarazuka Revue and the 'State Theatre' Movement in Japan." *Anthropological Quarterly* 64(Oct.):165–176.

———. 1997. "Miss Japan: Beauty, Blood, and Body in Imperial Japan." Paper presented at Cornell University.

———. 1998. *Takarazuka: Sexual Politics and Popular Culture in Modern Japan*. Berkeley: University of California Press.

Robinson, Gwen. 1995. "Sunset Strip." *Times*. Newspapers Limited. Lexis-Nexis. 3 June. Features.

Rohlen, Thomas. 1974. *For Harmony and Strength: Japanese White-Collar Organization in Anthropological Perspective*. Berkeley: University of California Press.

———. 1975. "The Small Work Group." In *Modern Japanese Organization and Decision-Making*. Ezra F. Vogel, ed. Berkeley: University of California Press. 185–209.

———. 1980. "The *Juku* Phenomenon: An Exploratory Essay." *Journal of Japanese Studies* 6(2):207–242.

———. 1983. *Japan's High Schools*. Berkeley: University of California Press.

———. 1996. "Building Character." *Teaching and Learning in Japan*. Thomas P. Rohlen and Gerald K. Le Tendre, eds. Cambridge, England: Cambridge University Press. 50–74.

Rosaldo, Renato. 1989. *Culture and Truth: The Remaking of Social Analysis*. Boston: Beacon Press.

Rosenberger, Nancy. 1992. Introduction to *Japanese Sense of Self*. Nancy Rosenberger, ed. Cambridge, England: Cambridge University Press. 1–20.

Saga, Junichi. 1987. *Memories of Silk and Straw*. Tokyo: Kodansha International.

Said, Edward. 1993. *Culture and Imperialism*. New York: Vintage.

Sato, Ikuya. 1991. *Kamikaze Biker: Parody and Anomy in Affluent Japan*. Chicago: University of Chicago Press.

Scott, James. 1985. *Weapons of the Weak: Everyday Forms of Peasant Resistance*. New Haven: Yale University Press.

———. 1990. *Domination and the Arts of Resistance: Hidden Transcripts*. New Haven: Yale University Press.

Scraton, Sheila. 1992. *Shaping Up to Womanhood: Gender and Girls' Physical Education*. Philadelphia, PA: Open University Press.

———. 1994. "The Changing World of Women and Leisure: Feminism, 'Post-Feminism,' and Leisure." *Leisure Studies* 13(4):249–261.

Shank, J. 1986. "An Exploration of Leisure in the Lives of Dual-Career Women." *Journal of Leisure Research* 18(4):300–319.

Shaw, Susan M. 1994. "Gender, Leisure, and Constraint: Towards a Framework for the Analysis of Women's Leisure." *Journal of Leisure Research* 26(1):8–22.

Silverberg, Miriam. 1991. "The Modern Girl as Militant." In *Recreating Japanese Women, 1600–1945*. Gail Lee Bernstein, ed. Berkeley: University of California Press. 239–266.

———. 1995. "Advertising Every Body: Images from the Japanese Modern

Years." In *Choreographing History*. Susan Leigh Foster, ed. Bloomington: Indiana University Press. 129–148.

Skov, Lise, and Brian Moeran. 1995. "Introduction—Hiding in the Light: From Oshin to Yoshimoto Banana." In *Women, Media and Consumption in Japan*. Lise Skov and Brian Moeran, eds. Honolulu: University of Hawai'i Press. 1–74.

"Slim Down! Shape Up! Change Your Body! Magical Underwear, Slim Down in Aerobics [Yaseru! Shimeru! Karada o Kaeru!: Mahou no Andaauea, Earobikusu de Yaseru]." 1995. *Body Impact* (Tokyo). 10 July. 30–79.

"Slimmer Fitness Sector Woos Older Crowd." 1998. *Nikkei Weekly*. 16 Nov. 8.

Smith, Robert J. 1987. "Gender Inequality in Contemporary Japan." *Journal of Japanese Studies* 13(1):1–26.

Smith, Stephen R. 1992. "Drinking Etiquette in a Changing Beverage Market." In *Re-made in Japan: Everyday Life and Consumer Taste in a Changing Society*. Joseph Tobin, ed. New Haven: Yale University Press. 143–158.

Sobo, Elisa J. 1997. "The Sweetness of Fat: Health, Procreation, and Sociability in Rural Jamaica." In *Food and Culture: A Reader*. Carole Counihan and Penny Van Esterik, eds. New York: Routledge. 256–271.

Stanlaw, James. 1992. " 'For Beautiful Human Life': The Use of English in Japan." In *Re-made in Japan: Everyday Life and Consumer Taste in a Changing Society*. Joseph Tobin, ed. New Haven: Yale University Press. 58–76.

Suematsu, Hiroyuki. 1993. "Current Perspectives on Eating Disorders [Seshokushogai Saikin no Doukou]." *Psychiatry* [*Seishin Igaku*] 35(1):6–17.

Sugawara, Sandra. 1996. "The Office Problem Japan Winks At: Women Challenge Harassment and a Business Culture That Tolerates It." *Washington Post*. 1 May. A1, A25.

Takabe, Kyoko, and Hiroshi Miura. 2000. "More People Burning Fat along with the Midnight Oil." Asahi News Service. 19 Dec.

Takeda, Aya, Kenji Suzuki, and Sachio Matsushita. 1993. "Prevalence of Bulimia Nervosa (DSM-III-R) among Male and Female High School Students [Danjokoukousei ni okeru Shinkeiseikakyokubyou no Shutsugen Hindo]." *Psychiatry* [*Seishin Igaku*] 5(12):1273–1278.

Taussig, Michael. 1993. *Mimesis and Alterity: A Particular History of the Senses*. New York: Routledge.

Thompson, Allen. 1986. "Professional Wrestling in Japan: Media and Message." *International Review of Sport Sociology*, 21(1):65–80.

Thompson, Becky. 1994. *A Hunger So Wide and So Deep*. Minneapolis: University of Minnesota Press.

Tobin, Joseph. 1992a. "Introduction: Domesticating the West." In *Re-made in Japan: Everyday Life and Consumer Taste in a Changing Society*. Joseph Tobin, ed. New Haven: Yale University Press. 1–41.

———. 1992b. "Japanese Preschools and the Pedagogy of Selfhood." In *Japa-

nese Sense of Self. Nancy Rosenberger, ed. Cambridge, England: Cambridge University Press. 21–39.

Treat, John Whittier, ed. 1996. *Contemporary Japan and Popular Culture*. Richmond, England: Curzon Press.

Tsurumi, Patricia E. 1984. "Female Textile Workers and the Failure of Early Trade Unionism in Japan." *History Workshop* (18):3–27.

———. 1990. *Factory Girls: Women in the Thread Mills of Meiji Japan*. Princeton, NJ: Princeton University Press.

Tung, Jennifer. 1997. "Thigh Hopes: Will Women Slather on the New Thigh Creams—Even Though There's No Real Cure for Cellulite?" *Allure*. Feb. 74, 79.

Turner, Bryan S. 1982a. "Recent Developments in the Theory of the Body." In *The Body: Social Process and Cultural Theory*. Mike Featherstone, Mike Hepworth, and Bryan S. Turner, eds. London: Sage. 1–35.

———. 1982b. "The Discourse of Diet." In *The Body: Social Process and Cultural Theory*. Mike Featherstone, Mike Hepworth, and Bryan S. Turner, eds. London: Sage. 157–169.

———. 1996. *The Body and Society*. 2d ed. London: Sage.

Ueno, Chizuko. 1990. *Theater in the Skirt: Why Do People Care about Underwear?* [*Sukato no Shita no Gekijo: Hito wa Doshite Panti ni Kodawarunoka*]. Tokyo: Kawada Shobo Shinsha.

The Underwear Expert: Becoming More Beautiful [*Shitagi no Tatsujin: Motto Utsukushiku Naru*]. 1997. Tokyo: Sanshindo Shuppansha.

Vertinsky, Patricia A. 1994a. "Gender Relations, Women's History and Sport History: A Decade of Changing Enquiry, 1983–1993." *Journal of Sport History* 21(1):1–24.

———. 1994b. "Sport History and Gender Relations, 1983–1993: Bibliography." *Journal of Sport History* 21(1):25–57.

Vogel, Suzanne H. 1978. "Professional Housewife: The Career of Urban Middle Class Japanese Women." *Japan Interpreter* (12):16–43.

Wacquant, L. J. D. 1995. "Pugs at Work: Bodily Capital and Bodily Labour among Professional Boxers." *Body and Society* 1(1):65–93.

Wagner, Eric A., ed. 1989. *Sport in Asia and Africa: A Comparative Handbook*. New York: Greenwood.

Watanabe, Teresa. 1993. "Wild Dance Craze Cures 9-to-5 Blues." *Los Angeles Times*. 15 Dec. A1.

White, Merry. 1992. "Home Truths: Women and Social Change in Japan." *Daedalus* 121 (fall):61–82.

———. 1993. *The Material Child: Coming of Age in Japan and America*. New York: Free Press.

———. 1995. "The Marketing of Adolescence in Japan: Buying and Dreaming." In *Women, Media, and Consumption*. Lisa Skov and Brian Moeran, eds. Honolulu: University of Hawai'i Press. 255–273.

Whiting, Robert. 1990. *You Gotta Have Wa*. New York: Vintage.

Willis, Paul E. 1977. *Learning to Labor*. Aldershot, England: Gower.

Willis, Susan. 1991. *A Primer for Daily Life*. London: Routledge.

Wilson, Elizabeth. 1985. *Adorned in Dreams: Fashion and Modernity*. Berkeley: University of California Press.

Winship, Janice. 1987. "Handling Sex." In *Looking On: Images of Femininity in the Visual Arts and Media*. Rosemary Betterton, ed. London: Pandora. 25–39.

"Wise Women's Schemes and Places for Tea-time and Lunch-time Fitness [Teiibureku to Ranchitaimu Fuittonesu wa Kenpujin no Kufuu no Shidokoro]." 1989. *Fitness Journal* (Jan.):10–11.

Wolf, Naomi. 1991. *The Beauty Myth: How Images of Beauty Are Used Against Women*. New York: Morrow.

"Wonderful Diet Goods. [Daietto Gutsuzu Kore Ga Sugoi!]." 1996. *Ray Magazine Special Edition*. Tokyo: Shufu no Tomosha.

Yamaoka, Yumiko. 1996. "Why Did Aerobics Become a Boom? [Naze, Earobikusu wa Buumu ni Natta no ka?]." *Fitness Journal* (Nov.): 13–15.

Yato, Tanotsu. 1967. *Young Samurai: Body-Building in Japan*. New York: Grove.

"You Will Never Be Fat Again! Seven Absolute Ways to Lose Weight [Kore de Mou Futoranai! Zettai Yaseru Nanatsu no Houhou]." 1996. *Fytte* (Tokyo). Dec. 4–37.

Yuasa, Yasuo. 1987. *The Body: Toward an Eastern Mind-Body Theory*. Thomas Kasulis, ed. Nagatomo Shignori and T. P. Kasulis, trans. Albany: State University of New York Press.

Zarilli, Phillip. 1990. "What Does It Mean to "Become the Character": Power, Presence, and Transcendence in Asian In-body Disciplines of Practice." In *By Means of Performance*. Richard Schechner and Willa Appel, eds. Cambridge, England: Cambridge University Press. 131–148.

Cellulite cream. *See* Dieting
Chaney, David, 49, 103
Chapkis, Wendy, 167
Chernin, Kim, 143
Cherry, Kittredge, 74
"Chiba club," 13-15, 77-81, 125-126,
    129-130, 196, 208, 210
Chinese medicine, 163, 182
Chow, Rey, 37
Clammer, John, 7
Clark, Scott, 216 n.11, 217 n.17
Class, 41-43, 123, 148; consciousness,
    119; beauty ideal based upon, 145.
    See also Smoking; Tanning
Cleaning, 23-24, 72, 77-81, 219
    n.11. *See also* Aerobics instructor;
    Hygiene
Clifford, James, 19
Coakley, Jay, 55
Cole, Cheryl, 8
Consumption: and fitness clubs, 46-
    47, 218 n.2; in postwar Japan,
    22, 26-27, 41-49, 175; and thin-
    ness, 186-187; and women, 30-
    32
Cooper, Kenneth, 50-51, 52
Cosmetic surgery, 167-168
Counihan, Carole, 193
Creighton, Millie, 16-17, 64, 156
Cultural relativism, 19-20
Cuteness, 7, 44, 132-133, 153. *See also*
    Beauty ideals; *Burikko;* Youth, and
    appearance

Daimatsu, Hirofumi, 50
Dalby, Liza, 147
Daycare facilities, 196, 216 n.10
DeVault, Majorie, 201
Diaspora, 4-5
Dieting, 32, 174-205; acupuncture
    and weight loss, 163; and aerobics
    instructors, 184-187; and calorie-
    cutting, 179-180, 182-184; and

Chinese medicine, 163, 182; defi-
    nitions of, 174, 179; the dumbbell
    diet, 183; and indulgence, 181-182,
    185-187; perfect weight, 176-
    179; in postwar Japan, 174-175;
    products, 1, 142, 158-164, 171,
    179; as resistance, 8, 32, 191-194,
    195, 198-202; selfish versus self-
    less, 32, 192-202, 204-205, 212;
    the *tamago* diet, 183-184. *See also*
    Anorexia nervosa; Food; Thinness
Diet slippers. *See* Dieting
Discipline, 7, 23-25, 26, 66; and
    body size, 88-94; through coordi-
    nated action, 104-107; through fat
    talk, 110-113; militaristic, 23-25,
    51-52; monastic, 23-25, 80, 87,
    211-212; through self-reflection,
    87, 108-110; and sexuality, 98-
    104; and space, 61-62; through
    surveillance, 67-68; and tanning,
    95-98. *See also* Foucault, Michel;
    Seishin kyouiku; Service industry
Doi, Takeo, 116, 117, 131. See also
    Amae
Dole Cup, 56
Domestication, of the West, 4, 16-
    17, 36-39. *See also* Globalization;
    Westernization
Douglas, Mary, 48, 76, 81, 82
"Downtown Fitness," 11-13, 29, 45,
    68, 73, 80, 89-90, 107, 153, 155-
    157, 203, 210, 216 n.8, 219 n.7,
    224 n.5. *See also* Roppongi
Dumbbell diet. *See* Dieting
Duncan, Margaret Carlisle, 219 n.3

Eating disorders. *See* Anorexia ner-
    vosa
Economic recession, 26-27, 48, 89,
    207, 211
Edwards, Walter, 181, 203
Eichberg, Henning, 61, 62-63, 77

Girdle, 101, 165–167
Globalization, 4–5, 36–39, 49, 181, 207
Goffman, Erving, 18, 69, 70, 79, 128, 221 n.5. *See also* Onstage/offstage
"Good wives, wise mothers." See *Ryosai kenbo*
Guttmann, Allen, 33, 35, 50

Hair, 146–147, 148, 149, 150, 153, 158
Hansei. See Self-reflection
Harajuku Counseling Center, 188
Hargreaves, Jennifer, 100
Havens, Thomas, 41, 42, 76
Health: definition of, 21–22, 94; folk theories of, 63; of the nation, 76, 94–95; and preventive care, 3, 93; and productivity, 39–41, 76, 195–198; and smoking, 137, 139–140; and thinness, 93. *See also* Beauty ideals; Body; Fitness
Health club, 21. *See also* Fitness club
Health, Labor, and Welfare Ministry, 43, 89, 188, 189, 225 n.2
Hendry, Joy, 70
Hip-hop aerobics, 49, 98–99
Hisano, Eiko, 50
Homosexuality, 181–182, 202–204
Honde, Christina, 168
Honne/tatemae, 116, 117
Hostess clubs, 75–76, 123, 133–134, 138
Hughes, Marvalene, 201
Hygiene, 72; and body pollution, 81–83; and Buddhism, 80–81; and spatial pollution, 77–81. *See also* Cleaning; *Seishin kyouiku*

Ideology: of beauty, 145, 150; of class, 42–43; and relationship between Japan and the United States, 4–5, 33–41, 150
Igarashi, Yoshikuni, 39, 41

Ivy, Marilyn, 43
Iwao, Sumiko, 103

Jacobson, Bobbie, 139
JAFA, 89. *See also* AFAA
Japan, stereotypes of. See *Nihonjinron*
Japan Aerobics Fitness Association. *See* JAFA
Jibyou, 112
Jogging: aversion to, 160; boom, 51, 63–64

Karoshii, 45
Kasulis, Thomas, 25, 144
Kata. See Seishin kyouiku
Kaw, Eugenia, 225 n.6
Kawahara, Kazue, 9, 51
Kelly, William, 35, 36, 41, 42, 102, 220 n.1
Kenko. See Health
Kimono, 147, 149, 150
Kinsella, Sharon, 44, 153
Kinue, Hitomi, 50
Kirei. See Hygiene
Kitanai. See Hygiene
Klein, Alan, 55, 73, 202–203, 203–204, 217 n.13, 218 n.2, 222 n.11, 225 n.3, 225–226 n.4
Kondo, Dorrine, 118, 194, 195

Lebra, Takie, 136–137
Legs: and beauty ideals, 148, 149, 154, 164–172; *daikon ashi*, 168; and modesty, 53. *See also* Body
Leisure, 20–22; and fitness clubs, 2, 20, 26–29, 74–76, 82; Health, Labor, and Welfare Ministry, 43; and postwar Japan, 41–49; and women, 54–56. *See also* Consumption; Fitness club
Leotard, 1, 52, 53, 59, 68, 98–104, 137, 213
Lifestyle. *See* Consumption
Lo, Jeannie, 8
Lock, Margaret, 168, 197

Laura Spielvogel is Assistant Professor
of Cultural Anthropology at Western
Michigan University.

Library of Congress Cataloging-in-Publication Data

Spielvogel, Laura.
Working out in Japan : shaping the female body in
Tokyo fitness clubs / Laura Spielvogel.
p. cm.
Includes bibliographical references and index.
ISBN 0-8223-3037-7 (cloth : alk. paper) —
ISBN 0-8223-3049-0 (pbk. : alk. paper)
1. Physical fitness for women—Social aspects—
Japan. 2. Physical fitness centers—Japan—Tokyo.
3. Body image—Japan.   I. Title.
GV482 .S67   2003
613′.0424′0952—dc21   2002012949